Verma reminds us again that the project management than mast. Understanding people in organizations is crucial. In his latest book, coauthored with his wife, Shiksha Verma, attention focuses on the importance of using influence and power to achieve outcomes that lead to project success. The authors offer practical guidance and a good read!
 —The late J. Davidson Frame, PhD, PMP, PMI Fellow
 Former CAO, University of Management and Technology
 Arlington, VA 22209, USA

Long-standing author Vijay Verma presents his latest book but with a difference. This time, Shiksha Verma, his wife, joins him as coauthor to focus on the more ephemeral aspects of conducting projects in our new world of high technology. Together, their thoughts and recommendations cover elusive topics such as how to engage peoples' support, practicing influence without authority, and ideas for next-generation leadership. To this end, they present frequent illustrations and focus lists to emphasize their written recommendations and act as organized reminders for a call to action by the reader. The future is in your hands.
 —R. Max Wideman, FCSCE, FEIC, FICE, FPMI, FCMI
 (Retired owner of www.maxwideman.com)
 AEW Services, Richmond Hill, ON © 2017
 Email: maxw@maxwideman.com

Another significant addition to leadership and project management literature by Vijay Verma with his wife, Shiksha Verma. A comprehensive and well-prepared treatise that all business leaders and project management professionals should have on their

shelves. The inclusion of ideas about using power and influence positively is indeed practical and exciting.
—Mahesh K. Upadhyaya, PhD
Professor Emeritus
University of British Columbia

Influencing without authority is a key skill set for the professional project manager. The people approach and emphasis that Vijay and Shiksha Verma provide in this book make a great difference for the reader.

This book is a must for every leader and project manager. Stories, examples, and best practices covered in this book are easy to read and understand. Read it, share it, and practice it to empower your people and Lead with Purpose.
—Alfonso Bucero, MSc, PMP, PMI-RMP, PfMP, PMI Fellow
Managing Partner, BUCERO PM Consulting

Leadership is about people and purpose. Vijay and Shiksha have created a stimulating masterpiece that is a must-read for every project manager. With clarity, this book skillfully places the onus of success on a person's internal drive to succeed through teamwork, psychology, and goals connected with your innate drive to create value through hard work, determination, and personal resolve.
—Nemy Banthia, PhD, PEng, FACI, FCSCE, FICI, FCAE, FRSC
Professor, Distinguished University Scholar and Canada Research Chair in Infrastructure Rehabilitation
CEO and Scientific Director, Canada-India Research Center of Excellence (IC-IMPACTS)
Dept. of Civil Engineering, The University of British Columbia

Best-selling author and highly revered thought leader Vijay Verma teams up with his wife Shiksha Verma to offer new insights in their latest book on leadership and influencing without authority. They also elucidate the interrelationship among power, politics, and influence and demonstrate how leaders and project managers can leverage them to deliver successful projects. Peppered with pearls of wisdom, the book is priceless for organizational leaders and project management practitioners in all industries.

—Dr. Prasad S. Kodukula, PMP, PgMP
Founder and CEO, Kodukula & Associates, Inc.
Adj. Faculty, University of Chicago and Illinois Institute of Technology

Vijay Verma is a leader and practitioner of project management tools and developments and a sought-after teacher and book author. Here, he teams with his wife, Shiksha Verma, to show how it is done in the real world, making connections between leading by example and inspirational philosophies—a true recipe for success and very timely for modern organizations and the next generation. This is how you lead people and get projects done, but it goes beyond the direct application. Very effective and motivational reading for all leaders and project managers.

—Jens Dolling, PhD
Associate Laboratory Director, Physical Science of TRIUMF (Canada's Particle Accelerator Centre)
Adj. Professor of Physics, University of British Columbia

Most project management books are written about how projects work, but projects are about people. There remains a gap in the project management literature that Vijay and Shiksha Verma fill with this essential

read about how people are motivated and influenced to work in different environments. Without this knowledge, project managers cannot steward the most important resources to any project: project team members, sponsors, and end users. They emphasize the positive side of power and influence creatively and practically.
—Dr. Dale Christenson, DPM, PMP, CMC
President, Project Management Centre of Excellence Inc.

It is a timely and important work as the world collectively imagines ways to build back better. Business leaders and project managers will find many useful suggestions to influence stakeholders and increase their overall performance and satisfaction.
—Mark Fattedad, CFA
Director and Portfolio Manager, Institutional Management,
Jarislowsky Fraser Global Investment Management

Many projects can easily turn into "herding cats," one where the project is heading in multiple directions with no focus or progress to meet the project objectives. On the other hand, to set up a project for success, one key skill for the project manager to have is the ability to influence without authority. At the end of the day, people make or break the project. Understanding people internally and externally to the project and the respective chemistry between them is crucial as part of the needed leadership. In his latest book, Vijay Verma, with his wife, Shiksha, focuses on the importance of using influence and power in a positive manner to achieve objectives that ultimately help pave the way to

project success. The Vermas discuss practical means of leading with purpose by using power and influence positively.
—G. Arthur Kanzaki P.Eng., MBA, PMP
Project Director, FortisBC Energy Inc.

Leading with Purpose: Positive Power and Inspirational Influence by Vijay K. Verma is a seminal work that masterfully dissects the nuances of purpose-driven leadership. The book's multidimensional approach resonates with the complexities inherent in modern project management, offering actionable insights for leading teams with vision and efficacy.
—Antonio Nieto-Rodriguez, PMI Fellow
Author, thought leader, professor
Former chair of the Project Management Institute

Leading with Purpose

Positive Power and Inspirational Influence

by Vijay K. Verma and Shiksha Verma

Oshawa, Ontario, Canada

Leading with Purpose: Positive Power and Inspirational Influence
Authors: Vijay K. Verma & Shiksha Verma
Contributing Authors: Jaimini Thakore & Krupal Patel

Managing Editor: Kevin Aguanno
Copy Editor: Susan Andres
Typesetting & Cover Design: Kiryl Lysenka
eBook Conversion: Charles Sin

Published by:
Multi-Media Publications Inc.
Box 58043, Rosslynn RPO,
Oshawa, ON, Canada, L1J 8L6.

All rights reserved. No part of this book may be reproduced or transmitted in any form or by any means, electronic or mechanical, including photocopying, recording or by any information storage and retrieval system, without written permission from the publisher, except for the inclusion of brief quotations in a review.

Copyright © 2024 by Multi-Media Publications Inc.

Paperback ISBN-13: 978-1-55489-181-8
eBook Formats ISBN-13: 978-1-55489-182-5

Published in Canada. Printed simultaneously in Canada, the United States of America, Australia and the United Kingdom.

CIP data available from the publisher.

Dedication

To our late parents and uncle (Taya Ji) for inspiring us.
   To our children—Serena; Naveen and his wife, Anita; and Angelee—for constantly encouraging us.

To our grandchildren, Nikhil, Neel, Rohnik, Jaya, Reyva, Rahi, and Veeyan, for their love and smiles. They teach us the importance of listening to better understand and empower one another to achieve extraordinary results together.

Leading with Purpose

Table of Contents

Foreword 17
Preface 23
Acknowledgments 27
Introduction 29

Part I. People and Project Management 37
Chapter 1. From Strategies to Results 41
Chapter 2. Achieving the Most from People 65
Chapter 3. People—The Key to Project Success .. 97

Part II. Power and Project Management 129
Chapter 4. Dynamics, Characteristics,
and Outcomes of Power 133
Chapter 5. Components and Use of Power 157
Chapter 6. Eight Sources of Power 189
Chapter 7. The Project Manager and Power 213

Leading with Purpose

Part III. Influence and Project Management 237
Chapter 8. Dynamics of Influencing 241
Chapter 9. Influencing Models, Styles, and Skills 267
Chapter 10. Achieving Successful Influencing ... 293
Chapter 11. Influencing by Increasing Power 313

Postscript 349
Appendix: Case Studies and Exercises 361
Notes 379
References 393
About the Authors 401

Table of Illustrations

Figures

Figure 1.1. Levels of power and influence in project management.
Figure 1.2. From strategies to results with power, influence, politics, and leadership.
Figure 1.3. Three skills for effective project management integration.
Figure 2.1. Model for achieving the most from people.
Figure 2.2. Communication components.
Figure 2.3. Power and politics in project management.
Figure 3.1. Three categories of elements for successful project management.

Leading with Purpose

Figure 3.2. Relationship between project complexity and a champion's positional power.
Figure 4.1. Outcomes of use of power.
Figure 6.1. Eight sources of power.
Figure 6.2. Typical organizational structure showing legitimate power.
Figure 6.3. Information power and number of links for four participants.
Figure 6.4. Information power and number of links for six participants.
Figure 8.1. Influencing by affecting thoughts and actions.
Figure 8.2. Thought coconut (representing extrinsic and intrinsic thoughts).
Figure 8.3. Influencing by using power.
Figure 8.4. Increasing circle of influence.
Figure 9.1. Two dimensions of influencing.
Figure 9.2. Influencing styles depending on connecting and convincing.
Figure 9.3. When to use different influencing styles.
Figure 11.1. Three characteristics of high-performance teams.

Tables

Table 1.1. Improving Project Management Value
Table 2.1. Differences Between a Leader and a Manager
Table 2.2. Improving Attentive Listening
Table 2.3. Major Elements of Culture
Table 3.1. Four Steps to Find and Sustain a Champion
Table 4.1. Power (in a Nutshell)
Table 4.2. Characteristics of Power
Table 5.1. Four Advantages of Informal Power

Table 5.2. Possible Outcomes of Using Power in a Formal or Informal Way
Table 6.1. Persuasion (in a Nutshell)
Table 7.1. Sources, Types and Bases of Power
Table 10.1. Influence (in a Nutshell).
Table 11.1. Teamwork (in a Nutshell)
Table 11.2. Team Characteristics and Associated Influencing Strategies
Table 11.3. Ten Guidelines to Increase Power and Influence
Table 11.4. Four Guidelines to Build High-Performance Teams

Leading with Purpose

Foreword

The keys to understanding the challenges and techniques for managing projects have undergone an important sea change over the past decades. When I began my academic career, project management was a niche discipline with a small and rather narrow scholarly focus—optimizing planning and scheduling processes. Paper after paper was published—generally in hard-core management science journals—focusing on aspects of how to create optimal schedules under conditions of resource constraints; resource-leveling algorithms, modeling and linear programming; and so forth.

The program evaluation and review technique (PERT), the graphical evaluation and review technique (GERT), the critical path method (CPM), and activity-on-arrow diagramming were all the rage.

Although these have been important additions to the theoretical foundations of the project management field, we seemed stuck in a rut. The discipline's knowledge base advanced slowly, through small (some might argue "nearly undetectable") turns of the screw, but always within the confines of a scientific, operations research worldview.

Fortunately, by the 1980s, this management science approach to project management broadened and extended beyond the purely quantitative and theoretical into a deeper understanding of how projects operate and, more importantly, what it takes to manage them successfully. Look at the evolution of the research and theory that supports project management, and you see a critical shift in focus, as the OR emphasis gave way to a new set of scholars—those who recognized that project management involves techniques and scientific methods where appropriate, but equally, it depends on fitting several additional pieces to the puzzle.

Pioneered by Professor David Cleland, among others, systems theory in projects opened new vistas for understanding the project development process's true dynamics. The interconnections between project methodologies and managerial and administrative practices were especially apparent. For example, scheduling involves scope management, which necessitates risk assessments that require identifying uncertainty and so forth.

The key actors in the project development process—the people whose behaviors, attitudes, motivations, and savvy ultimately determine the project's fate—are contextualized throughout these various interconnected systems. The "people," in this sense, reflect the stakeholders invested in projects, including the project team, top management, functional department heads, and the customer—anyone whose effects can be felt by the project.

Historically, we know this scholarly evolution reflected something important. Look at the current state of research on projects in the leading academic journals, and the keywords that leap from the page include those that leave no doubt about the emphasis on human behavior in projects: optimism bias, commitment escalation, deviance normalization, resiliency, ethical leadership, pluralism, . . . The list goes on and on but always arcs in the same direction —toward how the human element is central to the fate of projects as they work their way through their development cycles.

Vijay Verma was one of the earliest project management scholars and consultants to recognize and advance the criticality of people management in projects. Some twenty-five years ago, his set of three books on the human aspects of project management charted a new and essential course forward in the field. It opened the eyes of many researchers and practitioners to both the importance of people management and the myriad ways people matter to projects and their success. Exploring ideas such as project team formation and evolution, organizational culture, leadership, human resource management, and organizational design, these books have stayed on every serious project management researcher's shelf since their original publication.

What makes this book so exciting to me is the timeliness of its introduction. *Leading with Purpose: Positive Power and Inspirational Influence* represents the collective wisdom of Vijay and Shiksha Verma and scholars who have long understood that project

Leading with Purpose

managers face a unique challenge in the discipline of management. Unlike most other organizational settings, project managers are often given maximum responsibility but minimal authority to manage their projects. Ultimate responsibility for success or failure rests with them, whereas their parent companies rarely couple that with the direct supervisory authority to push their directives. Hence, the challenge—how do you succeed at managing processes that offer the risk of being blamed for failure but rarely the right to "command and control" the organizational resources to make the project succeed?

The Vermas' book is a unique blend of the academic theory and the practical how-to advice so rarely found in the project management literature. This book is full of practical ideas with real-life examples, stories, and case studies. It presents guidelines to influence without authority, lead people and projects with purpose, and develop skills to create high-performance teams. Its effect will be felt at many levels within project organizations; that is, it will help senior management empower managers at all levels, minimize the negative impact of politics often created by the misuse of power, and create a culture of more collaboration, teamwork, and synergy. Discussing and explaining what it means to "influence without authority" and lead with purpose are essential for project and personal success in any organization.

I applaud Vijay and Shiksha Verma's achievement in this book. I found it a critical update on what we understand to be the inner workings of organizational power and stakeholder dynamics, especially as they apply to project settings. I appreciated how they packed the pages with insights, always drawing on theory and case examples. It perhaps will unsettle readers, as they are asked to reconsider topics or viewpoints they have long held sacrosanct, for example, "power is always corrupting, and only schemers play political games," or "influencing without authority is difficult." Someone had to tell this story, and it is to our great good fortune that those people are Vijay and Shiksha Verma.

—Jeffrey K. Pinto, PhD
Black Chair in the Management of Technology,
Black School of Business,
Penn State University, USA

Leading with Purpose

Preface

"Sword" and "words" use the same letters with the same effect if mishandled. We can compare "sword" with formal power and "words" with communicating to influence. Many people associate power (especially formal authority) with autocrats. The misuse of power and lack of influencing skills derail many projects despite proper planning and scheduling. Managers only develop skills to use power and influence for successful projects after many scars. Successful leaders recognize that power and influence are interrelated. They are essential to achieving extraordinary results in any organization.

We present the positive side of power and influence. You will read about ideas for leading by influencing without formal authority to deliver successful projects. We discuss the importance of leading people and projects with purpose. This book stresses using power and influence to achieve more synergy and teamwork.

Today, internal purpose does not drive many business leaders. They lack a powerful vision, leading to low commitment. We emphasize power and influencing in leading organizations to optimize performance and stakeholder satisfaction. Most leaders and managers deal with these topics:

- The greater the level of power managers possess and can skillfully wield, the more efficiently they can perform their duties.
- What the sources of power are and how managers can increase their power.
- Power is an ability to influence, and communication is the key to successful influencing.
- Managers need to adapt influencing tactics and styles to people and situations.
- Successful influencing works more effectively than command and control to achieve the most from people.

We like to share our knowledge and experience because knowledge is power. The more we share it, the more we get. Books are excellent media to do this —they allow us to reach many people we might not meet in person.

Many project leaders' comments about being unable to influence without authority motivated us to write a book to help leaders and managers in all industries. We especially want to help portfolio, program, and project managers meet organizational strategies and goals.

Preface

Our grandchildren inspired us to simplify this book's theme by comparing it with *Star Wars*. The Force in *Star Wars* equals power in this book. Formal power is the Force's dark side, and informal power is the Force's light side, which focuses on the larger community's well-being.

Managers who act like Siths use formal power with manipulation, deception, threats, and greediness to gain more power. Managers who use informal power focus on caring, developing better understanding, and sharing others' interests to increase performance. These leaders are the Jedi who prove effective leaders. They use informal power because of its four advantages:

1. No one can take away informal power.
2. Managers can increase informal power immediately on their own.
3. The more managers share informal power, the more they get.
4. The stronger foundation of informal power leads to opportunities for formal power or promotion.

When we began this book, we relied on Vijay's work experience and existing writings, such as a *Guide to the Project Management Body of Knowledge (PMBOK Guide®)* (PMI 2021).[1] We thought they would give us ideas and research about the dynamics of power, practical influencing tactics and styles, and effective leadership. However, we quickly realized that we were wrong. We needed to research more, discuss this topic with many business leaders and project management practitioners and educators, and develop ideas based on our practical experiences.

The knowledge we present translates into behavior that increases project success in all business sectors. This book should help everyone at all experience levels:

- Manage projects and initiatives to meet organizational strategies and goals
- Influence people without authority through effective communication
- Build good working relationships
- Work with different stakeholders and create synergy among them
- Lead people and projects with purpose

This book offers practical guidelines to influence without authority. You will learn to develop skills to create high-performance teams. It should help leaders empower managers at all levels, decrease the adverse effects of politics created by misusing power, and foster collaboration, teamwork, and synergy. Vijay covered politics—their dynamics and strategies to manage them—positively in his book *The Art of Positive Politics: A Key to Delivering Successful Projects* (Verma 2018).[2]

Organizational leaders and portfolio, program, and project managers will understand the dynamics of power to influence all stakeholders to lead with purpose and deliver successful results. Academics and educators in business schools and project management programs can use this book to develop a course to teach practical ideas about using power and influence positively. The concepts, ideas, and guidelines apply to initiatives and projects in all industries.

Acknowledgments

This book was a fun and interesting challenge. Vijay started the book by himself but quickly realized Shiksha's input would be valuable. It became our first big project together after Vijay's retirement. We wanted to spend more time with our grandchildren, so we needed self-motivation, perseverance, and discipline to write. Most people find it difficult to adopt these characteristics, and we are no exception. Fortunately, our family and many others in our professional lives encouraged us to stay focused and supported us throughout this project. Jaimini Thakore and Krupal Patel later worked on this book, as we saw the value in their contributions because of their knowledge and experience.

We are grateful to our special friend, R. Max Wideman, for his moral support and encouragement in writing this book. Vijay thanks participants from his classes and seminars on the human aspects of project management. Their many ideas and discussions helped frame our thoughts for this book. These discussions inspired us to highlight and recognize the importance of power and influence to help managers at all levels and industries learn the art of influencing without authority to deliver successful projects.

We thank Kevin Aguanno of Procept Associates Ltd. He recognized that power and influence are major in delivering successful projects. He considered our idea of positively presenting power and influence unique and exciting. Based on his many years of project management and publishing experience, he suggested we had many new, interesting concepts and excellent ideas to compile in a book.

We thank Raso Samarasekera, who transcribed the original draft and went through several revisions cheerfully. We also thank Adrian Watt for his help in preparing the figures and tables.

Susan Andres, an outstanding editor at MultiMedia Publications, Inc., pushed us to the finish line. She edited our manuscript, expressing our messages and ideas precisely. We value the many excellent discussions that kept this book practical and easier to understand. In addition, she was amazing in encouraging many new ideas for this book. We cannot express Susan's tremendous help while writing this book; we are thankful she did it with the highest standards of quality and cheer.

Finally, we are grateful to our son, Naveen, and his wife, Anita Misri, and our daughters, Serena and Angelee, who encouraged us, offered brilliant suggestions about better understanding people, and gave us the freedom to complete this book.

Introduction

Global competition, rapidly changing technology, and limited human resources with the proper skill mix characterize today's business environment. Project management is critical to business organizations, transforming their strategies and goals into an appropriate set of portfolios, programs, and projects. Management by Projects (MBP) has become a successful way to lead and manage an organization. Effective leadership and project management integration require combined project management, industry-specific, and people skills, including the strategic use of power and influence.

Project managers are under constant pressure to complete projects on time, on budget, and within specified quality constraints. Many are bogged down in project management's processes, methods, and procedures and do not develop good people skills. They should pay more attention to people and their well-being because people, not software packages and processes, do projects.

This book has three parts focusing on influencing without formal authority. They include the concepts and applications of power and influence to deliver successful projects. They deal with using power and influence to do things through people over whom managers have limited authority.

The book starts with project management's human side and covers the importance and dynamics of power and influence, dealing with:

- Strategies to increase power sources
- Power characteristics and outcomes
- Influencing strategies
- Two main dimensions and four styles of influencing
- Ten guidelines to increase power and influence

This book helps project managers address the challenges they often face in influencing their stakeholders.

Power, influence, and politics interrelate because all three are important to produce high performance. Power and influence interrelate in that power provides the capacity to influence, and influencing focuses on gaining cooperation and commitment (rather than just compliance) from others through effective communication. Influencing requires using power appropriate for the people and situations. It is

Introduction

important for creating synergy and gaining support and collaboration.

Power and politics are inseparable in that power is an ability to influence others to do what we want when we want and how we propose or agree. Power is necessary to navigate organizational politics. Politics are associated with how people use their power to manage politics and deliver successful projects. Politics are about seeking, acquiring, and maintaining power by using it appropriately.

Power and influence are important in project management, yet they are still confusing in practical terms. Power's dynamics are complex because they are based on perceptions. Therefore, project managers must understand the dynamics, recognize when they have power over others, and realize how people respond when they exercise their power over people.

Influencing accomplishes things in the project environment because project managers usually lack direct formal authority over project personnel assigned to them on a matrix basis. Influencing is important for project managers to:

- Get information (to make decisions)
- Get resources (people and financial)
- Get timely approvals (to stay on schedule)
- Get agreements (that will be carried through)
- Solve problems
- Gain cooperation and commitment
- Position for the future

Project managers must evaluate the situations and use influencing strategies and styles described in this book.

Leading with Purpose

Learning Objectives

This book starts with basic concepts and builds a sound foundation with practical examples to enhance people's potential. The book's organization centers on an in-depth discussion of power and influence, describing their dynamics, characteristics, and outcomes. Project managers must use power appropriately and influence stakeholders to manage portfolios, programs, and projects. No previous knowledge of power and influence is required. However, a keen interest in people skills and a quest to achieve extraordinary results from all stakeholders are useful to understanding and applying the concepts covered in this book.

 We divided this book into three parts. Part I, People and Project Management, is divided into three chapters. Chapter 1 discusses how projects move from strategies to results through portfolio, program, and project management. It examines project management's technical perspective and the human, or holistic, views of a project and project management. Chapter 2 presents a model for achieving the most from people, discussing four key people skills and the need for awareness of power, politics, and cultural elements. Chapter 3 emphasizes the need for the right people, the right structures for the project and the project team, and the right tools.

 Part II, Power and Project Management, is divided into four chapters. Chapter 4 explains power's dynamics, characteristics, and outcomes. The components of power—formal as opposed to informal—and using power and the five issues that surround it are looked at in chapter 5. Then, chapter 6 explores eight sources of power. Finally, chapter 7 looks at power

Introduction

and the project manager—total power, strategies to increase the sources of power, and balancing power.

Part III, Influence and Project Management, is divided into four chapters. Chapter 8 examines influence—its dynamics, importance in project management, and relationship with power. Then, chapter 9 presents models, dimensions, and styles of influencing. Chapter 10 offers strategies for influencing. Chapter 11 discusses using influence to build an effective team by understanding its characteristics and exploring ways to increase power and influence.

The reader-friendly organization of the topics in all chapters will help readers find information relevant to their interests. Figures and tables illustrate the concepts and ideas, and we highlight the main points in lists. We have included review and critical thinking questions at the end of each chapter to facilitate the use of this book as a course textbook for business management and project management programs.

After reading this book and relevant reference materials, readers will better understand:

- The importance of people to turn strategies into results
- A model for achieving the most from people
- The importance of champions, their key roles, and steps to find and sustain a champion
- Power's dynamics, characteristics, and outcomes
- Two components of power (formal and informal)
- Advantages of informal power and issues related to using power formally and informally

Leading with Purpose

- Eight sources of power and strategies to increase total power
- Techniques to increase and balance power
- The relationship between power and influence and the importance of influencing in managing people and projects
- Two main dimensions of influencing (convincing and connecting) and nine influencing strategies
- An overview of influencing models and styles and choosing the best style to fit people and situations
- Influencing to build high-performance teams
- Guidelines to increase power and influence

Besides these learning objectives, we include the following case studies related to each part of the book:

- Case Study 1: For Part I (Chapters 1–3): From Strategies to Results
- Case Study 2: For Part II (Chapters 4–7): Evaluating Power Level and Strategies to Increase Your Power
- Case Study 3: For Part III (Chapters 8–11): Influencing in Project Management
- Case Study 4: For Part III (Chapter 11): Team Dynamics of a Dragon Boat Team

Introduction

Part I: People and Project Management

Chapter 1. From Strategies to Results
    1.1. Achieving Strategies with Portfolio, Program, and Project Management (PPM)
    1.2. The Technical Perspective of Project Management
    1.3. The Human, or Holistic, Perspective of Projects and Project Management
    Chapter 1 Summary
    Chapter 1 Review and Critical Thinking Questions

Chapter 2. Achieving the Most from People
    2.1. Four Key People Skills
    2.2. External Influences
    Chapter 2 Summary
    Chapter 2 Review and Critical Thinking Questions

Chapter 3. People—The Key to Project Success
    3.1. The Right People
    3.2. The Right Structures for the Project and the Project Team
    3.3. The Right Tools
    Chapter 3 Summary
    Chapter 3 Review and Critical Thinking Questions

Part I: People and Project Management

The reasonable man adapts himself to the world; the unreasonable one persists in trying to adapt the world to himself. Therefore, all progress depends on the unreasonable man.

—George Bernard Shaw

Businesses face intense global competition, fast-changing technology and markets, the need to speed up R&D to market times, and multiple regulations. In addition, high labor costs in developed countries have led to the need to outsource many business operations to deliver programs and projects successfully. These include manufacturing, information technology (IT) (development and operations), and customer services.

Project managers face challenges in managing culturally diverse teams geographically dispersed worldwide. They must manage a multigenerational workforce from baby boomers to millennials, leading to more interesting challenges with different cultures, work ethics, beliefs, and attitudes toward life. They encounter additional challenges because of power struggles and politics among different business units, departments, project teams, and stakeholders.

This part focuses on the dynamics of power and influence and people skills in helping project managers influence stakeholders, manage politics, and lead their projects successfully. This part does not discuss the technical side of portfolio, program, and project management (PPM), including the relationships and interactions.

Chapter 1 defines portfolio and program management, emphasizing that organizations should align portfolio and program management with business strategies. Most business organizations strive to optimize benefits from projects and project management processes in today's global economy. People, not just processes and software packages, do projects. Therefore, we describe the human or holistic perspectives of projects and project management.

Project managers are primarily responsible for overall project integration, which requires good people skills. People are the backbone of most projects. Chapter 2 describes a model for achieving the most from people. This model has two components: (1) four key people skills (teamwork, leadership, communication, and negotiation) and (2) the awareness of external influences (power, politics, and cultural factors).

Chapter 3 illustrates how and why people are crucial to project success. People make things happen and prevent things from happening. This chapter describes successful project management's basic elements: (1) people, (2) project and project team structure, and (3) project management tools. The people category includes having the right project champions, project managers, and team members. We describe issues and challenges in having the right champions, project managers, and team members to optimize everyone's performance to deliver successful projects.

Power and influence are important topics in project management. However, the *Guide to the Project Management Body of Knowledge (PMBOK® Guide)* (PMI 2021)[1] does not discuss them in depth. *Power* is the ability to influence others to do things. Therefore, program and portfolio managers must learn to influence all stakeholders to reach desired outcomes for their organization.

The dynamics of power and influence are complex and vary from organization to organization. Project managers must understand their importance and learn the art of using them to deliver successful projects—this book's principal theme—along with effective leadership skills.

Leading with Purpose

Chapter 1

From Strategies to Results

> *Make no little plans; they have no magic to stir men's blood—make big plans, aim high in hope and work.*
> —Daniel H. Burnham

Business success depends on aligning programs and projects with strategies in the next decade. Therefore, Management by Projects (MBP) is becoming popular in managing an organization. Project management is meeting challenges and leading organizations in today's global economy. Business unit performance depends on:

- Creative leadership
- Strategic planning
- Effective execution
- Synergy among diverse project stakeholders

Leading with Purpose

Business leaders must first develop the organizational vision, mission, and strategies. Next, they should select a portfolio of programs and projects aligning with strategies and goals. The key to successful results is effectively managing the right portfolios, programs, and projects. To improve project management value, competent people must lead the project. *Resources* must be *assigned and improved continually*.

A *project* is a temporary effort to create a unique product, service, or result. "Temporary" implies a definite start and a definite end. "Unique" implies that the product or service distinguishes itself from similar products or services (PMI 2021).[1] People, not processes or software packages, do projects. Project managers must consider the holistic view of the project and project management.

This chapter defines portfolio and program management. It discusses effectively managing portfolios, programs, and projects to fit an organization's strategies and using a project management office (PMO). We examine the relationship between power and influence levels; portfolio, program, and project management (PPM); and the effect of power and influence, politics, and leadership on meeting goals and strategies in most organizations. We also look at project management from a technical perspective, three skills effective project management integration needs, and the human or holistic view of a project and project management.

1.1. Achieving Strategies with Portfolio, Program, and Project Management (PPM)

Good management consists of showing people how to do the work of superior people.
—John D. Rockefeller

Effective portfolio management with the right programs and projects is critical to meeting organizational strategies and goals. Senior management must ensure portfolios align with organizational strategies. Resources must be assigned and improved continually. The following are brief definitions of PPM (PMI 2021):[2]

1.1.1. Portfolios and portfolio management

Portfolio management is the key to meeting organizational strategies and goals.
—Vijay Verma

A *portfolio* is a collection of programs or projects and other work to efficiently manage all work needed to meet strategic business objectives. The portfolio's programs and projects might not tie directly to one another.

Portfolio management, a technique for centrally managing one or more portfolios, is an organizational approach to selecting, launching, and managing several programs and projects to meet goals. Each project must follow standard project definitions (temporary and unique) and may integrate with other projects in that program. As a result, a portfolio often provides benefits that would be unrecognizable with separately managed projects.

Typically, portfolios have several programs. The portfolio manager defines and oversees the assembly of programs and projects in that portfolio. Individual projects in portfolios often share strategic goals and might have dedicated project teams and project managers.

A *portfolio manager* focuses on the big picture or end state, not individual projects. In a health care institution, an IT portfolio might include three projects: (1) advance clinical uses, (2) integrate financial systems, and (3) manage the patient effect of the two large IT implementations. These projects affect different health care operations, yet they fit together in the same program and share an improved strategic vision.

1.1.2. Programs and program management

Program management is a centrally coordinated effort to achieve a program's strategic objectives and benefits.

—Anonymous

A *program* is a group of related projects coordinated to achieve benefits and control unavailable with individually managed projects. Programs may include related work outside the programs' discrete projects. A project might not be part of a program, but a program always has projects.

Program management refers to a program's centrally coordinated effort to achieve the program's strategic objectives and benefits. Program management focuses on projects' interdependencies and helps develop the best management approach.

1.1.3. Projects and project management

Operations keeps the lights on, strategy provides a light at the end of the tunnel, but project management is the train engine that moves the organization forward.

—Joy Gumz

A *project* is a temporary effort to create a unique product, service, or result. Project management applies knowledge, skills, tools, and techniques to meet project objectives. Programs and portfolios have projects that help achieve organizational goals. A group of projects in a program can have specific benefits. They can contribute to meeting program, portfolio, and organizational strategic objectives.

Some organizations use a PMO to coordinate and manage assigned projects centrally. Some organizations view a PMO as a body to manage projects throughout the business. The PMOs and their roles range from supporting project management roles (defining processes, guidelines, and standards) to controlling (requiring compliance for specific project management tools, methods, and frameworks) to directing (directly managing projects). A PMO's specific form, purpose, and structure depend on the organization's needs, maturity in project management, and commitment to MBP.

Leading with Purpose

Improving project management value

Senior management should address these questions to improve project management's value and benefits, (Norrie 2008, 18–31):[3]

- What are the desired outcomes?
- What areas should receive primary emphasis?
- What are the resource constraints?
- What should they do to encourage teamwork and make the best use of resources?

Table 1.1 outlines desired outcomes for most organizations and the focus on reaching those outcomes (Norrie 2008).[4]

	Desired Outcome	Emphasis/Focus
1.	Selecting the right programs and projects	Aligning with organizational strategies; timing and business opportunity
2.	Selecting PPM processes and practices	Aligning with organizational goals and priorities
3.	Doing projects the right way	Project management methodology and appropriate resource allocation (emphasis on managing budgets, schedules, and quality)
4.	**Doing projects with the right people**	**Proper skill mix, training, and teamwork**

Table 1.1. Improving Project Management Value

1—From Strategies to Results

Doing projects with the right people and stressing proper skill mix, training, and attitudes are important considerations to improve management value (Table 1.1 in bold). Several challenges arise in improving project management value and benefits. A strategy is key to selecting programs and projects to achieve the desired results. Prioritization, resource management systems, and project management processes must align with strategic goals. However, few organizations meet these challenges and address the items in Table 1.1.

Good project selection and the best project management practices are important guidelines for achieving organizational strategies. But managers rarely review the process and objectively transform strategies into significant projects. Little documented research exists on how business strategy translates into projects. Project management value and benefits improve with a better understanding of turning business strategy into PPM (Morris and Jamieson 2004).[5]

The project management approach differs in organizations. Most businesses run into problems when they try to fit one approach. However, project management processes and methods must start with organizational vision, mission, and strategies. A business must select programs and projects for the right reasons to meet corporate strategies and goals. Organizations face chaos and great financial losses when top executives' emotions and wishes decide on programs and projects. Poorly selected programs and projects lead to:

- Much negative energy
- Inefficient resource use

Leading with Purpose

- Frustration
- Lack of synergy
- Poor leadership

Unfortunately, this happens often in today's business environment.

Business leaders must first develop organizational strategies and then select programs and projects that align with them. Organizations must design strategies with genuine stakeholder participation to gain support and buy-in.

Total organizational human resources determine the capacity to meet goals and strategies. Businesses must use the strategies and goals to select and rank projects to enhance human and other resources. This approach leads to effective human resource management (HRM), creates unity of purpose, and better aligns with the big picture (Norrie 2008).[6] As Table 1.1 shows in bold, the right people are essential to delivering successful projects (Morris & Jamieson 2004).[7]

Leaders must understand the dynamics of power and politics. They need to channel people's energy positively, develop a culture of more collaboration and synergy, and develop project management processes and methods to meet corporate strategies and goals. Figure 1.1 shows how the levels of power and influence relate to PPM in most organizations. The levels of power and influence and requirements for leadership and political skills comprise four variables:

1–From Strategies to Results

1. Interaction among stakeholders
2. The frequency of interaction among stakeholders
3. Stakeholders' competing demands and agenda
4. Stakeholders' desire to reach an agreement

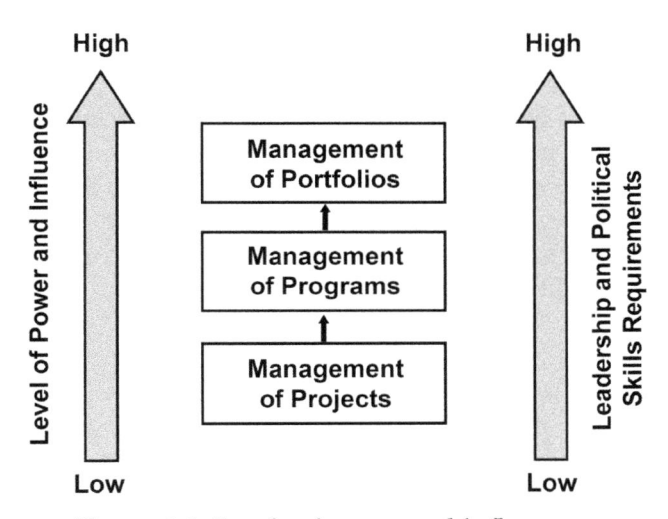

Figure 1.1. Levels of power and influence in project management.

Anytime people are involved, the dynamics of power are complex. Power and influence intensify as more people with diverse interests from different departments become involved and work in teams for various programs, and then for different portfolios. Leadership and political skill requirements also increase as you move from managing projects to programs to portfolios (Figure 1.1). Project managers face challenges in managing with some power and influence, which increases as they manage programs

49

Leading with Purpose

and then portfolios. The need to align with business strategies and improve resource constraints (quantity and skill mix) becomes more critical.

Figure 1.2 shows that power and influence, politics, and leadership affect PPM to get the needed business results. The dynamics of power, influence, and politics are difficult to understand. Their impacts and results are uncertain and complex, as the cloud illustrates. Therefore, effective managers must understand and analyze the dynamics of power and influence and develop proper political and leadership skills to manage portfolios, programs, and projects. Businesses must create an environment to lessen the inappropriate use of power and influence, negative politics, and ineffective leadership to compete in today's global economy.

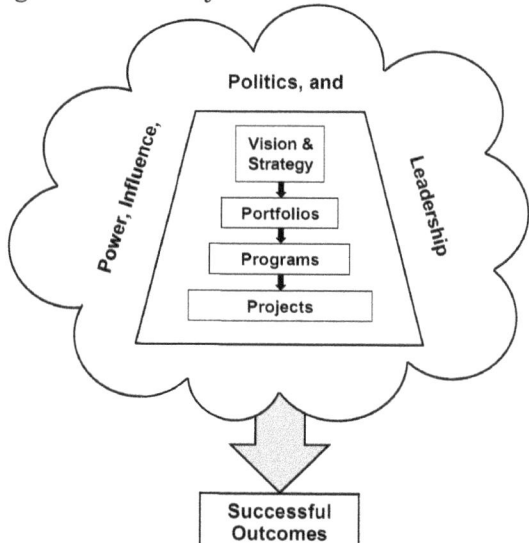

Figure 1.2. From strategies to results with power, influence, politics, and leadership.

1.2. The Technical Perspective of Project Management

> *Expect the best, plan for the worst, and prepare to be surprised.*
>
> —Denis Waitley

A good project manager tries to meet the requirements and exceed stakeholders' needs and expectations. Exceeding these expectations might involve balancing many competing demands, including the following (PMI 2021):[8]

- Scope, time, cost, quality, resources, and risk
- Stakeholders with differing needs and expectations
- Identified requirements (needs) and unidentified requirements (expectations)

A sincere effort to exceed identified requirements is the best strategy for success. The positive result leads to an improved reputation and increased opportunities for future business (PMI 2021).[9] Although organizations must address all demands, managing them in projects differs from managing them in ongoing operations. Therefore, MBP treats many pieces of ongoing operations as projects to apply project management principles and methods.

Project managers carry out project management by correctly applying and integrating five major process groups (PMI 2021):[10]

1. Initiating
2. Planning

3. Executing
4. Monitoring and controlling
5. Closing

Project management involves combining project management, business and industry-specific, and people skills. The *PMBOK® Guide* (2021) describes project management skills. Project managers gain industry-specific skills from practical experience working in a particular industry. Chapter 2 focuses on people skills. People skills include interpersonal skills:

- Influencing
- Communication
- Team building
- Motivation
- Conflict management
- Coaching
- Leadership

Project managers must understand these skills. They should educate and influence their stakeholders to gain their commitment. They should learn, develop, and practice these skills to manage and integrate projects effectively.

Competent project managers consistently integrate various project personnel and stakeholders' activities and efforts to meet project objectives. Figure 1.3 shows three skills needed to integrate project management successfully and three factors (organizational culture, project politics, and

1—From Strategies to Results

organizational politics) that influence proper execution of the skills (PMI 2021).[11]

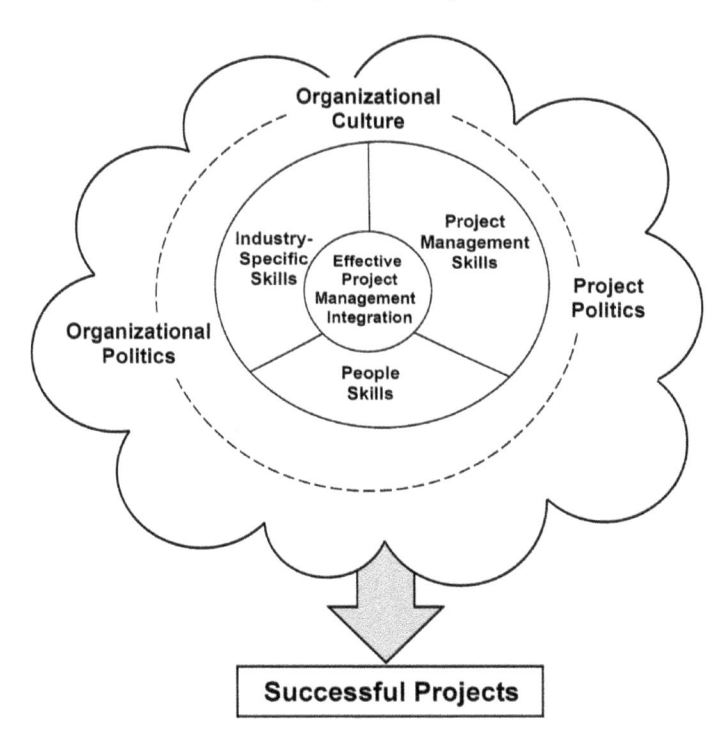

Figure 1.3. Three skills for effective project management integration.

1. Project management skills

In principle, project management skills are transferable. However, project managers must know the organization's internal and external cultures when applying these skills to manage work packages and project interfaces with stakeholders.

Internal culture refers to general practices and methods and varies by organization. For example, what works in a military organization might not work in a research environment. Stakeholders' *external culture* influences their opinions, beliefs, attitudes, and general viewpoints about communications, work ethics, and teamwork.

2. *Industry-specific skills*

These skills relate to specific industries and businesses, such as construction, utilities, information technology (IT), insurance, finance, pharmaceuticals, and airlines. Project managers develop these skills by working in these industries and applying them under company policies and procedures. Specific management practices and constraints often influence how projects are selected and managed. Project managers must also understand the internal culture to learn the organization of projects and how stakeholders work together to meet overall goals, constraints, and boundaries.

3. *People skills*

These skills are the most challenging project managers must learn, but they are critical to success. Good project managers recognize that people, not just project management processes and software packages, do projects. Politics are unavoidable because wherever there are people, there are politics. Project managers must recognize the dynamics and importance of power and politics and develop people skills to manage politics at all levels.

1–From Strategies to Results

These simple observations describe career progression for project managers in most corporations:
- Project managers are hired for their technical skills.
- Project managers are promoted for their interpersonal skills to integrate project activities and manage stakeholders.
- Project managers are fired because they lack leadership skills.

Awareness of internal and external cultures and general politics (Figure 1.3) influences the depth and breadth of each skill needed and its use in delivering successful projects. Therefore, project managers must understand these factors' basic concepts and dynamics and use them effectively to deliver successful projects.

1.3. The Human, or Holistic, Perspective of Projects and Project Management

*To accomplish great things,
we must not only act, but also dream;
not only plan, but also believe.*
—Anatole France

People, not processes or software packages, do projects. Therefore, project managers need to understand the human, or holistic, perspective of the project and project management.

1.3.1. The human, or holistic, perspective of a project

The quality of people and their thoughts, feelings, and actions influence the quality of project deliverables.

—Doug DeCarlo

Human connections mostly comprise projects. De Carlo (2004, 28–46) suggests we can think of projects as fields of *energy, actions, possibilities*, and *experiences* combined with verbal and nonverbal communications, negotiations, and relationships among project stakeholders. *Energy* represents the power and potential to do the work; actions are project stakeholders' tasks. *Possibilities* represent the results or project deliverables. *Experiences* represent either pleasant or unpleasant effects of good or bad or productive or nonproductive interactions with other project stakeholders.

Projects are a journey or a process throughout which people exchange thoughts and emotions to produce project deliverables. A project's physical output has two lives: (1) thoughts, emotions, and interactions, and (2) a tangible reality of deliverables. Deliverable quality depends on how harmonious and encouraging the project environment is to nurture high-quality thoughts, emotions, and interactions.

Projects are dynamic and alive. People prevent or enable accomplishments throughout a project. Project failure is likely if the project has a good plan but does not have enough positive energy—stakeholders lack sincere cooperation and collaboration. Therefore, project managers must create a collaborative environment that improves project success and the quality of thoughts, feelings, actions, and interactions.

Synergy is a key to project success. Project managers should focus on increasing the ability of team members and stakeholders to work effectively as a team to create synergy. When a project environment becomes toxic through negative thoughts, emotions, and interactions, the team members' ability to perform effectively decreases, leading to problems and poor deliverables (DeCarlo 2004, 28–46).[12]

The human, or holistic, perspective of project management stresses that project managers steer a project toward a successful conclusion by managing and helping the flow of these engagements (DeCarlo 2004, 28–46).[13] Thoughts produce:

- Ideas
- Decisions
- Facts
- Data
- Information
- Discoveries

Feelings can produce happiness, anger, and frustration. Negative feelings might drive people to engage in nonproductive behavior:

- Writing an aggressive email
- Criticizing people
- Cutting off communication with team members
- Not cooperating with team members

Leading with Purpose

Conversely, happy people interact effectively and find new ways to work together and support one another. Good thoughts and feelings lead to positive actions and outcomes. These might be productive meetings with creative ideas on flip charts, good hallway discussions leading to better decisions, and good bar conversations, producing diagrams and equations on napkins. These all lead to better:
- Project plans
- Project documents
- PowerPoint presentations
- Project deliverables

Interactions refer to communications in different forms that occur among project stakeholders to convey a message and information:
- Written memo or email
- Face-to-face
- Phone
- Audio/video conferencing

These communications increase emotional engagement and highlight creative thoughts, actions, and interactions of all team members and stakeholders, leading to the following (DeCarlo 2004, 28–46):[14]
- A unified, shared vision
- Synergy
- Enhanced performance
- High-quality deliverables

1.3.2. The human, or holistic, perspective of project management

The "P" in PM is as much about 'people' management as it is about 'project' management.

—Cornelius Fichtner

Holistically, project management is the art and science of facilitating and managing the flow of thoughts, feelings, interactions, and actions that produce valued outcomes (DeCarlo 2004, 28–46).[15] Projects in today's environments must operate under turbulent and complex conditions that feature:

- High speed
- Significant risk
- Long time to market
- Stress
- Constant pressures to change processes and products

Members with different backgrounds, norms, and expectations make up teams. Challenges further increase because of many geographically dispersed teams and the need to manage a multigenerational workforce. Project managers must also understand team members' cultures and capitalize on cultural differences.

High speed and high levels of change, uncertainty, and anxiety, and longer lead time to achieve desired results depict research environments. DeCarlo (2004, 28–46) developed an *extreme project management model* to get the best project results in R&D and uncertain environments.[16] Extreme project management is a technique to manage complex and unconventional projects constrained by uncertainties and ongoing changes in scope and politics.

Project management is not just about establishing a PMO that compiles a list of projects, develops a governance process, and establishes enormous methodologies, tools, and practices. PMOs are also excellent support systems. However, they should not create burdensome bureaucracy, project documentation, and overwork with little or no significant tangible results useful to customers. In an organization with ineffective PMOs, there is often much structure, bureaucracy, and paperwork but no actual results (DeCarlo 2004, 28–46).[17]

The quality of people and their thoughts, feelings, and actions influence the quality of project deliverables. The project environment is unhealthy without collaboration, cooperation, and trust among team members. Idea flow and communication effectiveness are restricted. Stakeholder interactions rapidly decline and turn to gossip, finger-pointing, withholding information, and sabotaging. The emotional states of the project team and stakeholders determine project output quality.

Pretty Gantt charts or rigidly defined processes threaten the product's quality and the project outcome. Stressing project management's human side means focusing more on creating an environment that fosters:

- Teamwork
- Cooperation
- Creativity

- Effective communication
- Positive politics

Projects should be guided from the top and managed from below, as stakeholders continually adjust to meet desired project results (DeCarlo 2004, 28–46).[18]

The people side is critical to innovation by establishing trust and confidence among stakeholders while addressing business questions and using tools, skills, and the environment to succeed (DeCarlo 2004, 28–46).[19] Emotional quotient (EQ) is more important than intelligence quotient (IQ) for project managers and leaders to succeed. This book underscores the importance of people skills, especially leading people and projects, by developing and using influencing skills rather than enforcing them. In addition, leadership through *commitment* (with proper support) is more critical to success than *command and control* are.

Chapter 1 Summary

Rapidly changing technology, economic uncertainty, and global competition characterize today's highly competitive and ever-changing business environment. Within this environment, organizations must deliver successful results continually to satisfy their investors and customers. High speed; high levels of change, risk, and stress; and longer lead time to get desired results also describe research environments. Organizations are adopting Management by Projects (MBP), which adds accountability and a systematic framework for planning and executing projects, to meet strategies and goals.

Leading with Purpose

Organizations feel constant pressure to develop sound strategies and the right portfolios to meet those strategies. As a result, business leaders must evaluate project management benefits and properly analyze cost benefits to optimize project management value organization-wide.

Some organizations use a project management organization (PMO) to manage assigned projects. A PMO's roles can range from supporting project management functions to controlling and directing the overall project management approach.

Political intensity increases as management moves from project to program and portfolio to the business strategy. Whenever and wherever people are involved, power dynamics are complex. The intensity of power and influence increases as we include more people with diverse interests from different departments and expect them to work in teams.

Portfolio managers must develop negotiating and people skills to influence stakeholders from different departments. In addition, they must raise their informal power to navigate politics positively and enhance their leadership skills to achieve synergy among stakeholders.

Effective project management integration requires combined industry-specific, project management, and people skills with a good understanding of internal and external culture and politics.

Project management's technical side includes structures, processes, and methodologies, but we must appreciate the human, or holistic, side. The people side is critical to successful project management by establishing trust and confidence among stakeholders.

Chapter 1 Review and Critical Thinking Questions

1. What questions should senior management address to improve project management's value in their organizations?
2. Identify desired outcomes and associated factors we should focus on to improve public investment value.
3. How do the levels of power, influence, and political skills change as project managers progress to portfolio managers?
4. Identify three important skills for project management integration. Describe external factors that must be considered.
5. Describe five major process groups in project management and the competing demands that must be balanced while managing projects.
6. How would you describe the holistic perspective of projects and project management? How does it differ from the traditional viewpoint of project management?
7. In your project management experience, identify your projects' fields of energy, actions, possibilities, and experiences.
8. How does a holistic project management perspective foster teamwork, creativity, cooperation, and commitment?
9. Why is the emotional quotient (EQ) more important than the intelligence quotient (IQ) for leading people and projects?

Leading with Purpose

Chapter 2

Achieving the Most from People

All things are created twice; first mentally, then physically. The key to creativity is to begin with the end in mind, with a vision and a blueprint of the desired result.

—Stephen Covey

People make things happen and prevent things from happening. They determine a project's success or failure. Verma (1995, 32–42) described an effective human resource management (HRM) model with three skills: (1) teamwork, (2) leadership, and (3) communication.[1] However, we cannot overlook the fourth skill of negotiation because negotiation is an important people skill to deliver successful projects. Negotiation is also important in developing and leading high-performance teams and communicating effectively with all stakeholders.

Leading with Purpose

In today's business world, good leaders, effective communicators, and strong team builders must have excellent negotiation skills to achieve win-win results and extraordinary results from ordinary people. To compete in today's global economy, we must optimize everyone's output in an organization. Unfortunately, most projects fail because of a lack of effective teamwork, leadership, communication, and negotiation. Besides these people skills, we should not overlook the external influence of power, politics, and cultural factors. The dynamics of these external influences are complicated.

People with diverse skills, personalities, and cultural backgrounds do projects. Power struggles, politics, and cultural differences will exist wherever people are involved. This chapter describes a model to achieve the most from all stakeholders using four skills, especially considering external influences.

A model for achieving the most from people

As shown in Figure 2.1, a model for achieving the most from people comprises two components:

1. Four people skills (teamwork, leadership, communication, and negotiation)
2. External influences (power, politics, and cultural factors)

The four people skills are easy to understand and learn. But the power, politics, and cultural factors are difficult to define, analyze, and manage because of their complex dynamics. Therefore, we show them in a cloud. Project managers must recognize external influences on all four people skills.

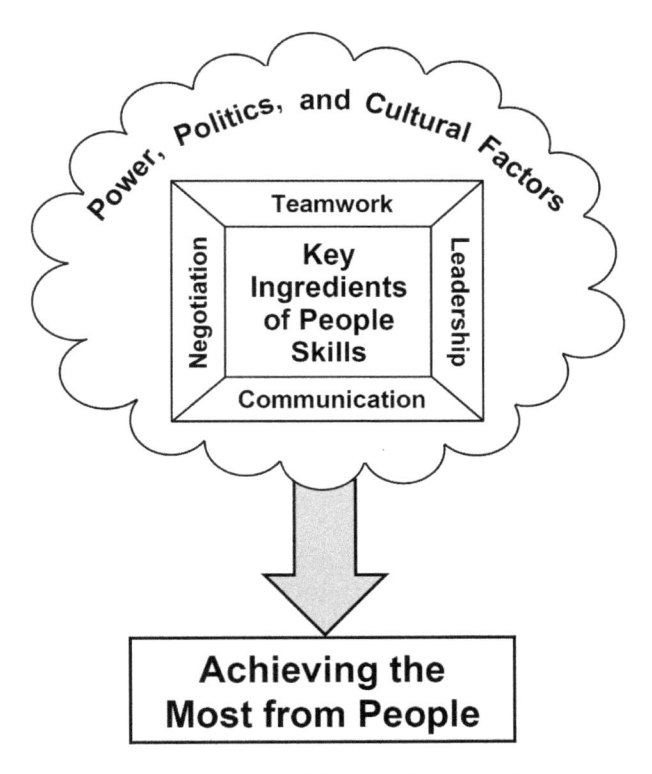

Figure 2.1. Model for achieving the most from people.

2.1. Four Key People Skills

> *I will pay more for the ability to deal with people than any other ability under the sun.*
> —John D. Rockefeller

Teamwork, leadership, communication, and negotiation, with politics and cultural aspects, are important because these factors' combined effect influences

Leading with Purpose

project stakeholders' performance. To achieve the most from people, project managers must understand the importance and concept of the four people skills mentioned in Figure 2.1. They must learn to apply these to fit people and situations to deliver successful results:

2.1.1. Teamwork

Snowflakes are one of nature's most fragile things, but just look at what they can do when they stick together.

—Anonymous

Teamwork varies by organizational culture, with an emphasis on working independently instead of interdependently. In addition, power struggles and politics affect cooperation quality, information sharing, and overall synergy among team members.

Teamwork provides unity of purpose, making it critical to achieve synergy among various stakeholders. Team members often come from diverse backgrounds, skills, and expertise. We must integrate this diverse mixture into an effective unit—the project team. Project managers must recognize the importance of team building to enhance team performance and nurture creativity and innovation.

Groups and teams differ. In a *team*, people work interdependently. Whereas in *groups*, people work independently. A team is an energetic group committed to achieving common objectives and working well together interdependently to produce high-quality results (Francis and Young 1992).[2]

2–Achieving the Most from People

Verma (1997, 89–101, 133–146, 194–195, 214–221) described major concepts related to the importance of teamwork and managing project teams:[3]
- Team dynamics and cultural diversity
- Team building and practical guidelines for effective team building
- Drivers and barriers to effective team building
- Inspiring top team performance
- Managing communication and leadership challenges in developing effective teams

Project teams are composed of members with diverse personalities and attitudes toward working as a team. Experienced project managers must identify constructive and destructive roles different team members play. Stuckenbruck & Marshall (1985, 48–49) described these roles:[4]

Constructive team roles:
- Initiators: "Let's do this . . ."
- Information seekers: "Don't we have better information?"
- Information givers: "My experience is . . ."
- Encouragers: "That was of great help."
- Clarifiers: "I believe we are saying . . ."
- Harmonizers: "I believe we are all saying the same thing."
- Summarizers: "I believe we can now agree on this."
- Gatekeepers (help others take part): "We haven't heard from the back of the room."

Destructive team roles:
- Aggressors (criticize and deflate others' status): "This is not a practical idea."
- Blockers (reject the views of others): "This will never work."
- Withdrawers (hold back and do not take part): "If you don't agree, you can do what you like."
- Recognition seekers (seek attention by monopolizing discussions): "I have done this many times successfully."
- Topic jumpers (continually change the subject): "Let's look at other options."
- Dominators (try to take over the discussion): "I am sure this is a way to go."
- Devil's advocates (bring up positive or negative alternative viewpoints): "Let's analyze the situation from this perspective . . ."

Working relationships affect individual and team productivity and the ability to satisfy the client. Project managers create an effective team and must develop the proper skills to do so. Project managers must motivate their teams and create an environment that facilitates cooperation by minimizing barriers to teamwork and synergy. They must also recognize and understand interpersonal and group dynamics to increase performance at individual and team levels. Most project personnel prefer to associate with a successful team. Most project managers are professionally satisfied if they create high-performance teams.

2.1.2. Leadership

The pessimist complains about the wind.
The optimist expects it to change.
The leader adjusts the sails.

—John Maxwell

Leadership varies by organizational culture (autocratic or participative). The dynamics of power and politics and the use of power and politics influence leadership quality. Leaders must develop their informal powers and mostly use their power informally. They should learn to manage politics at all levels to achieve better results.

Most project managers know through experience that different organizations have different work cultures. For example, the leadership styles that work in a university likely would not work in a post office because of the rigid structure. Similarly, the styles that work in a research organization cannot work in the military.

Project leadership is the ability to do things well through others and requires:
- A vision of the project goal
- Commitment and support from everyone to accomplish the goal
- A well-thought-out plan with a realistic schedule and budget
- Sufficient resources
- The ability to attract a good team and make it work throughout the project life cycle (PLC)

Leading with Purpose

Most researchers agree that vision is an important part of leadership. However, good leaders realize that a good vision without proper execution leads to disasters.

Pinto and Millet (1999) synthesized various leadership studies and indicated these important characteristics of good leaders:[5]

- Communicate well
- Are flexible and can respond to ambiguous situations while staying calm
- Work well with and through their team
- Influence and persuade well
- Capitalize on cultural differences
- Negotiate well
- Develop people

Verma (1996, 220–230) describes interesting issues about leadership:[6]

What makes successful leaders in terms of their attributes and skills?

Successful project leaders should have a well-balanced and appropriate set of attributes and skills:

Attributes (natural but also developable):

- Confident in envisioning and comfortable in leading
- Team player/leader
- Emotionally stable
- Trustworthy
- Accessible

2–Achieving the Most from People

Skills (can be learned and must be practiced properly):
- Communication and motivation
- Team building
- Creative problem-solving
- Analysis and conflict resolution
- Administration

Differences between a leader and a manager

Project management is a subset of project leadership. To be effective, project managers must have excellent leadership skills, especially emphasizing people skills to manage project stakeholders. Leadership and management are interesting topics in project management literature. The following are three important questions in this context:

1. What are the differences between a leader and a manager?

Verma and Wideman (1994, 627–633) concluded that leaders and managers mainly differ in that leaders emphasize effectiveness (doing the right things), and managers emphasize efficiency (doing things right).[7] The other differences between a leader and a manager are shown in Table 2.1.

Leading with Purpose

Leaders Emphasize	Managers Emphasize
• Being effective	• Being efficient (doing things right)
• Goals and results	• Processes and tools
• Long term	• Short term
• Top line (people)	• Bottom line (budgets and schedules)
• Unidentified requirements (go beyond the project scope and specifications)	• Identified requirements (just meet the project scope)
• People and relationships	• Tasks and methods
• **Doing the Right Things**	• **Doing the Things Right**

Table 2.1. Differences Between a Leader and a Manager

2. Which one is more important, and why?

Both leadership and management are important to delivering successful projects. However, if we must choose which is more important, we choose leadership. Leadership is more important because it emphasizes doing the right things. If we do not have good leadership but only good management, we might do the wrong things efficiently, leading to chaos and disaster. The key is to balance leadership and management to deliver successful projects.

Both qualities in a person are rare but highly desirable. Leadership traits come from the brain's left side, and management comes from the right side. To achieve good balance, good leaders should learn to be good managers or fill that gap by having good managers work with them. Similarly, effective managers should learn people and leadership skills to develop a vision and inspire team members to achieve high performance. To develop the art of balancing both, we must lead from the brain's right side and manage from the left side.

3. How do leadership and management relate to the PLC?

We must balance leadership and management to achieve project success. To relate this to the PLC, we must emphasize leadership during the conceptual and development phases when we define the project vision and develop the front-end plan. However, we must emphasize management more during the execution and finishing phases, where we must use resources efficiently to meet quality standards and schedules.

Often, even when well-run, 95 percent of the project finishes on schedule, and the last 5 percent is never finished or takes much more time, money, and effort. Companies must deliver 100 percent of the project (not just 95 percent) to be paid and earn a high reputation to get repeat business. Therefore, to be more practical, we need managers as strong administrators toward the project's end to ensure it does not slip in cost and schedule during the last 5 percent.

Leadership and management differ. We should emphasize leadership more during the conceptual and development phases and management more during the execution and finishing phases. To meet competition in today's tough global business environment, we must be first good leaders, then good managers. First, define the right things to do, then develop a plan to do the right things the right way.

Leading with Purpose

2.1.3. Communication

The kind words can be short and easy to speak, but their echoes are truly endless.

—Mother Teresa

Communication is affected by the organization's internal culture and the external culture of employees from different nationalities and cultures because of the high nonverbal component. Politics and communication are highly interrelated. We must be careful about written or verbal communication and plan how we say things to avoid political trouble.

Communication—exchanging and sharing information with a common set of symbols, signs, or behavior—is critical to a project's success. Project managers use communication more than any other skill to ensure team members work together to resolve issues and inspire participants' high performance. Sievert (1986, 77) emphasized communication's importance in project management and suggested that a breakdown in communication causes most friction, frustrations, and poor working relationships among stakeholders.[8]

Project managers must create communication channels to allow open communication and foster creativity, team spirit, openness, and integrity. Project managers should avoid negative and absolute statements. Instead, they should use positive, collaborative, or open-ended sentences to increase cooperation and better working relationships. Styles of communication include:

- Free form as opposed to following the chain of command
- Formal as opposed to informal
- Sharing information freely as opposed to withholding information

Project managers must evaluate the situation and use an appropriate communication style to communicate effectively with various project stakeholders. Project managers must evaluate the barriers to effective communication Verma (1996, 24–25) described and act to avoid them.[9]

Importance of communication's nonverbal component

Communication effectiveness varies with the cultural backgrounds of people from different nations, regions, and ethnicities. One reason is that three factors (words, vocal tones, and body language) contribute to the message's impact. Albert Mehrabian (1968, 53–55) asserted:[10]

Total message impact =
Verbal or Words (7%) + Nonverbal (93%)

The nonverbal component that accounts for 93 percent breaks down as

38% (vocal tones) + 55% (body language)

as shown in Figure 2.2.

Leading with Purpose

Verbal	Nonverbal
Content/Words	Vocal Tone · Body Language
7%	38% · 55%

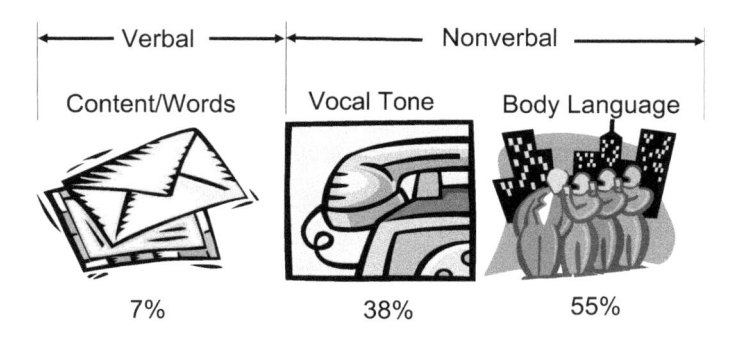

The Verbal (7%) is understood better if the Nonverbal (93%) conveys the same message.

Figure 2.2. Communication components.

Mehrabian's findings imply that the major impact is from nonverbal factors (up to 93 percent), and words count only 7 percent. Most of us have experienced that body language signals, which account for the highest impact (55 percent), vary in different cultures. Therefore, we must have as much FaceTime as possible when interacting with people to understand their message well by properly paying attention to their vocal tones and body language.

With today's technology and pace of change, most of us communicate with our project stakeholders by email. Project managers must compensate for losing 93 percent (38 percent for vocal tones and 55 percent for body language) of the total message impact when communicating by email. Many project managers have a set of guidelines for writing effective emails.

Face-to-face communication is better than email to clarify the situation when conveying a message about poor performance or raising an issue that people might interpret as finger-pointing. However, when emotions are high, some might like to vent by writing an aggressive or angry email, which they should not immediately send. The chances are that after they read it calmly, they will decide not to send it. Most people recognize this technique as good therapy and a way to cool down and handle such situations more carefully than meeting face-to-face.

Email can be useful for documenting project issues to track later. However, we should use emails carefully, as aggressive emails can affect working relationships negatively.

Importance of listening

Communication has four major components:
1. Speaking
2. Reading
3. Writing
4. Listening

Contemporary education continuously reinforces speaking, reading, and writing. In contrast, communication's most important component, listening, gets the least formal education and training. Verma (1996, 40–48) described the importance of listening, verbal and nonverbal listening behaviors, barriers to effective listening, and guidelines for active listening.[11]

Listening is communication's most important component. Attentive listening is crucial for successful project management. Often, companies hire project managers for their strong technical skills. However, they require excellent communication skills, especially active listening skills, to manage their projects effectively. Project managers should

Leading with Purpose

spend more time listening and less time speaking to their stakeholders, clients, and team members to better understand their issues and concerns (Verma 1996, 40–48).[12]

Table 2.2 illustrates that to improve attentive listening, we must keep our EARS open:

- Evaluate the message
- Anticipate actions to be taken
- Review the message with the sender to confirm the meaning and intent
- Summarize to confirm the message is understood correctly

	Keyword	Addresses the Question
E	Evaluate	Is the information relevant and valid?
A	Anticipate	What does the presenter want done?
R	Review	What did the presenter mean?
S	Summarize	Does the receiver understand the whole message correctly?

Table 2.2. Improving Attentive Listening

Communication is complex, but good communication leads to effective leadership, interface management, integration, and top team performance. Therefore, project managers should remove barriers to communication and choose a communication style based on the other party's preferred style and the situation. This approach ensures the sender delivers a clear message that the recipient receives.

2.1.4. Negotiation

We must learn to explore all the options and possibilities that confront us in a complex and rapidly changing world. We must learn to welcome and not fear the voices of the dissent.
—J. W. Fulbright

Cultural factors influence negotiation. Therefore, we must learn and capitalize on cultural differences to reach win-win solutions. The power we have and its use influence the negotiation process and strategies. The dynamics of politics and the quality of relationships with stakeholders also contribute to negotiating styles. Negotiation is essential to achieve good teamwork and effective leadership.

Negotiation is a process through which parties with shared and opposing interests agree through communication and compromise. Negotiation, to get what we want from others, is part of life in most business environments. Negotiation is critical to all project managers because negotiating involves bargaining with people about resource transfer, information generation, and accomplishment of activities in project environments. Project managers negotiate with these stakeholders:

- Functional managers, work package managers, upper managers, and other project managers (about resources, responsibilities, and project priorities)
- Clients (about changes in scope, schedule, budget, and performance standards)

- Team members (for issues about project management processes, methods, and results throughout the PLC)
- Suppliers (about delivery and prices of materials and services)

Effective negotiation is a fact of life. Therefore, all leaders and managers must learn the art of negotiation — persuading people through effective communication to agree with other stakeholders—as an important people skill. We must understand the principles of negotiation, common methods of negotiation, and the negotiation process (Fisher & Ury 2011; Verma 1996, 146–153, 161–162):[13]

Principles of negotiations

Project managers should follow these four principles to reach successful negotiations:

1. **Separate people from the problem.** Avoids misunderstandings and the endless cycle of actions and reactions.
2. **Focus on interest and not on position.** Position means what we want; interest means why we want it.
3. **Generate options that advance shared interests.** Encourages both parties to work together to develop options for mutual gain.
4. **Base results on objective criteria.** Avoids positional bargaining and pressure.

Common methods of negotiations

There are two dimensions of negotiating: (1) goal emphasis and (2) relationship emphasis. There are three common methods of negotiating based on these two dimensions:

1. **Hard negotiation.** Both parties take strong positions, often as adversaries. The primary goal is to win, with less emphasis on relationships.
2. **Soft negotiation.** There is more emphasis on relationships and avoiding conflicts. During negotiations, the atmosphere is friendly, sensitivity is shown to feelings, and confessions are readily made to maintain relationships.
3. **Principled negotiation.** This negotiation method implies being hard on merits and soft on people, using a problem-solving approach that can usually be applied.

Negotiation process

The process of negotiation involves three stages:

1. **Pre-negotiation stage.** Focuses on planning how to conduct negotiations. We should take these actions at this stage:
    - Gather information (represents requirements of both parties)
    - Analyze and evaluate information (for risks, strategies, and tactics)
    - Prepare for negotiation (determine location, timing, and so on)

2. **Negotiation stage.** Refers to working out details and agreeing. Take these actions during this stage:
    - Protocol (physical environment, dress, and cultural issues)
    - Probing (identify issues, interests, and options)
    - Tough bargaining (move from position to interest)
    - Closure (written agreements with implementation plan)
    - Agreement (clear, fair, and free of threat, fear, and coercion)

3. **Post-negotiation analysis.** Refers to evaluating how successful the process and outcome were. Actions during this stage:
    - Evaluate how well we did in the pre-negotiation stage and negotiations and how we can improve
    - Evaluate how well prepared we were and what preparation was needed

Tips for successful negotiations
Negotiation is persuading or influencing the other party to accept our terms, which requires gaining information about the other party's interests and needs. Therefore, preparation and effective communication are the keys to successful negotiations. The following are a few tips for successful negotiations:

- Use the four principles of negotiation to manage projects and initiatives.

2–Achieving the Most from People

- Use principled negotiations.
- Follow actions related to the three stages of the negotiation process.
- Analyze culture's impact on negotiations.

Project managers must use an appropriate mixture of four people skills to deliver successful projects in a comparative global economy. Different generations like to communicate differently (written, verbal, informal, electronically, emails, text messaging, and so on), feel motivated differently, and like to be rewarded differently. Project managers and leaders must consider the workforce's traits, characteristics, strengths, and limitations from different generations. In this work environment, they must develop and use skills to achieve good teamwork, effective communication, successful leadership, and win-win negotiations.

2.2. External Influences

If everyone is thinking alike, someone is not thinking.
—General George Patton, Jr.

International politics and today's global economy pose interesting teamwork, leadership, communication, and negotiation challenges. Virtual teams with team members at different sites do extensive project work in today's global economy. Sometimes, team members are in the same country, and sometimes, companies outsource work to personnel in different countries. In such cases, project managers face challenges associated with different cultures, time zones, work ethics, quality standards, expectations, and motivational factors.

Project managers must identify communication, teamwork, negotiation, and leadership challenges and learn skills to manage and lead virtual teams. Workforce diversity also influences teamwork, leadership, communication, and negotiation issues. For example, a multigenerational workforce (from baby boomers to Generation Y) differs in mindset, outlook, work-life balance, expectations, curiosity, and knowledge and proficiency in using modern technology.

Effective project managers have various people skills in their toolbox, and cultural factors greatly affect leadership styles. For example, in some cultures, such as dictatorships, autocratic leadership is acceptable and often expected. This acceptance contrasts with North American or Western European cultures, where a participative style is preferred. People expect their leaders to seek input, then evaluate and incorporate it to prepare final plans and decide. Project leaders must appreciate and capitalize on cultural differences to optimize different stakeholders' performance. They must understand the dynamics of power, influence, and politics. They must develop skills to use their power effectively and manage politics at all organizational levels to achieve better outcomes.

Cultural factors are important in conducting negotiations. Therefore, project managers must follow the discussed principles and actions for each of the three negotiation stages and capitalize on cultural differences to achieve win-win solutions.

2.2.1. Power and politics

> *Pay special attention to powerful stakeholders.*
>
> —Vijay K. Verma

Project managers must understand the dynamics of power and politics to meet challenges when dealing with stakeholders because politics are inevitable when managing projects. Figure 2.3 shows that power combined with politics results in successful project management (Verma 2018, 52–53).[14]

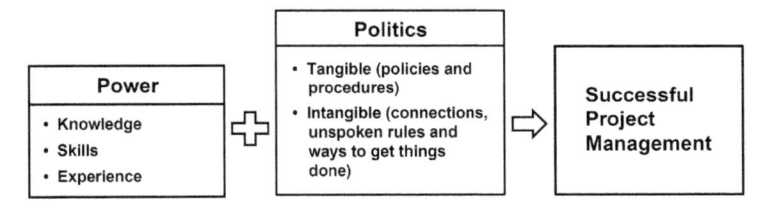

Figure 2.3. Power and politics in project management.

Politics are complex because influencing skills for managing conflicts are individualized. Power enables project managers, who usually have great responsibility but no formal authority, to influence stakeholders. Unfortunately, politically naive project managers depend too much on the tangible component of politics and believe knowing policies and procedures is sufficient.

Project managers must increase their total power composed of formal and informal power. *Formal power* refers to the power granted by position in the organizational chart, whereas *informal power* refers to what project managers earn based on their knowledge and experience.

To manage politics, project managers must remember the three steps of seeking, acquiring, and maintaining power. Project managers lose their power and cannot maintain it if they use it inappropriately (Verma 2018, 54–61).[15]

Project managers must analyze their political landscape and understand stakeholders' three political positions (Naives, Sharks, and Politically Sensibles) in viewing and dealing with politics and managing their people and projects (Verma 2018, 212–241).[16] Project managers should understand and manage various political behaviors with their impacts on project performance (Verma 2018, 243–302).[17] They should have the skills to manage politics related to organizational, leadership, and project management issues at the senior management level. They should also learn to manage politics regarding project management and team leadership issues, stakeholder management issues, and issues related to managing upward (Verma 2018, 331–413).[18]

2.2.2. Cultural factors

*People have one thing in common;
they are all different.*

—Robert Zend

The cultural environment can affect project managers' ability to optimize project stakeholders' performance. It influences the effectiveness of the four people skills: teamwork, leadership, communication, and negotiation.

2–Achieving the Most from People

Many global projects involve joint ventures and team members from various countries, increasing the complexity and challenges of managing global projects. Project managers must develop project management styles and strategies for global projects. Management of any project requires effective planning, organizing, and controlling. Managing international projects poses additional teamwork, leadership, and communication challenges because of team members' diverse cultural backgrounds and geographic placement. Project managers must know the major elements of culture, including material culture, language, aesthetics, education, religious beliefs and attitudes, social organizations, and political life.

Dean Martin (1981, 450–453) identified seven major elements of culture that project managers should know, as shown in Table 2.3.[19]

Project managers must identify and manage cultural differences when dealing with global team members, focusing on cultural diversity rather than ignoring cultural differences. Verma (1997, 89–100) summarized various factors influenced by culture:

- The power distance index (dealing with inequality and dependence in relationships)
- Individualism as opposed to collectivism
- Masculinity and femininity
- Uncertainty avoidance
- Time horizon[20]

Leadership and management are important in project management. Effective project leaders must learn the art of balancing both to achieve overall project success. Team building should focus on

	Elements of Culture	Examples
1.	Material organization	• Physical objects or technologies created by people. • Tools, skills, work habits, attitudes toward work and time.
2.	Language	• Mirror of culture and primary medium of communication. • Phrases, gestures, and expressions that others might interpret differently (even within a language).
3.	Aesthetics	• Art, music, dance, literary traditions, related customs, and artifacts.
4.	Education	• Transmission of knowledge. • How people approach problems and relate to others.
5.	Beliefs and attitudes (including religion)	• Vital component of culture. • "Mainspring" of culture; it influences other elements of culture, including dress, eating habits, attitudes toward work, punctuality, and work site.
6.	Social organization	• Organization of negotiators into groups and structuring of activities to accomplish goals. • Family relationships, labor unions, social clubs, other social groups that influence attitudes and values. • Classes of society.
7	Political life	• Government's concerns related to the project, such as profit, legality of transactions, number of jobs created, treatment of its people, safety, environmental concerns, and immigration issues. • Important when governments are involved.

Table 2.3. Major Elements of Culture

developing the skills, attitudes, and potential of team members with diverse backgrounds, experiences, and interests by sharing information, cross-training, and creative leadership. The cultural environment and organizational politics influence how people work together, with differing perceptions about work, project management function, and human relationships.

Communication is the key to successful project management through managing cultural diversity and politics. Project managers must recognize the importance of verbal and nonverbal and formal and informal communication components. In addition, they must develop active listening skills to gain stakeholder cooperation and commitment.

Chapter 2 Summary

People with diverse skills, experiences, and cultural backgrounds do projects. Therefore, project managers must optimize all project participants' output with project management and people skills to deliver successful projects. This chapter describes a model with the principal components of four people skills and external influences to achieve the most from people.

The dynamics of external influences are complex and unpredictable. Because these affect the four people skills, project managers must understand these dynamics and adapt their team building, leadership, communication, and negotiating strategies to fit people and situations.

The combined effect of teamwork, leadership, communication, and negotiation, with politics and cultural aspects, influences project stakeholders' performance. Therefore, project managers must understand the importance and concept of the four people skills and apply these to fit people and situations to deliver successful results.

Teamwork integrates diverse backgrounds, skills, and expertise into an effective unit. This chapter described major concepts related to the importance of teamwork and managing project teams.

Project leadership requires a vision of the project goal, commitment and support from everyone to accomplish it, a well-thought-out plan with a realistic schedule and budget, sufficient resources, and the ability to attract a good team and make it work throughout the project life cycle (PLC). This chapter shared Pinto's synthesis of the important characteristics of good leaders and Verma's issues about leadership.

Leaders and managers differ mainly because leaders emphasize effectiveness, and managers emphasize efficiency. The key to successful projects is balanced leadership and management. Leadership and management relate to the PLC. We must emphasize leadership during the conceptual and development phases and management more during the execution and finishing phases.

Communication is critical to a project's success. An organization's internal culture and the external culture of the people working in the organization who come from different nationalities and cultures affect communication. Project managers use communication more than any other skill, and a breakdown in communication causes most friction, frustrations, and poor working relationships among stakeholders.

Project managers must create channels for open communication. They must also choose appropriate styles and avoid barriers to effective communication.

Both verbal and nonverbal components are important for effective communication. Nonverbal is composed of vocal tones and body language. Therefore, three main factors contribute to the total message impact. Total message impact = Verbal or Words (7%) + Nonverbal (Vocal Tones (38%)) + Body Language (55%)). We must interact with people face-to-face as much as possible to understand their message by properly paying attention to their vocal tones and body language. Most of us communicate with our project stakeholders by email. Email can be useful for tracking project issues, but aggressive emails can affect working relationships negatively.

The most important component of communication is listening. Yet, it gets the least attention in formal education and training. To improve listening, we must keep our EARS open.

All leaders and managers must understand the principles of negotiation, common methods of negotiation, and the three stages of the negotiation process discussed in this chapter.

International politics and today's global economy pose interesting challenges, and project managers must learn skills to manage and lead virtual teams. In addition, today's diverse workforce influences teamwork, leadership, communication, and negotiation issues. As a result, effective project managers have various people skills in their toolboxes.

Power, politics, and cultural factors greatly affect leadership styles. A project manager's total power comprises formal and informal power. Therefore, they must understand the three political positions stakeholders may hold.

Leading with Purpose

The cultural environment in today's project world influences the four people skills and stakeholder performance. Project managers must know this chapter's major elements of culture and the factors they heavily influence.

Chapter 2 Review and Critical Thinking Questions

1. Describe four key people skills and external factors covered in this chapter with the most from people in your projects.
2. What are the constructive and destructive team roles played by team members? How would you capitalize on constructive roles and minimize the impact of destructive roles?
3. What is the difference between leadership and management? Which one is more important and why?
4. How are the leadership and management related to the project life cycle (PLC)?
5. Identify three main types of communication and their relative importance in evaluating the total message impact and effectiveness.
6. Why is listening important for effective communication? How would you improve attentive listening to communicate effectively with stakeholders?
7. What is negotiation? Describe four principles, three common methods, and five types of negotiations.

8. What are the three stages of negotiation? Identify the key items covered in each stage and how you would prepare for each stage to negotiate effectively and reach win-win solutions.
9. Identify external influences and their importance in project management.
10. What is the importance of power and politics in project management? What political skills do you need, and how would you improve those in managing your projects effectively?
11. Why are cultural factors important in managing projects? Identify the major elements of culture. What would you do to capitalize on the cultural differences among your stakeholders?

Leading with Purpose

Chapter 3

People: The Key to Project Success

Get the right people. Then, no matter what else you might do wrong after that, the people will save you. That's what management is all about.

—Tom DeMarco

People are the backbone of any organization and its most important resource. People define and execute organizational strategies, market products and services, and manage any organization's finances. Therefore, one of the toughest challenges in managing a project is managing the people.

The most important skill is managing people, including communicating, motivating, negotiating, and managing conflict. Experienced project managers with good people skills can use their influencing, team building, and creative leadership skills to motivate people and produce extraordinary results. People overcome challenges and issues associated with

Leading with Purpose

organizational structures and software packages to manage projects if they are committed and work as a team.

This chapter describes important elements of successful project management. These elements are critical because they emphasize special skills are required to anticipate and handle people issues. Most projects fail not from a lack of good software packages and organizational structures but because of politics and the lack of people with the right skills and attitudes. Politically sensible managers with good people skills believe successful project management's elements relate to people, project and project team structures, and project management tools.

Elements of successful project management

Effective project managers recognize that successful management requires more emphasis on people than on project and project team structures and tools. Successful project management's elements (Figure 3.1 (Verma 2000–2013))[1] can be divided into three categories:

1. People (project champions, project managers, and team members)

Having the right project champions involves understanding champions' key roles, finding and keeping them, and recognizing that they need the appropriate positional power to be effective. Having the right project managers relates to understanding how project managers are perceived and what makes a successful project manager. Project managers should always have people with skills that best match their assigned tasks.

2. Project and project team structures (functional, matrix, and projectized)

Project team members must have the proper skill mix and attitudes toward teamwork, regardless of the project's structure. Team members must commit to helping one another improve overall project success.

3. Tools (processes, methods, and project management software packages)

Experienced project managers recognize that although processes, methods, and software are important, they cannot substitute for people skills, practical knowledge, and experience to manage a project.

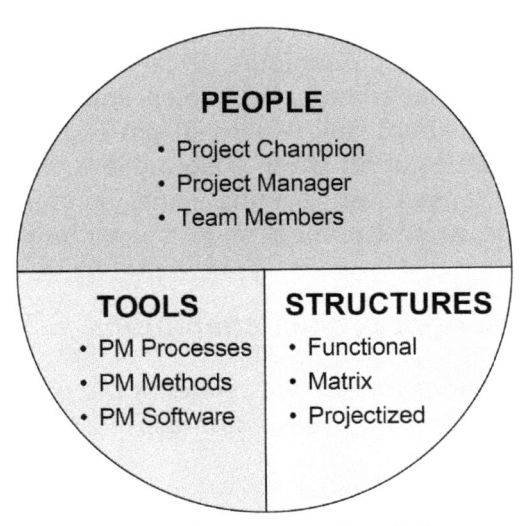

Figure 3.1. Three categories of elements for successful project management.

3.1. The Right People

Of all the things I have done, the most vital is coordinating the talents of those who work for us and pointing them towards a certain goal.

—Walt Disney

As shown in Figure 3.1, the importance of people for successful projects creates a need for the right people. The right people come in three forms (Verma 2000–2013):[2]

1. The right project champions
2. The right project managers
3. The right team members

This section discusses the people category, including project champions, project managers, and project team members, their roles and responsibilities, and practical tips to strengthen each. It covers the importance of all three stakeholders with associated challenges in finding and keeping good champions, project managers, and team members.

3.1.1. The right project champions

Champions are the backbones of the project and project manager.

—Vijay Verma

Most project managers think champions find funding for the project, and they often consider project sponsors for their champions. However, this is not necessarily true. The right champion is key to successful project management, especially from a political viewpoint. In reality, sponsors might not be good champions.

Key roles of a champion

The champion's position is not labeled in a box on the organization chart, but a champion must fulfill these two key roles (Verma 2000–2013):[3]

1. **Have a vested interest.**
   Project champions must have and show a vested interest in the project. They should want the project and the project manager to succeed.

2. **Remove obstacles and roadblocks as needed.**
   Champions must use a combination of organizational authority, power, and persuasive skills to remove roadblocks the project manager faces. They should have enough formal and informal power or connections with those with the right power mixture to "go to bat" for the project manager to remove project obstacles. In addition, they must help manage the project scope and fight for the main concerns and right resources to meet project objectives quickly.

Both roles are important, but the second is more crucial to dealing with politics that might derail the project. Project managers often encounter issues with project champions' roles and political savvy, especially their ability to remove project roadblocks. They must understand champions' responsibilities and their strengths and limitations.

Project sponsors naturally fit the first role of project champion—having a vested interest in the project outcomes—because they usually secure project funding, and the project's outcome affects them. Their interest in the project should motivate them to help the project manager succeed. However, project managers must be cautious because sponsors might not always be effective champions, especially when filling the second role of removing obstacles. Sponsors might be ineffective because they:

- Lack proper positional authority
- Lack the appropriate mixture of interpersonal and influencing skills
- Do not know how to use their power effectively
- Lack network power

Often, project managers face many challenges and difficulties in managing their projects and stakeholders if they do not have a good champion. Project managers must realize when their sponsors cannot resolve the project's problems and are too weak to be real champions. Project managers recognize such situations when encountering difficulties, commonly when organizational politics are outside their expertise and authority. In such cases, they should develop alternative strategies to resolve their problems.

Besides having the right interpersonal skills, project champions must know when and how to use these skills and their power effectively. Project champions should have good network power to gain support from the right people with enough positional power and influencing skills to remove obstacles.

They might not be directly involved in the project daily, but they must be informed regularly about the project to play both roles discussed when necessary.

Sometimes, project managers can be their project's champions. They must understand and manage politics effectively to meet project objectives rather than using them for selfish purposes. They must recognize that different project stakeholders have different priorities:

- The client focuses on the deliverables and outcomes.
- The project team focuses on quality, schedule, and cost.
- Contractors focus on payment and future business.

Steps to find and sustain the right champion

The lack of a good champion exposes us to political problems that might derail our project despite good planning and hard work. Therefore, project managers must find good project champions and maintain good relationships. Table 3.1 shows four steps to finding and maintaining a champion with suggestions (Verma 2000–2013).[4]

Leading with Purpose

	Steps	Suggestions
1.	Look for champions.	Look among senior management, advisory committees, and priority
2.	Convince them to be our champions.	Emphasize What's In It For Them (WIIFT).
3.	Groom our champions to advocate for us.	Give them proper data, facts, and analysis.
4.	Maintain a long-term relationship with our champions.	Thank them to cultivate and sustain a good relationship.

Table 3.1. Four Steps to Find and Sustain a Champion

1. Look for champions.

Where can good champions be found in an organization if an assigned sponsor is an ineffective champion? Champions must have extensive practical experience related to the project's business, even if they are not subject matter experts. Champions should have sufficient formal authority (positional or legitimate power) and influence decision-makers successfully to remove project obstacles. Effective champions should belong to the group or committee reviewing and evaluating the programs or projects, project priorities, and allocating scarce resources. By having a champion from such a group or committee, the project manager can influence the right people in the organization through their champions.

3–People: The Key to Project Success

In most organizations, such groups include:
- Senior management
- Steering committees
- Advisory committees and advisory boards
- Priority panel and resource management committees
- Program/project portfolio review committees

The project manager must find champions with positional authority and a functional role in the organization to resolve project problems related to decisions about priorities and resource allocation changes. In addition, project managers must gain their champions' continuous support to deliver successful projects.

Even project managers with strong technical project management knowledge and expertise cannot directly help their champions win project battles if their champions lack sufficient legitimate or positional power. Therefore, it is better if potential champions are decision-makers or belong to an influential committee or group responsible for making important decisions. Champions should also be powerful leaders whom senior management likes and respects.

The best strategy for project managers is to find champions at the appropriate level in the organizational chart. They should then sell them on becoming champions by describing the project and its benefits to raise their interest and support.

2. Convince them to be our champions.

To convince potential champions to become our real champions, project managers must remember a truth of life—most people usually do what is in their best interest. Before lending help and support, most people ask this question: What's In It For Me (WIIFM)? So, when project managers approach someone about being their champion, they should describe the project outcome and benefits, emphasizing these three points:

1. How their project aligns with organizational goals and strategies.
2. How the project benefits translate into benefits for the project champion, even if it is an indirect effect, such as elevating the image of the champion's department or group. Potential champions must be excited about the project.
3. What the shared interest is for us and the champion to work together.

These points help champions play their role more readily because they work toward organizational goals and objectives rather than their benefit or satisfaction.

After these issues are addressed, champions often advocate for the project managers in the right forums in the organization and influence the steering committees or high-level decision-makers. However, challenges often arise because of a lack of proper resources. Therefore, project managers must now prepare their champions to be effective by providing them with the right information to obtain sufficient resources with the necessary skill mixture.

3–People: The Key to Project Success

3. Groom our champions to advocate for us.

How can project managers develop good champions to address their concerns and advocate for meeting project goals? No one wants to take on battles they might lose. Therefore, project managers must help their champions handle challenges successfully. Project managers must do the preparatory work for their champions and provide:

- Useful data and valid facts about the project
- Valid information related to project issues
- The detailed analysis supported by figures, tables, graphs, and documentation
- The project's alignment with overall organizational strategies and goals

Project managers must give their champions everything they need to give convincing presentations. However, project managers should not expect their champions to prepare presentation materials independently from detailed project reports or documents because it adds to their champions' workload.

Project managers must provide concise, clear slides conveying the key message and persuasive arguments. These slides' contents and styles must match the champions' communication and presentation styles. Extra thorough and professional work to help with the champions' presentation motivates them to be more willing and prepared to find solutions and help their project managers succeed. This willingness and preparation create a win-win situation for project managers and their champions and better future relationships.

Leading with Purpose

4. Maintain a long-term relationship with our champions.

Project managers should thank their champions for their efforts as each milestone is completed. This show of gratitude maintains a good relationship and enhances it for the future. Cultivating this relationship is the key to maintaining our champions to help us long term.

Appropriate positional power for a champion

Project managers must find champions with appropriate positional power. The level depends on project complexity, defined by the number of organizational departments and disciplines involved. More politics are likely when more people from many departments are involved. They come with different personalities, attitudes, viewpoints, and beliefs about how to do things. Different people push their agendas and try to influence others to follow their viewpoints.

A more complex project (more departments are involved) requires a champion higher in the management hierarchy. For example, as shown in Figure 3.2, project A's complexity is the highest, followed by that of projects B and C. Therefore, project A's champion should be an executive VP, whereas a VP and director might suffice for projects B and C, respectively.

A director for project A is ineffective in removing roadblocks because of the lack of organizational influence and authority. The champions at this level are ineffective in fulfilling their roles unless they are well-connected with people at a higher management level. However, the situation becomes challenging when higher-level management people want to champion their projects. For example, an executive

3–People: The Key to Project Success

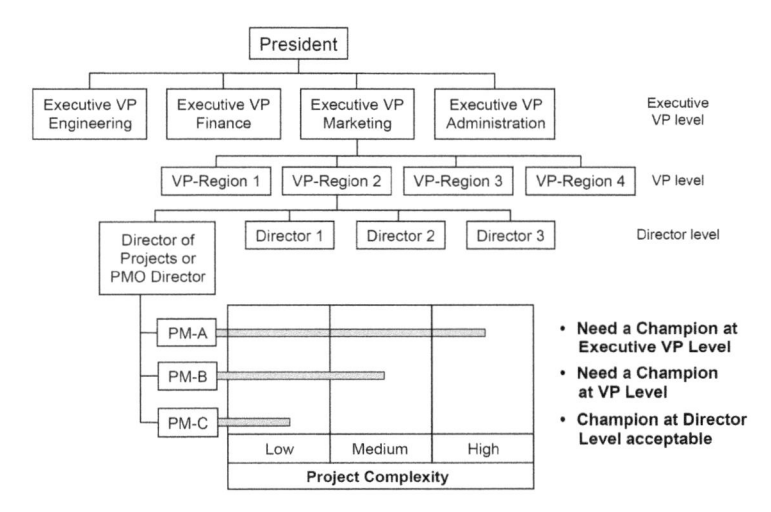

Figure 3.2. Relationship between project complexity and a champion's positional power.

VP for a project C would be overkill. Politically sensible project managers try to find champions from an appropriate level in the management hierarchy to influence other management people and stakeholders to remove roadblocks project managers encounter.

3.1.2. The right project managers

Project managers function as bandleaders who pull together their players, each a specialist with individual score and internal rhythm. Under the leader's direction, they all respond to the same beat.

—L. R. Sayles

Integration and effective communication are important skills for project managers because projects comprise several work packages different

Leading with Purpose

team leaders manage. *Integration* means tying loose ends. Project managers need not be the best at using all technology if they have people on their team to fulfill this role. However, they must understand the big picture, the program or project's main components, and the various interfaces' management. The major issues about having the right project managers relate to understanding how project managers are perceived and what makes a successful project manager (Verma 1995, 22–27, 109–113).[5]

A. How project managers are perceived

- Project managers are:
    a. Highly trained in technical skills.
    b. Undertrained in people skills.

- To succeed, project managers must:
    a. Cross organizational boundaries.
    b. Quickly develop the team into a cohesive organization despite many constraints.
    c. Combine technical and people skills.
    d. Create a physical and emotional environment to allow team members to achieve peak performance.

B. What makes a project manager successful:

- Thorough understanding of project management principles and best practices (*PMBOK Guide®*).
- An appropriate balance of technical, human, and conceptual skills.
- Fulfillment of roles and responsibilities with great commitment and professionalism.

3–People: The Key to Project Success

C. Key roles:
- Communicator—exchanges information.
- Influencer—gets things done.
- Negotiator—confers with others to reach an agreement.
- Problem-solver—defines problems and issues, explores and evaluates options, and decides.
- Leader—establishes direction, aligns people, motivates, and inspires.
- Interface manager—connects different phases.
- Trainer—trains team members to enhance their confidence and performance.
- Facilitator—gets the best input from others and establishes a common approach.
- Team builder and team player—builds and creates a high-performance team and commits to contributing to team efforts as a team member.
- Administrator—has a compulsion for closure.
- Ethical professional—follows the code of ethics: honesty, integrity, loyalty to the team, clients, and stakeholders.
- Integrator—brings together the people and processes to do the work.

Leading with Purpose

D. Key Responsibilities:
1. The project manager should ask these questions before starting the project:
    a. What is the project about (motivation to do the project)?
    b. What is it trying to accomplish (objectives)?
    c. What are the completion criteria (deliverables)?
    d. What are the real success criteria?
    e. Who cares about the project (who will benefit the most)?
    f. Who is responsible, and who is accountable?
2. Project managers should perform these tasks at the front end to avoid future problems:
    a. Get management support (Charter and champion).
    b. Identify all stakeholders (internal and external).
    c. Prepare and publish a Project Charter and send it to all stakeholders.
    d. Create a Statement of Work (SOW).
3. The project manager is responsible to the client and top management to meet project objectives within specified cost, schedule, and quality or technical performance constraints. In addition, the project manager carries out these steps:

3–People: The Key to Project Success

a. Prepare and maintain the project plan.
b. Collaborate and continuously plan.
c. Organize the project:
   - Work breakdown structure (WBS), organizational breakdown structure (OBS), and reporting relationships
d. Manage the project:
   - Interface with internal and external stakeholders.
   - Plan, assign, and control assigned resources.
   - Plan and communicate the work.
   - Use interpersonal skills to enhance project productivity.
e. Communicate the status and completion date:
   - Measure progress using proper metrics.
   - Monitor work against scope, budget, and schedule baselines.
f. Closure and post-project audit:
   - Lessons learned.

Senior management is interested in hiring project managers with technical skills who communicate effectively with different stakeholders, vendors, and contractors to achieve effective integration and deliver successful projects.

3.1.3. The right project team members

Head count is useful, but heads with brains and hearts are critical for delivering extraordinary results.

—Vijay Verma

Most projects are organized in a matrix to optimize limited resources. Managers first prepare a project plan that shows human resources required in full-time equivalents (FTEs) for the project throughout its life cycle. Then, they typically must negotiate with their functional managers to acquire the required FTE resources. Many project managers know a person with good skills and knowledge can do a task more quickly than someone with a lower skill level because people have varying skill levels.

Project managers should always have the right team members—people whose skills are the best match for assigned tasks. Therefore, besides getting enough people (head count in FTEs), project managers should negotiate for the best people with the best skills to complete the project tasks on time.

Project managers should get the heads with brains to complete projects successfully from the start. Team members must also have their hearts in the project. They should be committed to the project. Every project manager in the organization tries hard to get the best people for their projects, so these are the questions:

- Who gets the best people, and why?
- What can project managers do with the people they get from resource managers?

3–People: The Key to Project Success

The following scenario illustrates this:

> **Scenario: Who Gets the Best Resources?**
> Consider a situation in an organization in which Nikhil is an excellent information technology (IT) professional to do conceptual system design, and all six project managers —Neel, Rohnik, Jaya, Reyva, Rahi, and Veeyan—want Nikhil for eight weeks for their projects.
>
> Rohnik is an experienced manager and understands the importance and dynamics of power and influence. He realizes there will be tough competition and a battle to get Nikhil. But he recognizes that his life will be much more comfortable if he gets Nikhil for all eight weeks, as needed, to meet the project schedule.
>
> The main issue is who gets Nikhil. All six project managers want him because he is the best in system design. In this situation, the project manager who gets Nikhil is the one with a better champion and good influencing skills. This is part of developing network power and understanding the dynamics of power and influence.

Leading with Purpose

□

Most organizations have limited human resources, such as Nikhil. It is also difficult to get all team members who are the best in the organization. Therefore, project managers should be prepared to do their best with available resources. For example, in a project requiring ten FTEs, the project manager discovers that only four out of ten FTEs are competent and 100 percent effective in doing their tasks. Six out of ten FTEs are only 70 percent effective as Nikhil is. Here, project managers have only 8.2 FTEs [(4 x 1) + (6 x 0.7)] in terms of effectiveness instead of the expected 10 FTEs who are 100 percent effective.

After assembling the team, project managers must enhance their less-effective team members' skills by providing three types of training:

1. Technical training (to improve technical skills)
2. Interpersonal training (to improve people skills)
3. Mentoring and coaching (to improve leadership skills)

The project team is the most important power base for a project manager to succeed. Therefore, project managers should identify drivers and barriers to creating high-performance teams.

Drivers and barriers to high team performance

In a project environment, certain drivers and barriers influence project team performance. Understanding these drivers and barriers can help develop an environment conducive to high team performance. Verma (1997, 120–121) described important drivers and barriers to achieving higher team performance.[6]

Drivers

Drivers for effective team building represent positive factors associated with the project environment that enhance team effectiveness and increase performance. Building effective teams to achieve high team performance involves four factors:

1. Managerial leadership
2. Job content
3. Personal goals and objectives
4. Work environment and organizational support.

The following six drivers strongly correlate positively to project team performance:

1. Professionally interesting and challenging work, which shows confidence in people
2. Recognition of accomplishment, which provides positive reinforcement
3. Experienced technical management personnel, which improves integration and interface management
4. Proper technical direction and leadership, which reduces mistakes and inspires high performance
5. Qualified project team personnel, which ensures quality results
6. Professional growth potential, which motivates team members

These six drivers positively affect the project teams' tangible and direct performance in its technical success regarding the schedule and budget performance. But they are also positively associated with tangible and indirect team performance measures such as commitment to creativity, quality, change-orientation, mutual trust, effective communication, and high achievement needs.

Barriers
Barriers to high team performance include negative factors such as insufficient resources and unclear directions that reduce the project team's effectiveness and performance. We must analyze these factors and take action to minimize their impact and develop an environment encouraging teamwork. The following are six barriers to effective project team building:

1. Unclear project objectives and changing goals and priorities, which create confusion
2. Lack of team definition, structure, and environment, which leads to poor teamwork
3. Communication problems, which lead to destructive conflicts
4. Power struggles and conflict in roles and personnel selection, which lead to a lack of cooperation
5. Lack of team member commitment, which leads to poor quality
6. Uninvolved, unsupportive upper management

For an organization to succeed and manage its projects effectively, it must eliminate barriers to team performance by paying special attention to team management's human aspects. Project managers must foster a work environment conducive to innovative and creative work where people find professional challenges, receive proper recognition, and have

3–People: The Key to Project Success

personal and professional growth opportunities. Such an environment also lowers communication barriers, reduces conflict, and encourages team members to manage change and complex project requirements proactively. Project managers must concentrate on minimizing barriers and reinforcing drivers of teamwork to achieve human synergy and obtain team commitment and ownership to meet project objectives.

Project managers must create synergy among team members to create high-performance teams by:

- Supporting the project team
- Providing challenging opportunities for all team members
- Demonstrating trust and confidence in team members
- Nurturing creativity and innovation

We can achieve better results through creative leadership and an understanding of organizational dynamics, project environment, and relationships among various project stakeholders and team members.

Leading with Purpose

3.2. The Right Structures for the Project and the Project Team

Nobody knows how Honda is organized, except that it uses lots of project teams and is quite flexible.

—Kenichi Ommae

Verma (1995, 146–161) described several issues and challenges related to organizational and project structures. We can organize projects in any of three structures:[7]

1. *Functional structure*

   When there is no full-time project manager, and the project resides in the functional department, the functional manager is the sponsor and oversees the project. Project managers have no formal authority. However, they often work as project expeditors and prepare status reports for the functional manager.

2. *Matrix structure*

   In a matrix structure, team members are brought to the project part-time (percentage basis). They might work on other projects simultaneously. Their home base is their functional department, and their formal boss is their functional manager. However, they informally report to the project manager for tasks assigned to them on a matrix basis. Often, this leads to a two-boss situation that might create challenges and conflicts, especially if the project manager and functional manager have no good working relationship. It is difficult to get team members' full commitment to the project in such situations.

In matrix structures, a project manager might be assigned part-time. The percentage of time depends on whether the matrix structure is weak, medium, or strong. The project manager has little formal authority in a weak matrix and works more as a project coordinator. As the matrix structure becomes medium to high, team members are assigned to the project on a higher percentage level, and the project manager's formal authority increases.

Verma (1995, 146–161) described this authority continuum with the associated challenges and issues. Project managers are assigned full-time if the project is complex and has a high priority to meet organizational goals. In such cases, the project is organized as a strong matrix. The project manager is given more formal power over the budget, other resources, and making decisions.[8]

3. *Projectized structure*

This structure is used for large projects of five or more years where the continuity of teams and project managers is important. All people working on the project are often transferred to the particular project from their functional departments. They formally report to the project manager full-time for the project's duration. They are often physically on the project site to facilitate communications, participate in meetings, and participate in decision-making. This structure assigns team members and the project manager to the project full-time. A senior management team member sponsors and oversees the project.

Leading with Purpose

In projectized structures, there is only one boss. Therefore, the problems related to the two-boss situation do not exist. However, the project manager must have good people and leadership skills and balance the roles of a manager and a leader to achieve good results throughout the project life cycle (PLC) (Verma 1995, 146–161).[9]

If the project has the right people (champions, project managers, and team members) with high commitment, they resolve problems and achieve project goals, even if there are limitations and inefficiencies related to project and organizational structures.

3.3. The Right Tools

Data is like garbage—you'd better know what you are going to do with it before you collect it.

—Mark Twain

Sometimes, people believe their skills in following processes and effective use of project management software lead to success. But it is an illusion because people, not processes or software packages, do projects. Processes and methods are important and useful. The Project Management Institute (PMI) developed a *PMBOK® Guide—A Guide to the Project Management Body of Knowledge* that includes basic concepts and in-depth discussions of project management processes, tools, and methodologies (PMI 2021).[10]

Experienced project managers know people make or break a project. Therefore, people skills are much more important than processes and software. Managers with good people skills can design templates, processes, and methods with participation from stakeholders, increasing their buy-in and commitment to make the tools and processes work despite technical limitations.

Most project management software packages are conceptually the same, producing similar outputs (Gantt charts, status reports, etc.), which many project personnel do not follow. Some project managers print these reports in color to draw people's attention, often leading to a show-and-tell exercise, rather than spending their energy to motivate and inspire project team members to meet challenging deadlines.

Processes and tools can communicate project status and problems, but experienced project managers do not depend on these alone. Instead, they approach stakeholders personally, try to understand their main issues and concerns, and develop solutions by working with them.

Some project management organizations (PMOs) do not involve stakeholders while developing processes, tools, and templates. This oversight often leads to resistance during implementation and a lack of commitment to make processes work, even if they require simple modifications. Instead, PMOs must recognize that people issues are at the front and center of managing projects. Processes and tools work better by paying special attention to people and understanding the dynamics of power and politics at the project and organizational levels.

Leading with Purpose

Chapter 3 Summary

Politically sensible managers believe people, structure, and tools are the basic elements of successful. The right people come in three forms: (1) project champions, (2) project managers, and (3) team members. The most important issues with having the right project champions are understanding the champions' key roles, finding and keeping project champions, and recognizing the need for the appropriate positional power for the champions to be effective. A champion must fulfill the key roles of having a vested interest and removing obstacles and roadblocks. Project sponsors naturally fit as project champions, but they might be ineffective.

Project managers must find good project champions and maintain a good relationship with them, which involves four steps: (1) look for champions, (2) convince them to be their champions, (3) groom champions to advocate for them, and (4) maintain long-term relationships. Depending on the project's complexity, project managers must find champions with the appropriate positional power.

Integration and effective communication, not just technical skills, and having the right team members with an appropriate skill mixture are important for project managers. In addition, having enough head count (FTEs) is insufficient; they must have *heads with brains*, which means having the competence to complete the task successfully. In addition, project managers must cope with the resources they are given but properly train their team members to increase their technical and interpersonal skills to produce high-quality performance.

3–People: The Key to Project Success

Projects can be organized into three structures: (1) functional structure, (2) matrix structure, or (3) projectized structure. Practically, it matters little how the project organization is structured if the project has the right people.

People do projects, so people skills are much more important than processes and software. Paying attention to people and comprehending the power and politics involved in project and organizational dynamics can enhance the effectiveness of processes and tools.

Chapter 3 Review and Critical Thinking Questions

1. Review the three categories of successful project management elements covered in this chapter.

2. Identify the main stakeholders in the people category of successful project management elements.

3. What is the importance of project champions? Describe the four steps to finding and sustaining a project champion.

4. Did you have a good champion in your recent project management experiences, and how was it helpful? What would you do to improve the strength of your champions to help you achieve better project results?

5. Describe the concept of a relationship between the project complexity and the appropriate positional power of the champion to deliver successful projects.

Leading with Purpose

6. What makes a successful project manager in their key roles and responsibilities?
7. Identify the main drivers and barriers to high team performance. What would you do to create a team environment to maximize drivers and minimize the barriers?
8. Identify three types of project structures. What are the advantages and disadvantages of each structure?
9. What is the importance of project management tools and project management software packages? How would you improve project management tools' quality to achieve project success?

Part II: Power and Project Management

Chapter 4. Dynamics, Characteristics, and Outcome of Power
- *4.1. What Is Power?*
- *4.2. When Do We Have Power over Others?*
- *4.3. Understanding Automatic Responses*
- *4.4. Characteristics and Outcomes of Power*
- *Chapter 4 Summary*
- *Chapter 4 Review and Critical Thinking Questions*

Chapter 5. Components and Use of Power
- *5.1. Formal Power*
- *5.2. Informal Power*
- *5.3. Using Power*
- *Chapter 5 Summary*
- *Chapter 5 Review and Critical Thinking Questions*

Chapter 6. Eight Sources of Power
- *6.1. Legitimate Power*
- *6.2. Reward Power*
- *6.3. Coercive Power*
- *6.4. Referent Power*
- *6.5. Expert Power*
- *6.6. Information Power*
- *6.7. Network Power*
- *6.8. Persuasion Power*
- *Chapter 6 Summary*
- *Chapter 6 Review and Critical Thinking Questions*

Chapter 7. The Project Manager and Power
   7.1. *A Project Manager's Total Power*
   7.2. *Strategies to Increase the Eight Sources of Power*
   7.3. *Balancing Power*
   Chapter 7 Summary
   Chapter 7 Review and Critical Thinking Questions

Part II: Power and Project Management

The measure of a man is what he does with power.

—Pittances

Understanding the concepts of power is important to managing projects effectively. What separates project managers from the rest of the team? Certainly, they head the team, keep it on track, and influence and motivate members to get things done effectively. But what allows managers to influence and motivate their teams successfully? Power is the answer, and managers can use many power sources to influence people to do what is expected. Power is one thing, but managers soon feel stripped of their power if they do not use it effectively. Sometimes, they are even replaced by someone who can use it more effectively.

Leading with Purpose

This part has four chapters that deal with power dynamics, characteristics, and outcomes:
1. Components of power and issues related to using power
2. Eight sources of power
3. Strategies to increase the eight sources of power
4. Balancing power

Chapter 4 describes an overview of power and its dynamics in project management regarding when we have power over others and how to understand automatic responses to power. The chapter examines power, its meaning, and its importance to project management. We present seven qualities, or characteristics, of power that form a power base. A negative or positive response determines the dynamics of the power and its use. The chapter also points out that power is neutral—neither good nor bad—until it is exercised.

Chapter 5 describes power's formal and informal components with distinct advantages of informal power. Besides understanding power's components, we must understand the use of power and its impact. Project managers can use their power formally or informally. The important point is how the other party perceives it because the use of power is never binary. Project managers must understand and analyze the issues associated with power. The chapter describes the important issues associated with using power: people's feelings, possible outcomes, people's perceptions about their project managers, the effects on client relations, and the effects on future business opportunities.

Part II–Power and Project Management

Chapter 6 describes the eight sources of power: legitimate power, reward power, coercive power, referent power, expert power, information power, network power, and persuasion power. The chapter also describes the factors associated with each power source, tips to exercise each source, and practical guidelines to increase each source.

Chapter 7 defines a project manager's total power (formal + informal) and describes strategies to increase the eight power sources. Project managers should strive to increase their team members' power because the team is their most important power base. We discuss the importance of balancing power between project managers and functional managers.

Leading with Purpose

Chapter 4

Dynamics, Characteristics, and Outcomes of Power

Power consists in one's capacity to link one's will with the purpose of others, to lead by reason and a gift of cooperation.

—Woodrow Wilson

Power and authority are important in project management, yet they are confusing in practical terms (Verma 2000–2013).[1] Therefore, the dynamics of power in organizational settings are complex. Therefore, project managers must understand the roots of power, recognize when they have power over others, and how to use it to reach win-win solutions.

The concepts of power and its use influence project outcomes. Project managers must examine power, its meaning, and its importance to project management. For example, power can yield resistance, compliance, or commitment. These power outcomes correlate with employee motivation and potential effectiveness. Therefore, project managers must understand power's dynamics, characteristics, and outcomes to help them select the best way to use their power with people and situations.

This chapter describes power and its dynamics in project management as to when we have power over others and how to understand automatic responses to power. This chapter examines power, its meaning, and its importance to project management. We present seven qualities, or characteristics, of power that form a power base. A negative or positive response determines the dynamics of the power and its use. This chapter also points out that power is neutral, neither good nor bad, until we exercise it.

4.1. What Is Power?

Mastering others is strength;
mastering yourself is true power.

—Tao Te Chung

In simple terms, power is "the faculty or capacity to act, the strength and potency to accomplish something" (Covey 2013).[2] A deeper understanding is required to determine the roots of power and learn to use it, especially in a project management environment.

Power is the ability to do things by exercising leadership or control over people, situations, and events. Project managers derive power from the perception that project goals are realistic, achievable, and beneficial, and those working on the project benefit (Wideman 1998).[3]

4–Dynamics, Characteristics, and Outcomes of Power

Power is the ability to influence others to do what we want them to do. Influencing project stakeholders is almost the only way to do things in a project environment because project managers usually have no direct formal authority over project personnel or team members assigned to the project on a matrix basis.

More concretely, power is the capacity to influence. Therefore, we need power to influence stakeholders as a first and necessary condition. However, to influence successfully, we must exercise our power appropriately. Therefore, besides having power, we must know how to use it effectively.

Power is like a lottery system—we must buy a lottery ticket to win, but we must have the winning number drawn to win the lottery. Similarly, we must first have power (the ticket) to influence, but then we must use it appropriately (having a winning number drawn) to influence our stakeholders successfully. The difference is that how we use the power is in our control, whereas our ticket number drawn is not in our control; it depends on luck.

We have identified the strong connection between power and influence. In practical terms, power influences others to:

- **Do What We Want Them to Do** — Project managers have power only if they can get their team members to complete assigned tasks without scope, context, or detail changes. Sometimes, people alter their tasks if they do not interest them. Therefore, to gain compliance (or ideally a commitment), project managers must know their team members' interests. Following this, they should then facilitate the process of completing tasks. If team members can change tasks assigned to them or cannot do the assigned tasks, then the project manager has no "real" power over those team members in practical terms.

- **When We Want Them to Do** — Project managers are usually responsible for meeting deadlines and completing tasks by an overall schedule. However, because project managers must assign jobs to various work package managers, they must also ensure others meet project deadlines to stay on track to meet the overall project schedule. Some might not follow project schedules and change their deadlines for personal reasons rather than valid ones. Project managers have power when they can convince team members to adhere to their deadlines so they complete projects on schedule. Project managers will not meet their deadlines if they cannot do this successfully. If so, it again shows that a project manager lacks enough real power.

- **How We Want Them to Do** — Although project managers should provide clear guidelines for assigned tasks, project personnel often have excellent ideas to accomplish goals more efficiently with different processes and techniques. These ideas should be encouraged with the stipulation that the project manager must agree to all changes to the original assignment and how it should be done. This way, tasks are done in the proposed or another manner the project manager approves because it might be more efficient. If team members learn they can do their tasks any way they choose without repercussions, it leads to many

4–Dynamics, Characteristics, and Outcomes of Power

authority issues and again can show a project manager does not have enough real power.

Because project managers do not have direct authority, they must instead recognize the need to learn to influence project stakeholders to do things. The best way to do this is through power, especially informal power. Table 4.1 outlines key factors project managers who wish to gain and use power effectively must consider.

	Keyword	Focuses On
P	Perception	Understanding how to prepare for effective communication
O	Opinion	Respecting others' opinions
W	Wisdom	Having an ability to use power carefully
E	Example	Setting examples to increase personal and referent power
R	Reason	Using logical reasoning to convince people

Table 4.1. Power (in a Nutshell)

Many people perceive power differently. These are typical responses from participants in my many seminars about what power is and what power implies:

- **Power refers to a particular authority granted based on the hierarchical position in the organization chart.** This power is called *legitimate power*, which gives managers control over allocating budgets and resources. It also gives them the power to decide with or without others' input. In addition, this power refers to an ability to give rewards (monetary or otherwise) or remove rewards.

- **Managers earn their power from knowledge and experience based on their expertise or professional reputation.** This includes information they control or generate and their knowledge about the subject area and organizational policies and procedures.
- **Some managers gain power from personal charisma and characteristics, from which they earn others' respect,** which helps them create teamwork, synergy, and collaboration. This includes leadership skills in influencing others to meet organizational goals and objectives.
- **Power is all about *networking*** — whom we know well enough to call for help. It is all about close business contacts that greatly help accomplish many things.
- **Many managers get their power from their interpersonal and soft skills** and the ability to use these skills to persuade others and influence them to do things. These skills include motivation, effective communication, negotiation, and conflict management. Through effective interpersonal skills, project managers gain cooperation, trust, and agreement from other project stakeholders to help manage their projects successfully.

4–Dynamics, Characteristics, and Outcomes of Power

- **Power is neither good nor bad until it is exercised.** Power's effect is felt when someone uses their power over others, which is when the person acts based on how the power is applied.
- **It is not enough to have lots of power to do things.** The important thing is how well the power is used to gain cooperation and commitment.

Legitimate power refers to formal power, whereas all other types of power represent informal power. Some project managers believe having more power is sufficient to do things, but the important thing is how well the power is exercised to gain cooperation and commitment. So, using power effectively is necessary to deliver successful projects.

4.2. When Do We Have Power over Others?

*Perceptions about power are important.
Power perceived is power achieved.*

—Vijay Verma

We must understand the dynamics of power and recognize when we have power over others. The dynamics of power are complex because they might be based on perceptions. We have power over others when:

- We have something they want;
- We have access to something they want;
- They perceive we have, or have access to, something they want.

Leading with Purpose

Both sides of the equation must be satisfied; whatever we have or have access to should be something others want. If they do not want what we have or cannot get them what they want, we have no power over them.

Sometimes, we need not have something or be able to get something people want, but they may believe we can get them what they need. We also have power over others, even if they only perceive we can get them what they want.

Once project managers understand their power over other stakeholders, the next step is to leverage the power to negotiate whatever is most important to manage their projects more effectively. Sometimes, project managers might have more power than they think, based on their and others' perceptions of them.

4.3. Understanding Automatic Responses

I have never been able to conceive how any rational being could propose happiness to himself from the exercise of power over others.

—Thomas Jefferson

A manager can gain compliance using blatant methods such as stating a direct order or using psychology and making a casual suggestion. In his book *Influence: The Psychology of Persuasion*, Cialdini (2006) provides an interesting parallel in the animal kingdom that describes this concept.[4]

A grouper species eats all small fish stupid enough to cross its path. The one exception is a species of cleaner fish. When a grouper sees such a fish approach, it automatically opens its mouth. It

4–Dynamics, Characteristics, and Outcomes of Power

allows the fish to eat any fungus or parasites in the grouper's mouth, providing the grouper a great service while giving the smaller fish an easy meal.

Another species of fish, the saber-toothed blenny, takes advantage of the grouper's automatic response to the cleaner fish. After approaching a grouper, the blenny mimics the cleaner fish's movements, spurring the grouper to lower its guard and wait to be cleaned. Then, the blenny tears a large strip of flesh from the grouper and swims away quickly. The blenny recognizes and exploits this mental conditioning to its advantage because of the automatic response instilled in the grouper from the cleaner fish.

This comparison with the human world is imperfect, as the intention and result are far less sinister, but it illustrates the automatic responses people are conditioned to expect. These automatic responses play a significant role in how successful a person's attempt to exert power and influence over others will be. When people better understand different power, they can use the psychological conditioning in others to gain their compliance much more easily.

We know people who can go from one social encounter to another with a request for compliance and who achieve compliance with a high success rate. "The secret of their effectiveness lies in the way they structure their requests, the way they use the art of influencing that exist in the social environment" (Cialdini 2006).[5]

All this might sound like cold, calculating manipulation. However, the results can be positive or negative, depending on the intents of the people with power at their disposal, whether from a formal position or simply having great charisma.

Leading with Purpose

A negative application of power can result in unjust persecution. Yet, a responsible and positive application of power achieves compliance while motivating people to be their best. She expands on this idea with the example that Gandhi and Genghis Khan commanded multitudes with political mastery yet used different persuasive tactics. Gandhi influenced people positively and empowered them to join him in fighting for India's freedom. Genghis Khan used his formal power to make people fight to win the battle he was interested in. We could interpret Gandhi's strategy as motivation and Genghis Khan's strategy as manipulation (Hogshead 2010).[6]

4.4. Characteristics and Outcomes of Power

The golden opportunity you are seeking is in yourself. It is not in your environment; it is not in luck or chance, or the help of others; it is in yourself alone.

—Orson Swett Marden

There are eight forms or sources of power, which we discuss later in this book:

1. **Legitimate power**. Power granted based on hierarchical position.
2. **Reward power**. Power to reward people.
3. **Coercive power**. Power to remove rewards or punish people.
4. **Referent power**. Has two components:
    a. Based on identifying with high-profile people and projects.

4–Dynamics, Characteristics, and Outcomes of Power

    b. Based on charisma and leadership skills, which earn respect.
5. **Expert power.** Power based on knowledge, experience, and expertise.
6. **Information power.** Important to generate and control information.
7. **Network power.** Personal and business contacts we can call on for help. It is about first doing and then receiving favors.
8. **Persuasion power.** Interpersonal skills to persuade and influence stakeholders to win cooperation, trust, and agreement.

Each power source has specific characteristics. Project managers must know the characteristics to use suitable power to get needed results. Three common outcomes occur when power is exercised:

1. **Resistance.** When power is used authoritatively without sensitivity to others' feelings, people most likely resist and do not put forth their best effort.
2. **Compliance.** Sometimes, people cannot resist openly because of job insecurity or possible negative consequences. In those cases, they comply and make the minimum effort to stay out of trouble.
3. **Commitment.** Project managers should always avoid resistance, not compromise with compliance, and strive to gain commitment, motivating people to go the extra mile to produce better outcomes.

4.4.1. Characteristics of power

*Power always thinks it has
a great soul and vast views beyond
the comprehension of the weak.*

—John Adams

The characteristics of power refer to the qualities that form a power base. For example, to be seen as a professional, we must rely on a specific source of power, such as expert power. Each power can lead to different characteristics and outcomes, although they often overlap.

Another important point project managers should know is the possibility of temporarily and indefinitely losing power. When we use power improperly, others see it as negative, manipulative, and threatening. For example, if we provide information citing our professional reputation, and this information is false, we lose perceived expert power. The proper use of power helps avoid or correct this scenario. Therefore, we must understand the relationships between characteristics and sources of power well. Table 4.2 summarizes the key relationships between characteristics and different types of power.

We must consider characteristics of power while applying power to gain commitment and higher performance from stakeholders:

Degree of control, compliance, and resistance

When applying formal power to get a person to complete a task, we must strive for commitment or at least voluntary compliance. If a manager forces and intimidates a subordinate to do something, they are

4–Dynamics, Characteristics, and Outcomes of Power

Characteristics of Power	Forms of Power
Degree of control, compliance, and resistance	Reward, Coercive, Legitimate
Position in the organizational hierarchy	Reward, Legitimate, Referent
Professional reputation	Expert
Knowledge and experience (widely accepted)	Expert, Information
Leadership abilities	Referent, Expert
Organizational awareness	Information
Good contacts/working relationships	Network, Referent
High-quality results	Persuasion
Effectiveness potential	Referent, Expert, Persuasion

Table 4.2. Characteristics of Power

more likely to meet resistance than when they use other power bases. To produce quality outputs, we must believe in what we do. As the adage stresses, "A man convinced against his will is of the same opinion still" (Carnegie 2011).[7]

Legitimate power often leads to resistance, but if applied informally, the risk of encountering resistance is greatly reduced. Reward power can lead to commitment if the reward satisfies the needs people value the most. Conversely, a lack of suitable rewards might create resistance. Constructive feedback helps soften the blows of coercive power. The following list provides a good idea of the relationship between these characteristics of power and the source of power used:

Legitimate Power
- Commitment is possible if the request is polite and appropriate.
- Compliance is likely if the request is appropriate.
- Resistance is possible if the request is arrogant or inappropriate.

Reward Power
- Commitment is possible if used subtly and personally.
- Compliance is likely if used routinely and impersonally.
- Resistance is possible if used in a manipulative, arrogant, or threatening way.

Coercive Power
- Commitment is unlikely, regardless of how it is done!
- Compliance is possible if used helpfully and non-punitively.
- Resistance is likely if overused or used in a hostile or manipulative way.

Position in the organizational hierarchy

A project manager's position in the organizational hierarchy directly relates to how they may use reward, legitimate, and referent power. A higher hierarchical position means a manager has more authority to provide more and better rewards. Subordinates quickly realize just how much reward power particular managers have.

4–Dynamics, Characteristics, and Outcomes of Power

Legitimate power directly relates to the hierarchical position for the same reasons as reward power. The higher a project manager's organizational position, the more direct power (how many people are under them) and indirect power (perceived based on title, salary, etc.) belong to them. Referent power relies more on subtlety, primarily from informal power. Nonetheless, it connects with the organizational position. Referent power also comes from being admired and seen as a leader. With higher positional power, the chances of this happening increase.

Professional reputation

Our professional reputation relies on our possession of and ability to use expert power. Without the specific knowledge and experience that makes us an expert in our area who can apply this knowledge to help others, we will not have a strong professional reputation. However, a person who regularly shows expert power is widely regarded as irreplaceable, and they enjoy their colleagues' respect.

Knowledge and experience (widely accepted)

As characteristics of power, knowledge, and experience are like professional reputation, yet they differ. Professional reputation refers more to a specific set of expertise related to an area relevant to our profession, whereas knowledge and experience refer to a more general wealth of information a person has. For example, if someone has an engineering question, they go to an engineer with a strong professional reputation. On the other hand, if someone has a general question, they first seek a person widely seen as "someone with all the answers." It also reflects higher self-confidence and more confidence of management and others in us.

Leadership abilities

Many people are followers and are content when led by a competent leader. This gives people with strong leadership abilities an immediate leg up on others when competing for formal positions and informal power. A person is seen as more powerful by getting others to identify with people with leadership ability and gaining respect and admiration (the prerequisites of referent power). By cementing this reputation through expertise and interpersonal skills, we ensure the person keeps high informal power.

High-quality results

A manager's job is not just to earn compliance. Good managers earn commitment because, through commitment, they get optimum performance from their people. By empowering employees to feel appreciated and respected, managers coax out much higher-quality results than if they force them to complete tasks. Effective persuasion power, such as phrasing requests and assignments positively, can mean the difference between an adequately completed project and an excellent one.

Effectiveness potential

In the same way as high-quality results are achieved, effectiveness potential relies on gaining commitment rather than compliance. With different sources of power (referent, expert, persuasion), a manager can gain subordinates' respect, making them feel strongly obligated to them. If trust and commitment are achieved, team members want to see their leader and the team succeed almost as much as they want success. Happy, committed team members use their potential and produce results to the best of their ability. If a manager can bring this out in their team members, it reflects an effective use of informal power. Thus, all managers should strive toward this goal.

Each characteristic relates to specific forms or sources of power. Therefore, project members must understand the relationships among characteristics and forms of power and increase the appropriate powers to optimize their effectiveness in delivering successful projects.

4.4.2. Outcomes of power

Nearly all men can stand adversity, but if you want to test a man's character, give him power.

—Abraham Lincoln

Power is sometimes thought to be an ability to influence. However, it is the capacity to influence. How well we influence the outcome depends on how well our power is applied or exercised and how the other party receives it.

A more committed worker is more useful. Yet, many managers order team members around and enforce deadlines to ensure completion rather than using informal (personal) power to gain their commitment. The importance of gaining team members' commitment to a successful project outcome cannot be understated, as this is perhaps the key difference

Leading with Purpose

between good managers and great ones. Figure 4.1 shows a correlation between employees' resistance, compliance, and commitment, and motivation and potential effectiveness.

Each form or source of power and its use lead to different outcomes from project personnel for their level of ***resistance***, ***compliance***, and ***commitment***.

Resistance	Compliance	Commitment

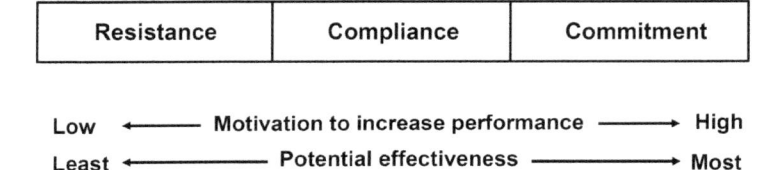

Low ←——— Motivation to increase performance ———→ High
Least ←——————— Potential effectiveness ——————→ Most

Figure 4.1. Outcomes of use of power.

Going up the management ladder can increase only formal or positional power. It does not help if managers do not gain their team members' respect and cooperation. Therefore, project managers and personnel should work on increasing their informal or personal power, as it is the most effective strategy. A project manager's team is their most important power base because a project manager's success depends on final team outputs. This is why project managers should recognize the importance of increasing their power and helping team members increase it. This way, a project manager's total power increases further, past the point they could reach alone.

$$\text{Power of Project Manager} = \sum \text{Power of each team member}$$

4–Dynamics, Characteristics, and Outcomes of Power

Skillful and thoughtful execution of power, which requires the following, leads to successful results:
- Better interpersonal and persuasion skills
- Effective communication, negotiation, and positive reinforcement
- Sensitivity to others' feelings, emotions, and beliefs
- Supportive environment and positive reinforcement

Even though these are all legitimate points, we can still ask many difficult questions about the outcomes of power, including:
- What power should project managers have?
- What kind should they acquire, and how?
- How should power be balanced to avoid conflict, power struggles, infighting, and politics?

These are all valid questions, yet the more legitimate power project managers hold, the more influential they are perceived, and the more influence they can exert over others. From an informal viewpoint, project managers earn others' trust and respect by using their talents and energy, being fair and sincere, and having knowledge and understanding of the whole project and organization. When these conditions are satisfied, others are more willing to listen, cooperate, and meet demands.

Project managers' total power is the sum of their positional (formal) and personal (informal) power. Therefore, managers without direct control over their personnel or low positional power must increase their personal power. This increases their total power directly and likely increases positional power because of the increased possibility of promotion.

Project managers should concentrate on increasing personal power because they can increase it. Project managers rarely have direct control over their advancement in an organization; thus, their positional power. Relying on formal power alone to control others fails because (1) project managers depend on people over whom they have no formal authority, and (2) few accept orders from someone just because they are the boss (Kotter 2008).[8]

Some managers have difficulty balancing informal and formal power, especially when people have most of the positional power and thrive on using it formally. On the other hand, most organizations accept power corruption risk if the power stays in a few people's hands. Therefore, some organizations like to flatten the organizational structure to distribute power more widely.

Chapter 4 Summary

Power is the ability to do things by exercising leadership or control over people, situations, and events. The perception that project goals are realistic, achievable, and beneficial gives project managers power. Project managers must understand their team members' interests and influence them effectively to gain compliance. Project managers are typically responsible for meeting deadlines and completing tasks following an overall schedule. Managers wield power when they can persuade team members to meet their deadlines.

4–Dynamics, Characteristics, and Outcomes of Power

The best way to accomplish this is through power, particularly informal power. Many managers derive their power from interpersonal and soft skills and the ability to persuade others. However, having a lot of power isn't enough to get things done. What matters is how well we use power to gain cooperation and commitment.

Based on their perceptions and the perceptions of others, project managers may have more power than they realize. Therefore, project managers must understand the characteristics of appropriate power to achieve the desired results.

The qualities that make up a power base are called power characteristics. We must rely on a specific source of power, such as expert power, to be seen as professionals. Legitimate power frequently elicits opposition; however, the risk of encountering resistance is reduced when applied informally. Resistance is likely if used excessively or in a hostile or manipulative manner.

The higher a project manager's organizational position, the more direct and indirect power (as perceived by title, salary, and so on) they have. Knowledge and experience are like professional reputation but not the same. A manager's job is to earn their employees' commitment, not just compliance, which good managers gain by making them feel valued and respected. Managers use various forms of informal power to gain team members' trust and respect.

A project manager's ability to gain team members' respect and cooperation is critical to their success. The most effective strategy is increasing their informal or personal power. The more power project managers wield, the more powerful they are perceived to be and the more power they wield over others. Project managers' total power is the sum of their positional and personal/informal power. Managers with low positional power must increase their personal power to gain trust and respect. Some organizations prefer to flatten their organizational structure to distribute power more evenly (Kotter 2008).

Chapter 4 Review and Critical Thinking Questions

1. Define power and describe the associated keywords and focus of these keywords.
2. From your project management experience, when do you feel you have power over others? Give examples of how you used your power in those contexts.
3. What are the different roles of a project manager? Describe how project managers should use their power to fulfill their roles effectively.
4. In your project management experience, what is the significance of power when interacting with various stakeholders?
5. Describe the characteristics of power and the sources of power associated with those characteristics.
6. What are the best outcomes of using power described in this chapter? How do these outcomes affect the motivation to increase performance and the potential effectiveness of team members?

4–Dynamics, Characteristics, and Outcomes of Power

7. Think of the recent projects you have managed but about the role of power and its dynamics when interacting with your team members and other stakeholders. What were the challenges, and how would you resolve them?
8. What would you do differently after reading this chapter about using your power to motivate your team members and gain their commitment on a long-term basis?

Leading with Purpose

Chapter 5

Components and Use of Power

But the relationship of morality and power is a very subtle one. Because ultimately power without morality is no longer power.

—James Baldwin

Power is an ability to influence others. Power has two forms or components: (1) formal and (2) informal. *Formal power* is granted by hierarchical position in the organization chart and derives from authority. Three types of authority are associated with formal power: (1) line authority, (2) staff authority, and (3) functional authority. *Informal power* is based on our knowledge, experience, and expertise. The many sources of informal power include referent power, expert power, information power, network power, and persuasion power.

Most project managers have enormous responsibility but limited formal authority over their project personnel. Therefore, they must strive to increase their informal power to increase their ability to influence their stakeholders positively to complete work assignments efficiently and deliver successful projects. Project managers can increase their informal power by working independently rather than depending on positional power. In addition, informal power has distinct advantages because it is permanent and increases by sharing. Therefore, a stronger foundation of informal power leads to better formal power and promotion opportunities.

This chapter describes power's formal and informal components with distinct advantages of informal power. Besides understanding power's components, we must understand the use of power and its impact. Project managers can use their power formally or informally. The important point is how the other party perceives it because the use of power is never binary. Understand and analyze the issues associated with power. This chapter describes with examples the important issues associated with using power: people's feelings, possible outcomes, people's perceptions about their project managers, the effects on client relations, and the effects on future business opportunities.

5.1. Formal Power

Speak softly but carry a big stick; you will go far.
—Theodore Roosevelt

We receive formal or positional power based on our position in the organization chart. It is closer to authority than informal power, as formal power often comes from authority. Three types of authority related to formal power are line authority, staff authority, and functional authority (Verma 1995, 102–105).[1]

Line authority

Line authority refers to the right to give orders and decide on the product, sales, etc. Project managers have line authority over personnel working on their projects only in a projectized structure. However, in a matrix structure, some team members may be assigned to a project part-time and temporarily, but those team members have someone else as their permanent boss. Therefore, project managers operating under the matrix setup have little or no line authority over these team members. Although we can make quick decisions with line authority, this method might neglect the input of specialists and overwork key people to meet deadlines.

Staff authority

Staff authority is the right to advise and help people with line authority. For example, an organization's accountants, lawyers, and personnel managers have staff authority. This authority allows specialists to give expert advice and help the line executive analyze where special in-depth expertise is needed. However, one disadvantage of staff authority is that it might undermine the chain of command.

Leading with Purpose

Functional authority

Functional authority refers to the right to give orders but usually only in specific tasks. It is valid only if the person with that functional authority stays in a specific position. Managers with functional authority make routine and specialized decisions. However, setting boundaries for each specialist is sometimes more difficult, which might lead to issues and challenges.

Authority refers to the right to command and represents only formal power. The organization usually grants it based on a person's positional status in the organization chart. Power, however, represents an ability to influence others' actions or decisions.

Authority stemming from formal power can be a potent force. Those wielding it find they can often achieve the desired results, but the compliance is often given without commitment or enthusiasm. Formal authority can help get only compliance and not commitment. The will to follow authority figures, sometimes blindly, is a heavily entrenched social condition traceable throughout human literature (Thomas Hobbes for the history of the feudal system) and religion (Adam and Eve eating the sacred fruit) (Cialdini 2006).[2]

Legitimate power is the only power that rests on authority because it gives project managers control over dispensing rewards and punishment. Yet often, people with less positional authority might influence project stakeholders better than those with greater legitimate authority because of their leadership skills, expertise, skills, or knowledge about the organization.

5.2. Informal Power

Respect commands itself and it can neither be given nor withheld when it is due.

—Eldridge Cleaver

Formal power is granted based on our position on an organizational chart and is more likely to get compliance. Informal power is all other powers that result from a person's knowledge, experience, contacts, and leadership skills. Formal power alone or with other informal power can often be applied formally or informally. Using formal power informally can lead to better outcomes rather than relying on formal power's strength alone. For example, formal power can involve forcing subordinates to accept a viewpoint. Still, it can also work with informal power to persuade others by drawing on their expertise or identifying with others.

Informal power aims not just to earn compliance but also to motivate people to want to engage in specific behaviors and to do so to the best of their abilities. Simple changes in tactics, such as requesting tasks of subordinates by convincing and persuading rather than imposing and commanding, and motivating others in a collaborative and empowering manner rather than belittling them, can make all the difference. Therefore, using informal power is increasingly seen as preferable to just using formal power, and in most cases, using only formal power (legitimate authority) should be a last resort.

Informal power's advantages are not limited to employees' favorable responses. Perhaps its greatest strength is based purely on personal skills and characteristics. Formal power might be lost or taken away suddenly (for example, when moved from a position), but informal power persists for life and can even be improved. Formal power is often limited to specific situations (a specific department, for example), whereas informal power can apply to many other situations, both inside and outside the department or organizational group.

Informal power has many advantages because it represents what a person earns. Table 5.1 summarizes the four major advantages of informal power.

	Advantages
1.	No one can take it from us.
2.	We can work to increase it right away.
3.	The more we share, the more we get.
4.	A good foundation of informal power increases our potential to get more formal power. (Sufficient informal power makes us better candidates for promotions with more formal power.)

Table 5.1. Four Advantages of Informal Power

1. Informal power is permanent (no one can take it away).

Informal power stays with managers because they earn it based on their knowledge, experience, expertise, charisma, and interpersonal skills. It becomes part of their strength, as opposed to positional power that might give them legitimate authority in the organization or department. In reality, positional power belongs to people only if they stay inside the box in the organizational chart. When managers with specific positional power transfer to another department, they lose the legitimate authority or power associated with that position or box.

We can observe from various organizational charts that presidents or CEOs have great legitimate power because many boxes connect to their box with solid lines. Conversely, when we look at project management on the organization chart, we see boxes of only a few project managers connected to the Project Management Office (PMO) Director or Director of Project Management Services.

Formal power belongs to the person inside the box. When that person moves out of the box by leaving the department or organization, they lose that power, whereas no one can take away informal power, even if the person transfers to another department or leaves the organization.

However, projects are mostly organized in a matrix; dotted lines link the resources assigned to project managers. For this reason, project managers do not have formal authority over several project personnel assigned to them in a matrix. When resources, or team members, are joined with the box of the project manager by a dotted line (with gaps), the project manager's legitimate or formal power is broken, and therefore, they should not depend on it. Instead, project managers should focus on developing their informal power, which allows them to influence and lead project stakeholders more effectively.

2. Informal power can be increased anytime (through independent effort).

Project managers can increase their formal power only if management promotes them to a new position. However, project managers can work to increase their informal powers whenever they want rather than waiting for a promotion. They can increase their informal powers by improving their expertise, social networks, access to information, persuasive skills, and charisma. They can accomplish these by reading journals and books about their profession, attending conferences and trade shows, and improving their communication, negotiation, interpersonal, and leadership skills. In addition, they can empower themselves to prepare and implement their plan to enhance their informal powers on their own.

3. Informal power increases by sharing with others (the more we share, the more we get).

Managers can increase their informal powers by sharing them with other managers, which is untrue of formal power because once we give it to someone else (such as our replacement in the organization), we lose that legitimate power or formal authority. By sharing knowledge in any area through publications and teaching courses and seminars, managers help others and help themselves develop more self-confidence and gain a professional reputation. More people recognize them for their knowledge, leading to respect and collaboration, and people are more likely to respond favorably to their attempts to exert their influence.

If managers do not share their knowledge widely by publishing books and papers on their subject, the only people who recognize their knowledge or perceive their expertise are those who interact with them. Thus, project managers can increase their expert power (knowledge power) by sharing it with others.

Sharing our knowledge and power with others shows we use professional values and that we are transparent, honest people. Many leading authorities on power, such as Robert L. Dilenschneider (2007, 155–63), agree, arguing that the most successful and respected users of power work for a cause larger than consolidating their power. They concern themselves with the importance of empowering others.[3]

4. A stronger foundation of informal power leads to formal power or promotion (provides opportunities).

Informal power serves as a ladder to attain formal power. If managers have formal power without a strong informal power base, people might not cooperate with or respect them as much because their power can be perceived as undeserved. If this is true, managers likely cannot effectively coach or lead their project personnel. These people believe the managers have not earned their respect and have only authority granted by their position on the organizational chart. In such cases, people wonder how a manager with little or weak informal power was promoted. They believe such managers do not deserve the promotion, so the managers do not win their cooperation and respect.

Leading with Purpose

Well-liked and respected project managers with a strong base of informal power (a combination of knowledge, expert information, network power, and leadership or interpersonal skills) have the upper hand over their counterparts whenever there is an opportunity for promotion. People who earn a promotion (formal power) because of their stronger foundation of informal power have greater respect and cooperation from their subordinates. Often, subordinates recognize and are glad the promotion was given to the most qualified candidate based on their informal power. As a result, they are more willing to work hard for someone they believe deserves the position.

A project manager's total power comprises both formal and informal components:

Total Power =
Formal/Positional Power + Informal/Earned Power

Project managers should have greater informal power because it stays with people even if they change their organizational position, department, or organization. The advantages of informal power outlined in Table 5.1 and that informal power stays with us regardless of organizational position make it clear that project managers should work harder to increase their informal power.

However, sometimes during a project, people do not cooperate and do not do the tasks assigned to them on schedule despite the project manager's best efforts to support and motivate them with informal power. In such circumstances, project managers need their formal (legitimate) power to exercise proper control and change their behavior to achieve desired outcomes. It would be better if project managers could do this by using their formal power informally, but they should not shy away from it formally. Of course, using any power (formal or informal) informally is more effective, but project managers might have to wield their power formally as a last resort.

5.3. Using Power

It is when people feel controlled, rather than in control, that they are likely to lose the motivation to work.

—Michael LeBoeuf

Most participants in my seminars believe that project managers can manage their projects more successfully if they have more power. However, analyzing this statement further reveals that having power without knowing how to use it effectively renders it ineffective. Project managers should use their power skillfully and thoughtfully to achieve desired outcomes. Project managers who do not use their power effectively might even lose their power because their subordinates feel unhappy, unsatisfied, and under pressure to do what they are told and as they are told. These negative emotions often lead to resistance and a lack of cooperation.

This next section deals with issues about using power and the outcomes (tangible and intangible) when project managers exercise their powers formally or informally (see Table 5.2) over their stakeholders. However, exercising power (formal or informal) is not binary (0 percent informal and 100 percent formal) or vice versa. Instead, it relates to the perceptions or feelings resulting from the process and communication used in exercising power. Often, the most important thing is not what we say but how we say it.

Often, project managers face situations in which they want their team members to do a task, but they might be unsure how to use their power effectively to best influence their team members to do things. For example, consider the following scenario, which highlights how using power in two similar but subtly different ways leads to different outcomes.

5–Components and Use of Power

	Issues	Formal	Informal
1.	How people feel?	· Disempowered · Disrespected · Belittled · Demotivated	· Empowered · Respected · Happy · Motivated
2.	Possible outputs?	· Bare minimum · Low quality · Low motivation	· More than we asked for · High quality · High motivation
3.	Perceptions about the manager?	· Autocrat · Arrogant · Inflexible · Manager	· Collaborative · Respectful · Flexible · Leader/Coach
4.	Client relationships?	· Contractor (short term) · More business emphasis	· Collaborator (long term) · Partner (long term)
5.	Business opportunities?	· Gets paid for present contract · Cannot be sued	· Gets paid for present contract · Better references · Future contacts · Repeat business

Table 5.2. Using Power in a Formal or Informal Way

Scenario: Using Power (related to issues 1, 2, and 3)

James's manager, Gillian, asked him to work on a proposal for new product development. After completing the project proposal, James anxiously awaits her feedback on his work. He spent much effort on this proposal, and he believes she will respond favorably after reviewing the document. Gillian meets with James to give him feedback on his proposal and uses her power to influence James. The following two dialogues illustrate how James feels after the meeting and the impact of using power formally and informally.

Gillian wants to communicate the following three points:

1. I have more expert power based on years of experience.

2. I have more authority in this area (published three books).

3. I want pages 150–165 to be incorporated from book 2.

Dialogue A: Using power formally

Gillian: "Oh, my God . . . Hmm . . ."

(Body language shows disapproval and lack of appreciation)

"It looks like you have spent a lot of time on this report. However, section 3.4 needs significant improvement. I would like to point out that I have written three books related to this

5–Components and Use of Power

area. I strongly believe my book 2 and, in particular, pages 150–165, would be very relevant to this section. I want you to incorporate material from those pages to improve this section. Could you finish it by Wednesday morning, and we can meet at 10:30 a.m. to review it?"

"Is that OK?" (Uses assertive body language)

Dialogue B: Using power informally

Gillian: "Looks great! Oh, my God . . . Hmm . . . You have certainly put lots of effort into this report."

(Body language shows approval and appreciation)

"I like most of your report. However, section 3.4 needs some polishing. By the way, I have written three books related to this area, and you might find my book 2 and, in particular, pages 150–165, very relevant to this section. You might like to incorporate material from those pages in this section. Could you please get it done by Wednesday morning, and we can meet at 10:30 a.m. to review it?"

"Will that work for you?" (Uses suggestive and assertive body language)

This scenario emphasizes the differing outcomes of using power informally and formally. Usually, outcomes are more likely to be positive when we use our power informally and negative when we use power formally.

Outcomes being more positive when we use informal power is not a novel concept. Many experiments, notably those by B. F. Skinner, show that animals learn much more rapidly when motivated by praise and rewards than when punished for bad behavior (Carnegie 2011).[4] The same is true for humans, and if we use informal power to criticize, learning will not be nearly as effective, and resentment often occurs.

These five issues describe the different feelings, outcomes, and impressions many associate with their managers in response to their use of power in a predominantly formal or informal way. Table 5.2 summarizes the issues and what happens when managers exercise their power formally or informally.

5.3.1. Issue 1—How do people feel?

> *When I was coaching, the one thought that I would try to get across to my players was that everything I do each day, everything I say, I must first think what effect it will have on everyone concerned.*
>
> —Frank Layden

How people feel is important because it affects the outcomes, attitude, and working relationships between the project manager (who is exercising power) and the team members or other project personnel (over whom we exercise power).

Using as examples the two types of interaction between the manager Gillian and her subordinate James in the scenario, we can describe the feelings as:

- **Power used formally:** James has negative feelings. He is frustrated and angry that all his effort was not valued and appreciated. He feels belittled and disrespected based on how the feedback was conveyed.

- **Power used informally:** James feels positive about how the feedback was delivered. He feels appreciated, valued, and respected for his effort in preparing the report. He feels motivated and empowered to do additional work on the report or similar tasks Gillian assigns.

Albert Mehrabian (1968, 53–55) maintained both verbal and nonverbal components must be considered because

Total Message Impact = Verbal (words) + Nonverbal (vocal tones and body language). The relative percentage of each is
Total Message Impact = 7% (words) + 38% (vocal tones) + 55% (body language)[5]

Facial expressions, gestures,[6] gender,[7] and dress[8] can all influence the impact of the overall verbal message (Gladis 1985, 35–38; Steckler & Rosenthal 1985, 157–63; DuBrin 1982, 127–34). The words (7 percent) work effectively if the rest (nonverbal part (93 percent)) work together to convey the same

Leading with Purpose

message. Neutral or positive-sounding words do not sink in if the speaker's expression and body language convey annoyance or anger. How we convey the message makes a difference bigger than the words used to convey the message. Therefore, while communicating, managers should recognize the importance of verbal and nonverbal components of message delivery and be cautious in delivering contradictory messages. James might feel disempowered and demotivated to do further work for Gillian.

5.3.2. Issue 2—What are possible outcomes or outputs?

If you treat an individual ... as if he were what he ought to be and could be, he will become what he ought to be and could be.

—Johann Wolfgang Von Goethe

Influencing with power's purpose is to affect others' thoughts and actions in the desired direction. So, in the scenario, Gillian's purpose should be to urge James to produce the best report. However, she is likely to get different outcomes depending on whether she used her knowledge power over James formally or informally:

- **Power used formally:** James's motivation level will be low because he feels belittled and unappreciated. He will modify the report because his boss Gillian asked him to, but he will only produce what Gillian specified (incorporate pages 150–165 of book 2). As a result, his creativity and innovation will be low.

- **Power used informally:** James would feel more motivated because of the positive feedback if Gillian used her knowledge power informally. He would feel more committed to improving the report and willing to do much more than Gillian asked or specified. James is likelier to read more pages of Gillian's book and look at other sources. He would be more creative and innovative in producing a high-quality report for Gillian.

We can compare James's different courses of action with how a project manager can respond to a client's requests. For example, the project manager might focus only on meeting the client's written specifications or go beyond written specifications to better meet the client's goals. A project manager who takes the latter action has high motivation and produces better results, which produces greater client satisfaction.

5.3.3. Issue 3—What are people's perceptions of the project manager?

Flatter me, and I may not believe you.
Criticize me, and I may not like you.

Ignore me, and I may not forgive you.
Encourage me, and I may not forget you.
—William Arthur Ward

This quotation is an interesting statement about the use of power. People have different impressions and perceptions about their managers' quality and styles depending on how their managers use their power over them. In the scenario, the subordinate's perceptions of Gillian, resulting from her use of power, can be described as:

- **Power used formally:** James is more likely to think of Gillian as an arrogant autocrat and inflexible manager who does not appreciate and value her team members. He might see her as uninterested in helping them grow because he felt unappreciated, disempowered, and demotivated. Such managers are considered dictators or taskmasters who do not care how their people feel. They are only interested in making sure others do whatever they ask.
- **Power used informally:** James will have high respect and regard for Gillian because he thinks she appreciates and values him. He would consider Gillian more of a flexible and respectful collaborator. He would consider Gillian an empathetic leader and coach who wants team members to develop and succeed in life and on the specific project.

When team members respect and like their project managers, they do more work with high quality and innovation. As a result, they create high-performance teams that lead to successful project management.

Therefore, project managers must pay more attention to soft skills and use interpersonal skills to empower and motivate their team members. This emphasis on the people involved in projects makes some project managers more effective than others. Showing genuine care for people is an important skill for a good leader.

5–Components and Use of Power

Issues 4 and 5 deal with how client relationships and future business opportunities are affected. The focus shifts from a relationship between project managers and their team members to the relationship between project managers and their external clients who initiated the project. Sometimes, project managers manage a project and act as consultants or contractors for the project undertaken for another client. At other times, they act as a client when they contract some work packages of their project to someone else because of a lack of internal resources.

Both situations require good relationships to be established and maintained. Interestingly, the use of power and interactions carried out formally or informally can influence the understanding between the client and a contractor and, hence, the quality of relationships between them. In addition, it affects their future business opportunities and relationships. Let us look at the following simple scenario to further illustrate the quality of relationships between the client and the contractor or consultant.

Using the following "Satisfying Unidentified Needs" scenario as an example, we can examine the implications of the fourth and fifth issues.

Scenario: Satisfying Unidentified Needs (related to issues 4 and 5)

Serena was in charge of a very large project to develop new software for her company. With the unavailability of in-house software engineers, she needed to hire a consultant to work on one of the work packages of this project, which involved software design and development. She hired Mark as a consultant for such projects several times in the past, and she was happy with his performance. However, Mark was unavailable this time, and she had to look for another consultant or contractor and hired George.

The scope and statement of work (SOW) that included all requirements Serena identified was agreed upon with six milestones, a total fixed price budget of $200K, and total project duration of six months.

George started working on the project and regularly met with Serena to review the project's six main items and milestones. Finally, George finished everything included in the scope document and the SOW two weeks ahead of schedule and 3% under budget. He was excited with his overall performance, especially with the overall budget and schedule, and wanted to share his excitement with Serena (his client) in a final meeting, expecting a bonus. The conversation in the meeting went like this.

5–Components and Use of Power

George: "Well, Serena, thank you for allowing me to work on this project, and I am really excited that all six milestones and deliverables included in the SOW are completed. Furthermore, I am happy to say that we are one week ahead of schedule and 3% under budget. Are you also happy and excited about this?"

Serena: "Good work, George! However, I am concerned about something I learned from my technical team leader Angelee who interacted a lot with you on this project. She indicated that for two of the six deliverables, we could have incorporated some flexibility for future expansion of our system, but now it will be very difficult to do so."

In this case, Serena thought George met all the requirements identified in the SOW, but he did not go beyond this to incorporate additional features that could provide flexibility for the software system's expansion. Saving two weeks on the schedule at this time was not important to Serena, especially at the cost of losing an opportunity to incorporate flexibility at this time for enhancements.

Leading with Purpose

> Question 1: What are Serena's main concerns?
>
> Question 2: How could George try to meet Serena's unidentified needs?
>
> Question 3: What are the advantages of pursuing unidentified needs in addition to just meeting identified needs?

5.3.4. Issue 4—How are client relationships affected?

There is a real magic in enthusiasm. It spells the difference between mediocrity and accomplishment.

—Norman Vincent Peale

The relationship between the client and the contractor is highly affected, depending on the client's approach—whether too much of a formal or an informal approach is used. We can describe both sides as:

- **Power used formally:** Serena felt George used his knowledge, experience, and expertise power too formally, meaning George focused on getting the short-term requirements specified in the Statement of Work (SOW) without thinking about the organization's future.

- **Power used informally:** George could have used an informal approach because he was doing well on the project's schedule and budget. He could have used his knowledge and experience to discover future requirements and initiate discussion in his interactions with the technical team leader (Angelee) to incorporate enough flexibility at this phase to make the overall system's expansion easier and less costly.

Now, many project managers might wonder how we should use our power because the different approaches lead to different outcomes, as described below:

- Some project managers think George should focus on that alone because the company hired him to work on a defined SOW. If Serena wanted flexibility for expansion, the present SOW should have shown it. We can consider this a formal business approach, and the relationship between Serena and George (client and contractor) might be short-term.
- Perhaps incorporating flexibilities for system expansion was not George's responsibility. However, had he made these efforts, he would have been viewed more as a collaborator, working with Angelee, Serena, and other team members to explore their "unidentified requirements" to help them advance their business. Going beyond the minimum would put George in a better position for future contract opportunities and strengthen future business relationships.

5.3.5. Issue 5—What are the effects on future business opportunities?

Someone's sitting in the shade today because someone planted a tree a long time ago.

—Warren Buffett

The purposes of influencing others are to do things with the highest quality and increase future business. Using the scenario described between Serena (the client) and George (the contractor), understanding how power is used can better explain this issue. The effects of using power formally or informally can be described:

- **Power used formally:** If George meets all the identified requirements as defined in the contract or SOW agreed upon by both parties, George gets at least these results:
    - George is paid for the contract.
    - George cannot be sued because he met all his obligations as specified in the signed contract or SOW. He alleges anything beyond this SOW, such as the "unidentified requirements" referred to by Serena, was not part of this contract, and he should not be penalized for not fulfilling them. However, the reality in business involves more than meeting contract requirements.
- **Power used informally:** Serena felt that George should have acted more as a collaborator than a contractor for this project, which would have meant tapping more into his

5–Components and Use of Power

informal power. Besides meeting his obligations as specified in the contract or SOW, he should have used his knowledge, power, and experience to initiate more discussions with Angelee and Serena to address flexibility for expansion, especially when he was early. George could use his communication skills more effectively by asking probing questions to uncover requirements not identified in the present contract. Once some of the "unidentified needs" have been discovered, they could discuss whether they should be incorporated into the present contract by evaluating:

- Is it technically possible to incorporate them at this phase?
- Do we have enough resources with the right skill mix?
- What is the impact on the overall budget and schedule?

Discovering unidentified requirements is challenging, especially in an IT environment where most clients feel challenged to define their identified requirements. However, we must do so because it leads to good references and future business. Unfortunately, many project managers give lip service to this concept yet do not follow it effectively. Although finding unidentified requirements seems difficult, consultants or contractors can do it by:

- Showing genuine concern for clients about their advancement, future business, competitive edge, and increased market share.
- Figuring out What's In It For Them (WIIFT).

- Speaking their language and touching their passions. People open and share their thoughts more freely when we share their passions and interests, which leads to better references, repeat business, and future contracts.

The dividends of discovering and addressing unidentified needs, or at least the client's perception of an honest attempt to do so, are high. It leads to a win-win situation for both. Here, the client gets flexibility or a detailed analysis of what incorporates the flexibility in the present contract for expansion. The contractor or consultant is a true collaborator or partner interested in enhancing the client's business. In addition, the contractor or consultant gets good references leading to repeat business and future contracts.

So, from the above scenarios, examples, and discussions, we cannot have power without knowing how to use it effectively. Managers must exercise their powers skillfully and thoughtfully to gain team members' commitment to the project. Using power in this way influences and motivates team members to achieve higher-quality outcomes and deliverables. Often, project managers work under tight deadlines. But the dividends of exercising power properly and informally by effectively using their communication and other interpersonal skills are high in overall business and long-term relationships with stakeholders.

Chapter 5 Summary

We receive formal or positional power based on our position in the organizational chart. It is more similar to authority than informal power because formal power frequently comes from authority. Line authority, staff authority, and functional authority are three types of authority related to formal power. Formal power can be a powerful source of authority. Functional authority managers make routine and specialized decisions.

Setting boundaries for each specialist is more difficult, which may cause problems and challenges. The desire to obey authority figures is a deeply ingrained social condition.

Informal power stems from a person's knowledge, experience, contacts, and leadership abilities. Using informal power informally can produce better results than relying solely on formal power. Therefore, project managers should focus on developing informal power rather than relying on formal authority. They can strengthen their informal powers by expanding their expertise, social networks, information access, and persuasive abilities. Managers can expand their informal powers by distributing them to other managers. More people respect and collaborate with them because of their knowledge. The total power of a project manager includes both formal and informal components.

Project managers who are well-liked and respected and have a strong base of informal power have an advantage over their counterparts. In addition, project managers should have more informal power because it follows them regardless of their jobs or positions.

Exercising power (formal or informal) is not binary; it refers to the perceptions or feelings arising from the process and communication used in exercising power. Project managers who do not effectively use their power risk losing it because their subordinates are unhappy, dissatisfied, and under pressure to do as they are told. People's feelings are important because they influence outcomes, attitudes, and working relationships. Managers must understand the significance of verbal and nonverbal message delivery components. Facial expressions, gestures, gender, and dress can all have an impact on the overall impact of the verbal message. Project managers must pay more attention to soft skills and use interpersonal skills to empower and motivate their team members.

Some project managers are more effective at demonstrating genuine concern for others. Depending on the client's approach, the relationship between the client and the contractor is greatly influenced. Once "unidentified needs" have been identified, they can decide whether they should be included in the current contract. Managers must wield power effectively to gain team members' commitment to the project. The benefits of identifying and addressing unidentified needs, or at least the client's perception of an honest attempt to do so, are substantial. Using power in this manner influences and motivates team members to produce better results.

Chapter 5 Review and Critical Thinking Questions

1. Describe two main components of power. Give examples of how and when project managers use each component in managing their projects.
2. Describe the three types of authority related to formal power.
3. What is informal power? Describe the four main advantages of informal power. Give examples of how you can achieve these advantages as a project manager.
4. Describe the five main issues and associated outcomes when using your power formally or informally when interacting with six of your project stakeholders.
5. Describe the issues project managers focus on when they are under pressure because of time, cost, and scope constraints in managing their projects. Give examples.
6. Describe the issues leaders focus on when using their power. Give examples.
7. In project management, what is the importance of defining the scope upfront and then managing the scope appropriately to deliver projects successfully?
8. How would you describe the identified needs of your customers and clients that must be satisfied to deliver successful projects?
9. How would you describe the unidentified needs of your customers and clients? What strategies should project managers use to address unidentified needs?

10. What are the benefits of satisfying the unidentified needs of your customers and clients? Illustrate with examples how you would balance the efforts required and the potential benefits in satisfying the unidentified needs of your customers.

Chapter 6

Eight Sources of Power

*Opportunities? They are all around us . . .
there is power lying latent everywhere waiting
for the observant eye to discover it.*
—Orson Swett Marden

Obtaining power and knowing how to use it effectively are crucial for a project manager to succeed. However, knowing their power sources is equally important for project managers to understand their abilities and limitations. By understanding the power sources and their characteristics, a project manager can influence and direct project stakeholders more effectively by making them want to do their best rather than just meet demands. Therefore, project managers must take two steps to manage their power effectively: (1) try to gain power and (2) learn to use power effectively.

To maintain their power, project managers must try to gain their powers ethically rather than steal power from others. They must also address issues related to exercising their power. To maintain their power, project managers should use it mostly informally rather than formally. However, project managers must only use their powers formally as a last resort. Informal use of power leads to successful influencing and helps gain commitment, whereas formal use of power refers to the command-and-control style.

This chapter describes the eight sources of power: legitimate power, reward power, coercive power, referent power, expert power, information power, network power, and persuasion power. This chapter also describes the factors associated with each power source, tips to exercise each source of power, and practical guidelines to increase each source of power.

Eight Sources of Power

There are eight sources of power, and most sources or types of power are informal. Project managers should focus primarily on increasing the informal powers because of their four distinct advantages:

1. Informal power is permanent (no one can take it away).
2. Informal power can be increased anytime.
3. Informal power increases by sharing with others (the more we share, the more we get).
4. A stronger foundation of informal power leads to opportunities for formal power or promotion.

Project managers should review all eight sources of power and work on them according to their strengths, interests, and long-term goals (Youker

6–Eight Sources of Power

1991, 36–40).[1] Figure 6.1 shows how these eight power sources are similar to a work breakdown structure (WBS) of power. The high-level characteristics are shown for each power source, and each source is labeled as formal or informal.

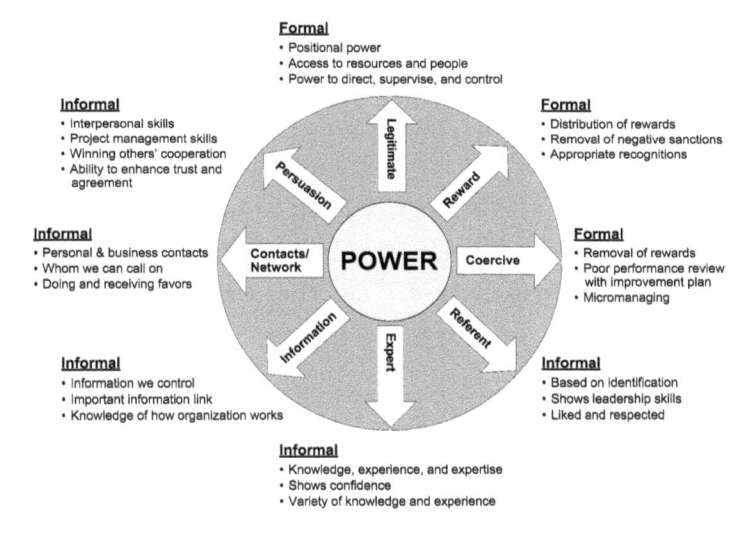

Figure 6.1. Eight sources of power.

The following are important points to note in Figure 6.1:

- There are only three formal powers (legitimate, reward, and coercive power).
- Legitimate power also gives the power to reward and punish. Therefore, to simplify, these three sources of power can be grouped into one source as a formal power.
- Most powers are informal (about 20 percent of sources of power are formal, and 80 percent are informal).

- Information power combines a small component of formal power and a large component of informal power.
- We can increase overall power by increasing any power.
- We must work to increase informal powers because of their advantages.
- We should typically use all powers (formal or informal) informally to gain more commitment and achieve better results.
- We should still be willing to use power formally, but only as a last resort.

The following describes the eight sources of power:

6.1. Legitimate Power

He who pays the piper calls the tune.

—Proverb

Legitimate power refers to the right to give orders and make requests, as required, to do things. It is formal authority but unreliable, as it can change as our position on the organizational chart changes. A powerful position (more people reporting to us means more legitimate power) can create a perceived right to make decisions and direct project personnel's efforts as the power holder sees fit. Project personnel often suspend their judgments and let power holders guide their behavior. This is not limited to the right to direct, supervise, and control but also might include the right to reward and punish, depending on the actions and outcomes.

Besides gaining legitimate power from formal authority, legitimate power can also come from the informal rule of reciprocity—if we do something for someone, they feel obligated to do something for us. Legitimate power limits how much influence we can exercise, and those using it should recognize the limits.

Figure 6.2 represents a typical hierarchical organization chart. It shows that a matrix assigns people from various functional departments to project managers A, B, and C.

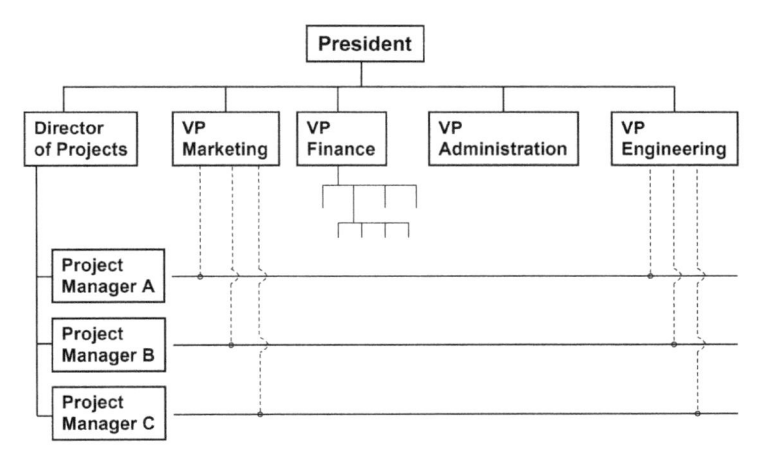

Figure 6.2. Typical organizational structure showing legitimate power.

There are important points to recognize about legitimate power. Legitimate power attached to a position belongs to the person occupying the box identifying that position on an organizational chart. This person loses their legitimate power if moved out of the box (transferred to another department or leaves the

Leading with Purpose

organization). For example, in Figure 6.2, the president is the most powerful person because many boxes come out of their box, and solid lines connect all those boxes.

If solid lines do not connect a box to other boxes, the person occupying that box has limited legitimate power. However, if dotted lines connect the box, as for Project Managers A, B, and C in Figure 6.2 with resources assigned on a matrix basis, their legitimate power is broken just like the dotted line. Project managers only have legitimate power over those who directly report to them and connect with their box by solid lines.

6.2. Reward Power

Encourage each other to become the best you can be. Celebrate what you want to see more of.

—Tom Peters

Reward power refers to managers' ability to offer their employees positive consequences such as monetary rewards, promotions, raises, and vacations. Conversely, subordinates sometimes may have reward power over their bosses through upward peer appraisals. Typically, this power refers to managers' ability to influence others by controlling the distribution of rewards valued by others and removing negative sanctions.

All people like rewards and feel motivated if they receive the rewards they want. Therefore, we must understand the effectiveness of rewards in terms of what, when, and why. People like rewards because they satisfy their needs and desire to be recognized and appreciated for their efforts. It is human nature to seek this satisfaction.

Managers must understand this important concept about the effectiveness of rewards. We must choose rewards for our employees to turn them ON (Nelson 2012).[2] When we use this approach, managers use their reward power effectively, which helps them motivate their project team members. Monetary rewards are not necessarily the most important rewards given. A review of eighty studies evaluated various motivational factors and their impact on productivity. Although they supported the importance of money in increasing productivity, these studies also highlighted these points about increasing productivity (Locke, Feren, McCaleb, Shaw & Denny 1980, 363–383):[3]

- Proper goal-setting led to a 16 percent increase in productivity.
- Employee involvement in decision-making increased productivity by less than 1 percent.
- Job enrichment increased productivity by 8 percent–16 percent.
- Monetary rewards resulted in up to 30 percent increases in productivity.

These studies' results show that a reward is only effective if it satisfies the employee's needs they value the most. All rewards might seem good to most people, but the most effective are those satisfying their most important needs. This being the case, managers must identify:

- What is the most important or valuable need?
- What reward will satisfy that need?

Both points differ for different people, and as a person's life circumstances change, their most relevant needs or rewards also change. Therefore, project managers must know their team members' most important needs and create rewards to satisfy them. Some senior executives suggest "managing by walking around (MBWA)" to understand project personnel better by learning their interests and passions.

6.3. Coercive Power

> *Being responsible sometimes means ticking people off.*
>
> —Maria Bartell

Coercive power is the ability to impose negative consequences on subordinates, such as suspending or reprimanding employees, docking pay, and assigning unpleasant tasks. Sometimes called old-style authority, it has been largely discouraged in recent years and labeled as predicated on fear. Coercive power is used horizontally (among team members), not just vertically (by managers and subordinates). For example, team members looking to increase their power in a group might use this power to ridicule, belittle, and ostracize their peers. Though, coercive power is the ability to influence others by controlling the distribution of punishment and removing rewards others value.

A positive view of coercive power is to think of it as power an employee might not want and might dislike, but its emphasis should be on understanding what is going wrong and how to improve it. This

exercise's most productive part is to have an honest discussion without pointing fingers and then create an action plan to improve the situation. Some project managers exercise their coercive power in different ways that include:
- Negative performance appraisals
- Micromanaging
- Taking away privileges (working from home, training, seminars, and conferences)

Most people feel uncomfortable about coercive power, especially when they use it formally. Project managers should turn team members' poor performance with constructive and timely feedback. The following are common tactics project managers can use to confront poor performers:
- Be neutral in giving feedback. State the facts; do not use judgmental statements, and do not rehash the past.
- Give constructive feedback promptly.
- Prepare an improvement plan with a timeline.
- Explain how performance improvements will be evaluated.

6.4. Referent Power

The leader's role is not to control people or stay on top of things, but rather to guide, energize and excite.

—Jack Welch

Referent power is the power project managers wield when subordinates admire and respect them. In this sense, a manager is viewed as a strong leader or a role model, which results in personnel willing to meet the project manager's demands voluntarily. This power has two components: (1) subordinates identify with someone with great power or a high-profile project, and (2) the manager's leadership skills.

If people closely identify with their managers, the managers have referent power through admiration, as team members like and respect them. This power can develop slowly over time and closely relates to the managers' leadership skills. Leaders are usually seen as having good charisma. Those with charisma can develop an interpersonal attraction with team members and, over time, build great trust and respect. Both identification and leadership skills are keys, as the combination results in high commitment, meaning team members want to follow the managers rather than just comply with orders and instructions.

6.5. Expert Power

*You cannot build a reputation
on what you are going to do.*

—Henry Ford

Expert power is earned personal power based on technical knowledge, skills, or expertise. If project personnel believe their project manager has extensive expertise, they voluntarily comply with the project manager's requests and assigned tasks. Managers with expert power pass their knowledge or skills to their team members, which helps them gain team members' support and commitment, leading to higher motivation for better performance. This is especially true when our expertise can help others accomplish their goals. As with most informal powers, expert power has the advantage of staying with us permanently. It cannot be taken away, regardless of organizational position or changing circumstances.

Expert power is commonly the power most easily associated with overall reputation. Most professionals build their reputations by showing knowledge and achievement in their field. Reputation can be described as the most important power an individual can possess, and it is sometimes called the cornerstone of power (Greene 2000).[4] Although it is perhaps the most respected power, it can be the most difficult to obtain because of the time and effort involved. It pays off, however, because senior management trusts people with expert power. As a result, they can benefit the organization through their experience, expertise, and knowledge.

6.6. Information Power

It is wise to disclose what cannot be concealed.
—Johann Friedrich Von Schiller

Information power is gained when a person is perceived to have control over the information flow. When someone has privileged access to information sources, they are gatekeepers with the power to distribute valued information selectively at their discretion. This power enables managers to address confidentiality issues and engage in secrecy (withholding information) and selective fact dissemination. Additionally, through privileged access to information, managers likely have the advantage of superior data interpretation, which allows them to focus on critical activities such as forecasting (predicting market changes, becoming marketing specialists) and company expertise (knowing how our organization works through policies).

In another way, project managers gain information power by understanding their organization's policies, procedures, strengths, and limitations. This helps them learn how the organization should work and how it works. They know how to ethically avoid bureaucracy and red tape to do things faster. All this information and organizational awareness give them the information power to achieve results more effectively. Therefore, the greater our information, the greater our power.

Exchanging and sharing information with other stakeholders increases project managers' information power. The greater the network of people sharing this information, the more communication lines increase each person's information power. The number of participants can be considered nodes in the communication network. As these participants exchange information with others, lines of communication among participants, or the number of links, increase by the following formula:

The number of lines of communication (total links) = N(N – 1)/2, where N = the number of participants or nodes.

For example, if the total participants are four, N = 4, including one project manager (D) and three participants (A, B and C), the total lines of communication will be 6, that is, 4(4−1)/2 = 6, as shown in Figure 6.3.

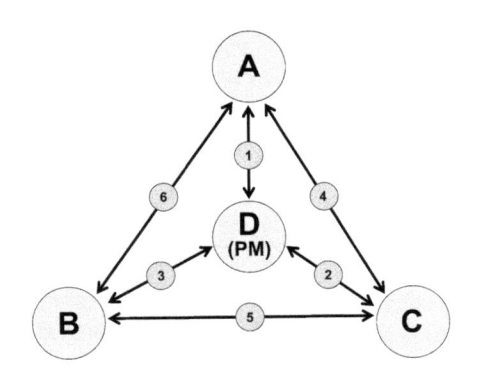

$$\text{Number of links} = \frac{N(N-1)}{2} = \frac{4(4-1)}{2} = \frac{4(3)}{2} = \frac{12}{2} = 6$$

Where N is the number of people exchanging the information

Figure 6.3. Information power and number of links for four participants.

Leading with Purpose

If the number of participants (N) increases from 4 to 6, the lines of communication equal 15, which represents a significant increase by adding only two participants. Figure 6.4 shows the 15 lines of communication with 6 participants, including the Project Manager (D) and 5 other participants (A, B, C, E and F). With these increased lines of communication among all participants, the information power of each dramatically increases as they share information. It reinforces the advantage of sharing information—the more information people share, the more information power they get.

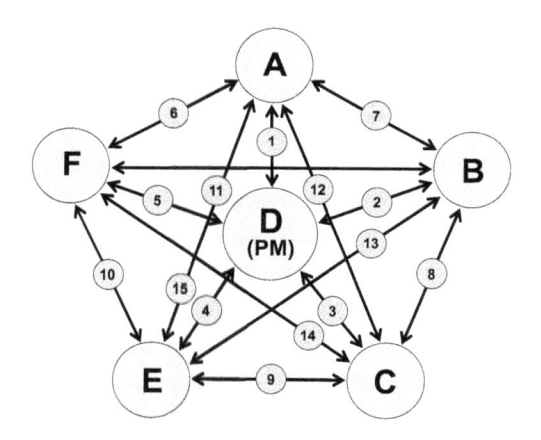

Number of links = $\dfrac{N(N-1)}{2} = \dfrac{6(6-1)}{2} = \dfrac{6(5)}{2} = \dfrac{30}{2} = 15$

Where N is the number of people exchanging the information

Figure 6.4. Information power and number of links for six participants.

When a project manager has information power that others do not, others depend on the manager to obtain the information they seek. The more people depend on a manager, the more indispensable the manager becomes. The more indispensable we become, the more can extend our power further, particularly information power.

Managers usually need at least a few people to get the information they need to maintain their information power base. But the fewer this number is, the better to control the information flow (Kotter 2008).[5] Some project managers use this concept to increase their power. They have a network of a few people from whom they get important information. Then, they process this information and increase their information power's quality and quantity.

Because many other project personnel depend on such a project manager to get various information to complete their tasks, they perceive the project manager as having significant information power. Additionally, as project managers depend on only a few people for information, they have more independence and stability, which are valuable assets (Dilenschneider 2007, 82–88).[6]

6.7. Network Power

If you make yourself valuable and memorable, others will want to make you part of their network.

—Jeffrey Gitomer

Network power is an important power project managers should increase. Unfortunately, many project managers think they are too busy and cannot find enough time for networking. Although we should expand our network to include as many people as

Leading with Purpose

possible, the quality of our contacts and the depth of honest and reliable relationships are the strengths of network power.

We can use network power when we have a large network of influential people in and outside the organization. It is a power base derived from knowing the right people. This network is based on both personal contacts and business contacts. The larger and deeper the network is, the greater power we can draw from it. These contacts are useful in making new connections and providing information, increasing overall network power. Network power is often gained through reciprocal relationships. Doing favors and being a useful resource for others make them feel committed and obligated to us, solidifying them as valuable contacts on whom to draw.

Managers who concern themselves more with acquiring many contacts often overlook cultivating relationships to expand and strengthen their network. They have as many contacts as possible but even fewer contacts who are close, genuine, and influential. It is difficult to pinpoint the best way to attract these golden acquaintances, but two general rules are worth following:

1. Be where the best and the brightest professionals in the sector or industry are, whether at meetings or seminars.
2. Exude confidence and charisma constantly and naturally to attract the admiration of followers and other leaders' respect and interest (Dilenschneider 2007, 125–38).[7]

The following are two practical strategies to enlarge and strengthen our network:

1. Nurture the network (keep our network alive).
Contact people in our network regularly and stay in touch. At a minimum, send them wishes on their birthdays and greetings on holidays or other special occasions.

2. Feed the network (do favors first for others).
Feed the network by doing favors before expecting anything in return or asking people for favors. This strategy conveys more sincerity in relationships and increases the depth of relationships. It is like a bank account in that we must make deposits first. Do favors for others; otherwise, our checks bounce. The rule of give and take is "Before you take, you gotta give" (Gitomer 2006).[8]

6.8. Persuasion Power

You have to believe that by persuading other persons, you are helping them and that after you have persuaded them, they will benefit.

—Jeffrey Gitomer

Persuasion power is persuading others to do what we want with communication skills rather than formal power. This practical power requires a person to have patience and effective communication skills to use properly. Persuasion power is largely based on interpersonal skills such as solid communication and negotiation techniques and people skills such as integration, facilitation, running or planning sessions or meetings, and enhancing teamwork. For example, a manager wins subordinates' cooperation and commitment through this power base and uses their power to enhance trust and agreement, leading to higher follower satisfaction and performance.

Persuading is like negotiating to get what we want. To persuade successfully, we must prepare, prepare, prepare. Preparation includes knowing or learning the following about the other parties:

- What do they want and why?
- How strongly do they feel about it?
- What would it take to sway them?
- How can we meet their interests?
- How can we add value if they go along with us?

Active listening is the key to successful persuasion because it properly understands the other parties' positions and interests. Once these are understood, project managers can develop a plan to prepare logical arguments to persuade others to accept their viewpoint. Project managers should communicate in the other parties' preferred communication styles because it often starts communication on the right foot, and the other parties are more likely to agree.

Like communication style, the other parties' professional background is important. For example, engineers, IT, or technical professionals can often be persuaded only by means such as logic, data, and statistics, whereas analogies, metaphors, anecdotes, and examples might sway people with softer backgrounds better. The strategy of persuasion is to analyze the situation from the other person's viewpoint, which requires empathetic listening. Follow one of the seven habits of highly effective people (Covey 2013): "Seek first to understand and then to be understood."[9]

We must analyze the issues (both tangible and intangible) and then develop a strategy to resolve them to achieve a win-win situation. Unfortunately, many people fail in persuading because they believe their viewpoint is better or more correct and impose their views too strongly. This leads to confrontation rather than collaboration to reach a win-win solution.

The objective of persuading people is to reach clear agreements and ensure they take accountability for carrying through those agreements. It is better done when there is open and honest communication, and genuine effort is made to convince them to accept the responsibility and accountability to produce good quality results. This gains accountability power, a valuable technique a manager can use to best access a person's potential.

Table 6.1 shows the keywords of persuasion concisely, highlighting various factors to focus on achieving successful persuasion. By examining these individual points, certain similarities, and patterns emerge. First, most require a project manager to use informal power to understand better and show respect for those they try to influence. Persuasive project managers understand those they wish to influence and have empathy and respect for them. They offer encouragement, ensure fair agreements, encourage cooperation, and pursue mutually beneficial outcomes. Second, a project manager must use interpersonal skills effectively to engage properly in factors leading to successful persuasion. Without a base of strong interpersonal skills, it becomes difficult to carry out the steps to achieve persuasion efficiently.

Leading with Purpose

	Keyword	Focuses On
P	Preparation	Prepare! Prepare! Prepare!
E	Empathy	Showing we care for others
R	Respect	Treating others with respect
S	Softness (in words)	Encouraging, not criticizing
U	Understanding	Creating mutual understanding between parties
A	Agreements	Ensuring agreements reached are fair and reasonable
S	Synergy	Emphasizing importance of working together
I	Interests	Focusing on interests rather than on positions
O	Organizational Awareness	Increasing knowledge about how organization works
N	Negotiation	Striving for win/win solutions

Table 6.1. Persuasion (in a Nutshell)

Chapter 6 Summary

To succeed, project managers must acquire power and use it properly. To do this, project managers must also know the eight power sources they have: (1) legitimate, (2) reward, (3) coercive, (4) referent, (5) expert, (6) information, (7) network, and (8) persuasion. Legitimate, reward, and coercive power are the only formal powers; the others are informal, with information power having a small component of formal power.

6–Eight Sources of Power

Informal power is the most advantageous, so we should work to increase informal power and use formal power as a last resort.

Legitimate power ties to our position in the organizational chart and refers to the right to give orders and make requests to do things. It is limited to those reporting to us and changes as our position changes. Reward power refers to our ability to offer positive consequences or rewards. However, the rewards must be valuable and important to the recipients to be effective. Coercive power is the ability to influence others by controlling the distribution of punishment and by removing rewards others value. It is used horizontally and vertically. Referent power derives from the admiration and respect of subordinates. This power has two components: (1) subordinates identify with someone with great power or a high-profile project, and (2) the manager's leadership skills.

Expert power is personal power earned by technical knowledge, skills, or expertise, and the power most easily associated with reputation. Senior management trusts people whose experience, expertise, and knowledge benefit the organization.

People with information power are perceived to control the information flow with privileged access to information. Information power is increased through access to information sources, understanding policies and procedures, and networking. The following formula illustrates the effect of increasing information power:

The number of lines of communication (total links) = $N(N-1)/2$, where N = the number of participants or nodes

Leading with Purpose

Managers derive power from others' dependence on information. Information power holders gain independence and stability from depending on only a few people for information.

Network power comes from knowing many people, but the quality of contacts and the depth of honest and reliable relationships are more important. Attract close, genuine, and influential contacts by being where the best and brightest professionals in the industry are and exuding confidence and charisma constantly and naturally. Nurture the network (keep the network alive) and feed the network (do favors first for others).

Persuasion power is persuading others to do what we want with communication skills rather than formal power. It requires patience and effective communication skills. Preparation, active listening, and understanding others' backgrounds are the keys to successful persuasion. Our objectives are to reach clear agreements and ensure others take accountability to carry through the agreements.

By understanding the power sources and their characteristics, a project manager can influence and direct project stakeholders more effectively by making them want to do their best rather than just meet demands.

Chapter 6 Review and Critical Thinking Questions

1. Review the eight sources of power described in this chapter. Identify which sources of power are formal and which ones are informal.

2. In your project management experience, which powers are you comfortable with and why? Give examples. Which powers are you uncomfortable with and why? Give examples.
3. In your project management experience, how and when did you use your formal powers? What were the outcomes? What personal and emotional challenges did you encounter while formally using your formal powers? How would you resolve them?
4. In your project management experience, how and when did you use your informal powers? What were the outcomes? What were challenges did you encounter while using your informal powers? How would you resolve them?
5. Which sources of power would you focus on as a leader and why?
6. Describe the two main components of referent power. How would you increase each component to increase your effectiveness in managing projects successfully?
7. What are the main features of network power? What strategies would you use to increase your network power to manage and lead projects effectively?
8. What are the main features of expert power? What strategies would you use to increase this power in delivering successful projects?
9. What are the main features of information power? How is it related to the number of stakeholders involved in exchanging the information? What strategies would you use to

increase this power in delivering successful projects?

10. What is the difference between persuasion and forcing and persuasion and influence? Describe when and why you would use these strategies while interacting with your stakeholders.

11. What are the main features of persuasion power? What are the main keywords for persuasion described in this chapter, and what is the focus of each keyword? What strategies would you use to increase your persuasion power in managing projects successfully?

Chapter 7

The Project Manager and Power

Those who succeed are the efficient few. They are the few who have the ambition and willpower to develop themselves.

—Robert Burton

Project management requires unique skills and techniques. Most project managers have great responsibility but often no direct authority over their team members because of a matrix structure. Therefore, project managers must increase their total power and balance it with other managers to achieve synergy and increase overall organizational performance.

Power and authority are important in project management, yet they are confusing practically. There are two forms, or components, of power: (1) formal and (2) informal. *Formal power* is granted by the hierarchical position in the organization chart. Formal power derives from authority. *Informal power* is earned based on knowledge, experience, contacts, and leadership skills.

Project managers' success depends on their acquisition of power and the ability to use it properly. As discussed earlier, there are eight sources of power: (1) legitimate power, (2) reward power, (3) coercive power, (4) referent power, (5) expert power, (6) information power, (7) network power, and (8) persuasion power, and most of these powers are informal. Legitimate, reward, and coercive power are the only formal powers.

We can use power formally or informally with different impacts. Project managers should understand each component of power, its use, and its impacts. Five issues arise in response to managers using power in either a predominantly formal way or predominantly informal way: (1) how people feel, (2) possible outcomes or outputs, (3) people's perceptions of the project manager, (4) how client relationships are affected, and (5) the effects on future business opportunities.

The purpose of influencing by using power is to affect others' thoughts and actions to achieve desired outcomes or outputs. People perceive their managers based on how the managers use their power. Project managers should use their powers informally and be willing to use them formally, but only as a last resort. They must recognize that their total power relies on knowing how to use it effectively to improve their performance.

This chapter defines a project manager's total power (formal + informal) and describes strategies to increase the eight power sources. Project managers should strive to increase their team members' power because the team is their most important power base.

We discuss the importance of balancing power between project managers and functional managers.

7.1. A Project Manager's Total Power

Nature arms each man with some faculty, which enables him to do easily some feat impossible to any other.

—Ralph Waldo Emerson

Project managers' total power combines their positional power and their personal power. Therefore, project managers should work to increase their total power by increasing any of the eight forms of power, depending on their interest and aptitude, resources available, and support from their organizations and network.

Project managers increase their power by leveraging their team members' power, especially by encouraging everyone to share their knowledge, expertise, and information power. To do this effectively, they must empower their team members continually and help them increase their powers. Referring to the situational leadership model (Hersey, Blanchard & Johnson 2012), this is like increasing the professional strength and maturity level every leader must do for their followers.[1]

Leaders become more effective when they try to increase their team members' developmental/maturity levels. Team leadership also relates to the maturity level of the team members (the followers). Team members' maturity or developmental level depends on three factors:

1. Competence: task-relevant knowledge and skills and transferable skills
2. Commitment: composed of the following:
    - Motivation: energy, enthusiasm, and commitment
    - Confidence: self-esteem and self-assuredness (allows people to trust in their decision-making)
3. Attitude: lasting beliefs and behavior tendencies directed toward specific team members, team ideas, issues, or objects

Different powers are interrelated. For example, legitimate power gives us the power to reward or punish. Powers also overlap, as network, information, and referent power have several things in common, especially related leadership skills. One common characteristic among all three powers is the importance of using them informally. Project managers get better results from their stakeholders and enhance their team members' productivity by using their communication, negotiation, team building, and persuasion skills while being culturally sensitive to their team members.

No one likes to take orders, so it pays to phrase requests informally when changes or decisions must be made. For example, rather than demanding employees work extra hours to meet a deadline, ask, "Is there any way we can adjust your hours or personnel assignments to better meet the deadline?" When workers feel involved in the process and think the ideas came from them, they will be much more eager to cooperate and accomplish the tasks (Carnegie 2011).[2] Developing a sense of obligation in other team members increases project managers' overall power, which is a desirable outcome. They should also make the organization believe they are experts, have others identify with the project manager, and develop the perception that team members depend on one another and the project manager.

The following are keys to the effective use of power:

- Project managers should choose their appropriate power base (their project team) because they only shine if their team members make them shine.
- Project managers must execute their power skillfully and thoughtfully by paying special attention to their team members' viewpoints, verbal and visual (body language) feedback, and cultural aspects.

Remember that the dynamics of power are complex. This complexity exists because of perceptions about whether we have or can get something the other person wants. Sometimes, we might have power and not even know it. Power can be derived from various skills, talents, habits, and personalities.

Depending on how we apply or exercise our power, our group or we can benefit. For example, if we make a presentation on a project or research to which our group members contributed, the group benefits from having expert power if we mention them specifically in our presentation. The first step for project managers trying to earn benefits for themselves and their team is to put themselves in a position to succeed. The best way to do this is to increase their power bases.

7.2. Strategies to Increase the Eight Sources of Power

> *In order to obtain and hold power,*
> *a man must love it.*
>
> —Leo Tolstoy

There are many ways to increase our power and how effectively we use the power already acquired. To do this, we must understand the types and bases of the eight sources of power, as shown in Table 7.1. Project managers can increase their overall power by increasing any of the eight sources of power.

The following list outlines techniques to help project managers increase each source of power efficiently.

7.2.1. Legitimate power

> *Authority without wisdom is like a heavy ax*
> *without an edge—fitter to bruise than polish.*
>
> —Anne Bradstreet

Based on: Power related to position in the organization chart

Means to attain:

- Develop relationships with senior managers and stakeholders.
- Increase project sponsor involvement.
- Get to know the manager and stakeholder interests outside work.

7–The Project Manager and Power

	Sources of Power	**Type of Power**	**Basis of Power**
1	Legitimate	Formal	· Positional power · Access to resources (money and people)
2	Reward	Formal	· Distribution of rewards · Developing effective rewards
3	Coercive	Formal	· Poor performance review with a plan to improve · Removal of rewards
4	Referent	Informal	· Identification with high-profile people and projects · Leadership skills
5	Expert	Informal	· Variety of knowledge and experience · Shows degree of confidence of management
6	Information	Informal	· Knowledge of how organization really works · Important information link
7	Network	Informal	· Personal and business contacts · Doing and receiving favors
8	Persuasion	Informal	· Winning others' cooperation (negotiation) · Ability to enhance trust and agreement

Table 7.1. Sources, Types and Bases of Power

Leading with Purpose

- Ask to clarify expectations, roles, and responsibilities.
- Know who is responsible for what.
- Volunteer to fill roles our organization lacks.
- Ask to work on high-profile projects.
- Restructure projects to gain more authority.
- Provide informal employee performance feedback.
- Serve on committees where decisions are made.
- Get involved in budget decisions.
- Take on leadership roles on teams.
- Take responsibility for producing project WBS and project plans.
- Build an alliance with our customers by satisfying expectations.
- Volunteer on boards and committees.
- Prepare a progression plan and a succession plan.
- Pay attention to internal and external politics to identify future opportunities.
- Be aware of major restructuring plans to position ourselves properly for the future.

7.2.2. Reward power

Encourage each other to become the best you can be. Celebrate what you want to see more of.
—Tom Peters

Type: Formal
Based on: Distribution of rewards
Means to attain:
- Do performance appraisals.
- Publicly acknowledge achievements (only if people like for use to).
- Give service awards.
- Grant flexible work hours.
- Approve training requests.
- Give more challenges, responsibility, and choice assignments.
- Send handwritten thank-you cards.
- Provide good feedback about our team members to their functional managers.
- Tailor rewards to the person—learn what they value.
- Influence senior management to get recognition or rewards for our people.

Nelson (1997) suggests many simple but effective rewards to energize people.[3]

7.2.3. Coercive power

> *The ideal of behaviorism is to eliminate coercion: to apply controls by changing the environment in such a way as to reinforce the kind of behavior that benefits everyone.*
> —B. F. Skinner

Type: Formal
Based on: Withholding rewards
Means to attain:
- Remove rewards and privileges.
- Give objective performance appraisals.
- Withdraw high-profile assignments and responsibilities.
- Address poor performance positively.
- Address the issues, not the person.
- Give honest feedback by staying neutral:
    - Use "I" statements, not "you" statements.
    - Do not editorialize; do not pass judgment.
    - Be silent and wait for an answer or feedback.
- Prepare an improvement plan with the employee.

7.2.4. Referent power

Your role as a leader is even more important than you might imagine. You have the power to help people become winners.

—Ken Blanchard

Type: Informal
Based on: Identification or affiliation
Means to attain:
- Listen without interrupting.
- Take time to network with those with power.
- Invite our customer to a project meeting.
- Be visible and available to the team; have face-to-face discussions.
- Show interest in team members.
- Protect our team.
- Make the team feel valued.
- Give meaningful feedback; copy functional managers.
- Acknowledge our team's strengths.
- Celebrate success!
- Be accessible.
- Lead by example.
- Align our project goals with organizational goals.
- Identify with powerful, influential, and respected people.
- Develop leadership skills by learning from our mentors.

7.2.5. Expert power

> *You cannot build a reputation on what you are going to do.*
>
> —Henry Ford

Type: Informal
Based on: Knowledge, experience, and expertise
Means to attain:

- Become certified in our field.
- Create opportunities to use our skills.
- Join professional societies.
- Communicate our skills; highlight our successes.
- Give formal presentations.
- Provide coaching/mentoring.
- Look beyond our project; get involved with other projects.
- Take varied assignments.
- Act like a consultant.
- Find a mentor.
- Mentor others (we learn by teaching).
- Write a white paper or report.
- Publish in reputable journals.
- Publish a book.
- Make presentations at reputable conferences in our field.

7.2.6. Information power

It is wise to disclose what cannot be concealed.
—Johann Friedrich Von Schiller

Type: Informal
Based on: Important information link, knowledge about our organization or our customer's organization
Means to attain:
- Know our customer's business.
- Know our organization's mission and vision statements.
- Join professional associations (Project Management Institute (PMI), International Project Management Association (IPMA), special interest groups, and societies in PMI and other relevant associations.
- Be thoroughly aware of our organizational policies and procedures (formal and informal).
- Make opportunities to know people and their roles.
- Attend other departments' meetings or other projects' meetings.
- Prioritize information to prevent information overload.
- Break down divisions and barriers among staff.
- Establish good rapport.
- Keep information simple (Grade 8 level).
- Encourage more verbal communication.

Leading with Purpose

- Create and distribute the project's distribution list.
- Establish and implement an effective communication plan.
- Implement knowledge management software.
- Share information with our network.
- Read outside literature and analyze (to identify future opportunities and challenges).

7.2.7. Network power

If you make yourself valuable and memorable, others will want to make you part of their network.

—Jeffrey Gitomer

Type: Informal
Based on: Personal and business contacts, doing and receiving favors
Means to attain:

- Remember the names and faces of those we meet.
- Ask for a business card.
- Acknowledge the person by name at meetings.
- Get involved.
- Join associations and societies; volunteer for service.
- Show interest in others' work and lives.
- Ask for help or advice.

7–The Project Manager and Power

- Share knowledge through courses, articles, and presentations.
- Feed the network (offer to help; do favors for others).
- Schedule regular lunch events.
- Join Toastmasters.
- Make conversation in the elevator.
- Organize social events.
- Attend and organize conferences and trade shows.
- Set aside two to three hours a month to nurture our network.
- Be culturally sensitive.
- Encourage face-to-face (personal) interactions rather than facts-to-facts (business).
- Analyze the political landscape and identify the strengths and weaknesses of our stakeholders, whom we can trust, and how much.
- Analyze and understand internal and external politics related to our project.

7.2.8. Persuasion power

To be persuasive we must be believable;
to be believable we must be credible;
credible we must be truthful.

—Edward R. Murrow

Type: Informal
Based on: Interpersonal skills, ability to gain trust and agreement

Means to attain:
- Spend time with the customer.
- Build a good working relationship.
- Conduct project kickoff meetings.
- Include the customer to clarify the project purpose and specifications.
- Use their words to persuade them.
- Make commitments and keep them.
- Solicit others' opinions.
- Motivate the team by giving rewards.
- Extend ourselves with goodwill.
- Use concepts of Myers-Briggs personality types to persuade people.
- Prepare well for persuasion (persuasion is like negotiation and needs good preparation).
- Gain trust by being consistently trustworthy.
- Use a logical approach.
- Identify a contact to help us in difficult situations.
- Listen actively and then present our ideas or approach.
- Focus on interests, not on position.
- Increase expertise about the subject matter of discussion.
- Have confidence, but do not be arrogant.
- Work with examples (match the style or preference of the person).
- Know past and previous examples.
- Show appreciation and gratitude.

- Be inspiring/have energy/passion.
- Be sincere and genuine.
- Maintain appropriate attire.
- Approach by clearly understanding What's In It For Them (WIIFT).

These lists can be used as guidelines to increase the eight sources of power. First, project managers must evaluate the organizational culture, understand their stakeholders, and then choose strategies to fit the people and situation.

7.3. Balancing Power

Make the best of what is in your power, and take the rest as it happens.

—Epictetus

Project managers should have both formal and informal power. Formal power is based on the ability to ascend the organizational ladder, which depends on time and opportunities. This being the case, we cannot emphasize enough that we should rely on increasing informal power to gain power. Organizations should encourage this behavior and support project managers trying to improve themselves, thus rewarding actions with promotions and increased responsibility.

Do not interpret this to mean that formal power is unnecessary because it is. Project managers should manage their teams and stakeholders primarily with informal power, but they should also be prepared to use formal power as a last resort. Even when they must use formal, it will probably produce a more positive outcome if they use it carefully and informally.

These points relate to how project managers interact with functional managers and how the two groups of managers differ from each other:

Project managers:
- Challenged to do more with less
- Have no formal authority
- Depend on informal power

Functional managers:
- Thrive on formal power
- Thrive on using power formally
- Enforce rules and regulations

Often, the project manager must meet project goals on time and within budget without having sufficient direct authority over project personnel. Therefore, the project manager must rely on functional managers' cooperation to assign enough team members with appropriate skill levels to have the human resources to do a good job. Power struggles and conflict arise in this environment, so we must understand managerial relationships in a project and achieve a balance of power to ensure the project's success. Project managers must balance interests and share power among themselves and functional managers. Shared power is often unbalanced because of the dynamics of power.

Equally splitting authority and responsibility between project and functional managers is theoretically possible but not always successful. Some managers have strong interpersonal, communication, and persuasive skills, whereas others depend on formal power. Often, everyone becomes involved in a power struggle to increase their power. Because projects are an important element of many businesses, project managers contribute greatly to their organizations' bottom line. However, functional managers are more powerful because they directly control human resources. Therefore, for a project to work, project managers must gain enough power to stand up to functional managers by getting top management's support.

How we acquire power or apply power matters. Power should be acquired legitimately and applied mostly informally to get the best results—the reason power, authority, control, and influence are interrelated. If applied formally, formal types of power (authority and control) lead to unsuccessful long-term influencing.

Chapter 7 Summary

Project management's matrix structure gives project managers great responsibility but usually no direct authority over their team. For this reason, project managers need to augment their total power (positional and personal), especially their informal power because of its four advantages: (1) it is permanent; (2) it can be increased anytime; (3) it increases by sharing with others; (4) a stronger foundation of it leads to opportunities for formal power or promotion. Furthermore, project managers must use their power effectively.

Project managers increase their total power by increasing any of the eight forms or sources of power: (1) legitimate, (2) reward, (3) coercive, (4) referent, (5) expert, (6) information, (7) network, and (8) persuasion. This chapter expounded on the complexity of the dynamics of power and its importance. Techniques were outlined for increasing total power using any of the eight forms or sources of power. Projects, project managers, and their teams benefit from how power is applied or exercised.

Leveraging team members' power is key to increasing power. This is done effectively by increasing team members' developmental, or maturity, level, which depends on competence, commitment, and attitude.

Powers interrelate and overlap, but their importance comes from using them informally. To use power effectively, project managers should choose their appropriate project team and execute their power skillfully and thoughtfully.

Project managers must balance formal and informal power, primarily using informal power and using formal power as a last resort. Power also must be balanced between functional and project managers, with cooperation being a key to project success.

Chapter 7 Review and Critical Thinking Questions

1. What is the role of power in project management? Give examples of why project managers should strive to increase their power.
2. Describe the components that constitute the project manager's total power. What kind of power should they primarily focus on, and why?

3. What is situational leadership? Describe three factors to determine your team members' maturity and developmental levels. What should project leaders do to increase their team members' developmental levels to increase their leadership effectiveness?
4. What are the differences in the roles of project managers and functional managers? How should project managers create a power balance with functional managers?
5. Evaluate your power level for each of the eight sources of power described in this chapter. Which power level do you lack that reduces your effectiveness as a project manager and project leader?
6. When and why should you use your formal powers? What strategies would you develop to increase your formal powers long term?
7. What are the main advantages of informal powers? What strategies should project managers use to realize the maximum benefits of using their informal powers?
8. When and why should you use your informal powers? What strategies would you develop to increase your informal powers long term?
9. What are the challenges in implementing the strategies to increase various sources of power? How would you resolve those challenges?
10. Illustrate from your project management experiences the importance and main features of networking. What strategies would you develop to increase your network power and maintain the quality of your network power?

Leading with Purpose

Part III: Influence and Project Management

Chapter 8. Dynamics of Influencing
   8.1. What Is Influencing?
   8.2. Influencing's Importance in Project Management
   8.3. Relationship Between Power and Influence
   Chapter 8 Summary
   Chapter 8 Review and Critical Thinking Questions

Chapter 9. Influencing Models, Styles, and Skills
   9.1. Two Main Dimensions of Influencing
   9.2. Overview of Influencing Models and Styles
   9.3. Influencing Styles Based on Convincing and Connecting
   Chapter 9 Summary
   Chapter 9 Review and Critical Thinking Questions

Chapter 10. Achieving Successful Influencing
   10.1. Influencing Strategies
   Chapter 10 Summary
   Chapter 10 Review and Critical Thinking Questions

Chapter 11. Influencing by Increasing Power
 11.1. Influence in Team Building
 11.2. Ten Guidelines to Increase Power and Influence
 Chapter 11 Summary
 Chapter 11 Review and Critical Thinking Questions

Part III: Influence and Project Management

We firmly believe that how people live, how they think, and how they act and react to life's situations can be positively influenced.

—Catherine Pulsifer

Power and influence interrelate, and both are important to manage projects successfully. Project managers must influence others' actions, and *power* allows them to do so. The job of project managers revolves around getting things done through others. Therefore, project managers succeed with the appropriate type and level of power and the skills to use it effectively to positively affect team members' motivations and actions.

The opposite is true for those with poor influencing skills because they do not get the best from their stakeholders. Some project managers primarily depend on their positional power and use formal authority or threats. This behavior likely demotivates people and leads to minimum effort rather than achieving their team members' potential.

Many people had the terrible boss who bullied them, demanded results, and became angry when expectations were not met. However, some also had a boss they loved who inspired them to do their best and expand their potential. The difference between these two bosses is their leadership style to influence their people. Autocratic project managers think the easy way is to use formal power and force their will on others to keep them on task with fear and authority. Conversely, the more difficult but effective strategy is to use various influencing techniques to ensure people meet requirements and do so because they *want* to, not because they *have* to.

Project managers build a cohesive, loyal, motivated, and happy team if they use their influencing skills rather than formal authority over their team members to deliver successful projects. The ability to influence others is a difficult skill to learn, but it is a valuable skill for project managers to have.

This part includes four chapters (chapters 8–11). Chapter 8 deals with the definition and dynamics of influencing, along with the influencing process's key components, emphasizing that the art of influencing becomes especially important in a project environment. Project managers have little or no formal authority over team members allocated to the project on a matrix basis. Project managers must influence their stakeholders because they need their help in many ways, including information, resources, agreements, approvals, support and buy-in, positioning for the future, and solutions to issues and problems. This chapter describes the dimensions of good networking—enlarging, strengthening, and validating the

Part III–Influence and Project Management

network—to increase the circle of influence.

Chapter 9 covers practical influencing strategies, including gathering relevant and updated information and developing strong network power. Project managers must understand and evaluate each influencing strategy's strengths and shortcomings and then use strategies depending on the people and situation.

Chapter 10 deals with influencing models, skills, and styles. This chapter describes two dimensions of influencing: (1) convincing (pushing) and (2) attracting (pulling). Based on these two dimensions, there are four styles of influencing: (1) persuasive, (2) collaborative, (3) disengaging, and (4) supportive. In addition, this chapter describes three influencing models. Model 1 deals with three executive personality types, model 2 deals with five influencing styles, and model 3 deals with five characteristics of influencing styles. Project managers must evaluate influencing models and styles and use the appropriate one depending on the situation and personalities of the people involved.

Chapter 11 deals with influencing's importance in creating synergy and teamwork and describes how influencing can help build effective teams. Ten guidelines are also described to increase overall power and influence to create high-performance teams, along with an influencing model for developing a sense of obligation to enhance commitment and motivation to deliver successful projects.

Leading with Purpose

Chapter 8

Dynamics of Influencing

The key to successful leadership is influence, not authority.

—Ken Blanchard

Effective influencing is the key to delivering successful projects. Influencing involves affecting stakeholders' thoughts and actions in the direction the project manager desires to meet project objectives effectively and efficiently. To influence successfully and long term, project managers must understand and evaluate two levels of thoughts: (1) extrinsic (expectations, beliefs, and opinions) that can be expressed and understood easily and (2) intrinsic (emotions, attitudes, and feelings) that are difficult to express and understand because they require active listening with empathy and compassion.

Project managers often have enormous responsibility but very limited formal authority over their project stakeholders. Therefore, they need to learn the art of influencing because they need cooperation from their stakeholders throughout the project life cycle (PLC).

Leading with Purpose

This chapter describes influencing's components and achieving successful influencing by understanding the extrinsic and intrinsic levels of thoughts before desirable actions can be expected. Project managers need help from their stakeholders continually for various purposes, such as information (to make decisions), the resources (financial and people to get things done), agreements (that will be carried through), timely approvals (to stay on schedule), support and buy-in (to gain collaboration and commitment), solutions to issues and problems (to increase efficiency and quality), and positioning for the future (when restructuring happens because of mergers and acquisitions).

This chapter also describes how power and influence interrelate and how project managers should increase their circle of influence by enlarging, strengthening, and validating their network.

8.1. What Is Influencing?

The greatest ability in business is to get along with others and to influence their actions.

—John Hancock

An interesting paper on influencing defines influencing and covers influencing models and styles (Saylor Foundation 2013).[1] The word *influence* comes from the Latin *floor*, meaning "to flow." In the fifteenth century, the word *influence* evolved as the meaning became "exertion of unseen influence by people." *Merriam-Webster* defines *influence* as "the power or process of producing an effect upon a person by

8–Dynamics of Influencing

imperceptible or intangible means." The *Oxford English Dictionary* defines *influence* as "the capacity to affect the character, development, or behavior of someone or something, or the effect itself."[2]

Influencing involves affecting a person's thoughts and actions in the direction favorable to the influencer. To influence successfully, project managers must understand and evaluate these two thought levels:

1. Extrinsic (expectations, opinions, beliefs)
2. Intrinsic (emotions, feelings, attitudes)

Project managers must recognize the importance of both and understand their effects. They should then plan and execute their communication and call for action clearly to the influenced to affect their action successfully and reach the desired outcome. Once the desired outcome is achieved, the influenced's actions must be recognized. Desirable behavior should be rewarded to continually understand the influenced's thoughts at both the extrinsic and intrinsic levels.

This influencing process is shown in Figure 8.1.

```
┌─────────────────────┐     ┌─────────────────────┐     ┌─────────────────────┐
│ Gather and analyze  │     │ Plan and affect     │     │                     │
│ thoughts of         │ ──▶ │ thoughts of         │ ──▶ │ Achieve desired     │
│ influenced at the   │     │ influenced by       │     │ actions and outcomes│
│ • Extrinsic level   │     │ • Communicating     │     │                     │
│ • Intrinsic level   │     │ • Calling for action│     │                     │
└─────────────────────┘     └─────────────────────┘     └─────────────────────┘
          ▲                                                        │
          │                  ┌─────────────────────┐               │
          └──────────────────│ Recognize/Reward    │◀──────────────┘
                             │ Behavior            │
                             └─────────────────────┘
```

Figure 8.1. Influencing by affecting thoughts and actions.

This execution might be as simple as influencing someone to respect teammates more or work harder. On the other hand, it might be a major shift, such as convincing people to support a project they initially opposed. It does not matter how we want to influence someone unless we know how to influence them effectively. Therefore, project managers must understand the differences between intrinsic and extrinsic thought components that help achieve a successful outcome from influencing.

We can often readily observe extrinsic thought components through the opinions and outward expressions a person shows. However, a person's intrinsic thoughts are more complex, as they are buried beneath the surface. Figure 8.2 illustrates this by comparing intrinsic and extrinsic thought components to a coconut's shell. On the surface is a readily observable husk, which represents extrinsic thoughts. Peeling the husk is somewhat time-consuming but not too difficult. It is much like understanding people's extrinsic thoughts by encouraging them to express themselves, listening to them actively, and observing them for a period.

The inner shell represents emotions, feelings, and attitudes (intrinsic components) supporting extrinsic thought components. However, the inner shell is difficult to crack and often warrants using a tool to break it successfully. Similarly, to "crack" into a person's intrinsic thoughts, the influencer needs tools—*better communication and understanding.*

Actively and openly communicating with someone, especially listening empathetically, leads to better understanding and more trust between both parties. Much as the valuable parts of the coconut (milk and cream) are accessible once the inner shell is opened, the valuable understanding of a person's thoughts and the reasons behind those thoughts show once the intrinsic layer is cracked.

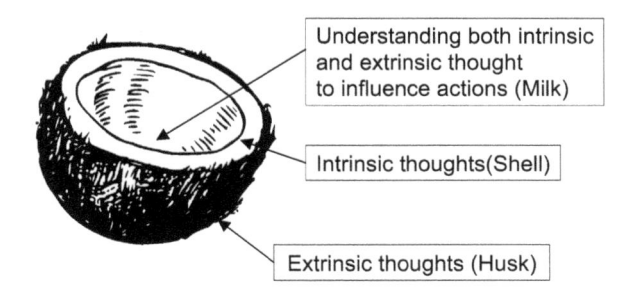

Figure 8.2. Thought coconut (representing extrinsic and intrinsic thoughts).

Coconut Graphic Source: http://downloadclipart.org/
f/coconut-clipart-black-and-white-3041

Manipulating and influencing differ. When people manipulate, they try to influence others to do something they would not do if both parties knew the outcomes and understood the implications. Influencing also refers to an attempt to convince someone to engage in behavior beneficial to the influencer, but the key differences are the method and intention used in the influencing process. An influencer, to maintain influence, acts primarily by providing information, support, moral actions, and positive behavior rather than deception used primarily in manipulation.

Three components form the influencing process:

1. **The Influencer** (the person who wants to influence someone)
   The influencer must use proper strategies and skills to influence.

2. **The Message** (what the influencer communicates)
   The message is important, but how we communicate it is more important.
   Communication is the key to successful influencing.

3. **The Influenced** (person to be influenced)

Ultimately, successful influencing should lead to desired actions and outcomes. We should evaluate and positively reinforce this process continually to get better results.

Successful influencers must have sensory sharpness, and to be effective, they must use these four guidelines (Laborde 1987):[3]

1. Pay attention to the concerns and interests of the influenced: What's In It For Them (WIIFT)?

2. Tailor the message for the influenced to get the desired effect by paying attention to both verbal and nonverbal parts of the communication process.

3. Recognize the preferences of both the influencer and the influenced, and use this information to develop skills to achieve flexibility and success in influencing.

4. Recognize and reward the desired behavior, and be flexible to change strategy, if needed, to achieve better outcomes.

Influencing is a complex process. Project managers must learn the art of influencing to get things done through their team members and other stakeholders over whom they have little or very limited formal authority. They must understand the process of influencing that involves understanding both extrinsic and intrinsic thought levels and pay special attention to the compelling reason people should do what they want. To achieve this, project managers must ask themselves and understand WIIFT to convince stakeholders and get their commitment to take desirable actions positively to help meet project objectives.

8.2. Influencing's Importance in Project Management

The influential man is the successful man, whether he is rich or poor.
—Orison Swett Marden

Influencing is an important skill for project managers because they have great responsibility and insufficient direct formal authority over their team members, especially in a matrix structure. Verma (1997–2020) emphasized that the art of influencing becomes important because project managers need help from their project stakeholders for the following seven purposes:[4]

Information (to make decisions)

Project managers should influence their stakeholders at various levels by communicating with them effectively. They can achieve this effectiveness by efficiently exchanging information with them. The groups of stakeholders and desired information exchanges with project managers include the following (Locke 1976, 1300):[5]

- **Top Management:** This relationship relies on providing top management, clients, and sponsors with information on a project's status and warnings when needed. The project managers expect support and honest feedback from top management.

- **Project Team Members:** Project managers can ensure the reception of their requests and expect quality and conformance to requirements by providing team members, contractors, subcontractors, and subordinates with appropriate leadership, direction, and control.

- **External Stakeholders:** When project managers responsibly provide external stakeholders, regulatory agencies, the public, and the press with ongoing information, they typically receive useful feedback and valuable support.

- **Functional Managers:** Project managers can expect increased technical support and cooperation by providing these managers with help and support during planning and coordination. Project managers should use their influencing skills to negotiate with functional managers for the best resources. This valuable information can help project managers better grasp their immediate surroundings and develop relationships with the people they work with side-by-side, resulting in greater and more open access to resources that might otherwise be unavailable.

Resources (financial and people with the proper skill set and attitude)

All organizations have limited resources, including time, people, and money. Most project managers face the challenge of procuring enough people in head counts and full-time equivalents (FTEs) and human resources with the proper skills and attitudes to do assigned tasks. Resources often come from functional and resource managers; we must develop amicable relationships wherever possible. We must consider:

- What, how many, and when resources are available
- What skill mix (technical and management) people bring to the table

Attitude is important because project managers might sometimes have enough head count, but the resources might not have the best attitude. Skill mix is important because if one person takes six weeks to do a job, another with better skills and experience can do the same job in three to four weeks. Therefore, intimate knowledge of the skills, strengths, and potential of the people available is greatly beneficial. This knowledge is most easily obtained through functional managers, resource managers, and other project managers. Once project managers know their team members' potential, they can enhance their skills by training, coaching, and mentoring, if needed, which equals increased resources by increasing their overall potential.

Project managers can improve their team members' skill levels by using these techniques:

- Subject matter training (to improve their technical skills)
- Coaching and mentoring (to improve their interpersonal skills)
- Visioning and inspiring (to improve their leadership skills)

Effective organizational leaders must emphasize the importance of these three techniques and should encourage and support their project leaders and project managers in applying them because of these observations. In most organizations:

- People are hired based on their technical skills and knowledge.
- People are promoted based on their interpersonal skills.
- People are fired because of a lack of leadership skills.

Therefore, project managers must increase their team members' overall competency level by providing them with proper guidance and support, as needed, and mentoring them to help them grow and develop their leadership skills.

Agreements (that will be carried through)

Agreements are one thing, but carrying them out is more important. To increase the probability that the agreements are carried out willingly, they must meet these three conditions:

1. Agreements should be free from fear, threat, or coercion.

If people agree through fear or coercion (for example, "Do this job, or you will be demoted"), they are not motivated to do their best, compromising output quality. Instead, they do a job grudgingly and put forth only enough energy to avoid a negative response or punishment. If agreements are free from fear or threats, people *want* to carry through the agreement wholeheartedly, which leads to better quality results.

2. Agreements should be fair and reasonable.

If people perceive agreements as unfair, they might try to get out of them. And if they cannot get out of them and are forced to go through with the agreements, they put in minimum effort, for example, to meet compliance criteria. So, the overall results are not high quality because the other party does not feel committed to giving their best.

Similarly, if people see an agreement as unfair, they resent both the other party and the agreement, and their outputs reflect it. And if agreements are unfair, and one party tries to take undue advantage of a situation, the other party cuts corners and takes shortcuts, leading to poor quality. If both parties interpret an agreement differently and consider it unfair, they will also be unhappy with each other's actions and outputs and might start blaming each other, leading to a lose-lose situation. If the agreement is fair and reasonable and perceived as such by both parties, they will commit to working together and carrying through the agreement, which will lead to better results and good working relationships.

3. Both parties should have a clear mutual understanding.

Creating mutual understanding is a meeting of the minds of both parties. It helps develop mutual trust, an important element in negotiating and reaching good agreements to be carried out. If two parties share great trust, resolving differences, reaching compromises, and avoiding costly confrontations are easier.

Developing mutual trust and respect is critical in project management. For example, the project manager might estimate a project completion time of twelve months. However, certain circumstances, such as global competition and quicker time to market for certain products, might require completing the project in nine months, which the project manager might consider too optimistic. Management should try to persuade project managers based on an overall big picture and explain logically why the schedule needs to be shortened (for example, to stay ahead of competition or get technical results to get funding) rather than imposing the over optimistic schedule on the project manager.

We should use influence rather than exercise formal authority. In such circumstances, explaining the "why" part and providing full support to project managers are critical to gaining their acceptance and, hence, their commitment to a nine-month schedule. Project managers must recognize that it will not be easy and require extraordinary performance from their project team members and them.

Management must develop trust and clear mutual understanding with no fear, threat, or coercion while requesting any extra effort from team members. These extra steps, if taken genuinely, convince project managers that everyone is "in it together." Senior management must approach in a problem-solving and collaborative manner and urge the project manager to explore all options to meet the nine-month constraint and commit to fully supporting the project manager.

Project managers feel more motivated and committed to accepting the challenge to meet an optimistic schedule, especially if all stakeholders commit to working as a team and solving problems rather than pointing fingers at one another when something goes wrong. With this approach, management has positive influence and is more likely to gain volunteer commitment from project managers and project team members, leading to higher chances for project completion in nine months.

Senior management should request such extraordinary performance only in genuinely special circumstances. Because if this request is a common management practice and used too frequently, the trust level goes down, project personnel feel burned out and disappointed, and no one will put forth extraordinary effort and push themselves again. Good leaders believe everyone has the potential to put in 100 percent–120 percent effort, but not always and not long term.

Approvals/green light (to stay on schedule)

Approvals are important because delays in making decisions delay the project schedule. Approvals give the green light to pass through the gate. Project managers must use foresight to determine when approvals must be granted to stay on schedule. They should clearly understand how difficult it might be to convince stakeholders to decide promptly and do their utmost to appeal to these decision-makers. Project managers might be challenged to appeal to people differently for the desired results.

Support and buy-in (to gain collaboration and commitment)

Project managers need support for ongoing activities to gain resources and approval promptly. They must ensure their stakeholders buy in to what they do and convince project stakeholders that the plans and processes they developed are realistic, which helps them earn support from stakeholders to succeed. As with approvals, earning support might involve appealing differently to people.

Job satisfaction (the pleasure or satisfaction we receive from work or job experience) is a key motivator. Therefore, support and buy-in from project stakeholders help get more collaboration and cooperation to achieve better organizational results and job satisfaction for project managers.

Solutions to issues and problems (to increase efficiency and quality)

Problem-solving and conflict resolution are two key skills all project managers should develop because many issues crop up that affect a team's efficiency:

- Personality problems
- Differing perceptions
- Lack of sufficient information (quality and quantity)
- Lack of mutual support
- Insufficient teamwork and a positive spirit

The ability to recognize these problems and use interpersonal skills to resolve them cannot be understated. These characteristics are important for a team to function efficiently and produce high-quality results.

Positioning for the future (to survive)

Planning for future events is often difficult, as politics can quickly change the landscape of an organization or department. Change is typical and should be expected, as changes occur whether we want them to. Mergers, acquisitions, and restructuring cause such changes, leading to uncertainty and stress. Because of the unpredictable nature of changes, the only general rule that can be stated is that we must look after ourselves and our immediate team. Properly analyzing and understanding the political landscape help project managers identify the right people to be influenced as a first step. Then, they must use their influencing skills to position themselves and their team for the future.

Project managers have limited or no formal authority over their project stakeholders. They need influencing because they need continual help throughout the PLC from their stakeholders for various purposes:

- Information (to make decisions)
- Resources (financial and people with the proper skill set and attitude)
- Agreements (that will be carried through)
- Approvals/green light (to stay on schedule)
- Support and buy-in (to gain collaboration and commitment)

Leading with Purpose

- Solutions to issues and problems (to increase efficiency and quality)
- Positioning for the future (to survive)

Project managers should develop interpersonal skills to get these things from stakeholders.

8.3. Relationship Between Power and Influence

A leader who has the vision and conviction that a dream can be achieved. He inspires the power and energy to get it done.

—Ralph Lauren

Some influencing strategies are more likely to achieve only compliance and no commitment. However, project managers should strive for commitment rather than compliance because commitment leads to long-term influence. Therefore, project managers must understand how to use their power to achieve commitment, which can be considered a long-term influence, rather than compliance, which can be only short term. In addition, project managers should increase their circle of influence through effective networking. The quality of networking is based on enlarging, strengthening, and validating the network.

8.3.1. Power and influence

It does not matter how much power and influence you have; what matters is how wisely you use it.

—Vijay Verma

Power and influence interrelate. Power provides the ability to influence, and the key to successful influencing is how we use our power. The following are the two components of power:

1. Formal, or positional, power granted or given based on the position on the organizational chart
2. Informal power earned based on one's knowledge, experience, and expertise

There are eight power sources:

1. Legitimate power (formal)
2. Reward power (formal)
3. Coercive power (formal)
4. Referent power (informal)
5. Expert power (informal)
6. Information power (informal)
7. Network power (informal)
8. Persuasion power (informal)

Interestingly, only three types of powers—legitimate, reward, and coercive—belong to the formal power category. The remaining five types of power—referent, expert, information, network, and persuasion—belong to informal power. For successful and long-term influencing, project managers should use these guidelines:

Leading with Purpose

1. Focus more on increasing informal power.
Informal power is more important because it constitutes a significant component (five out of eight) of the overall power pie. On the other hand, the formal power component is made of only three out of eight powers, and these three can be combined into one power—legitimate power because if we have legitimate power, we also have the power to reward and punish.

2. Mostly use power informally.
The real effect of power comes from how it is used. Therefore, when using power, mostly use it informally to gain commitment long term. Using power formally likely leads to only compliance and not commitment.

Further, using coercive power formally likely endangers long-term relationships. However, in certain situations, project managers should not hesitate to use their powers formally to emphasize certain policies and procedures but should do so only as a last resort. Power provides an ability to influence, and the quality of the outcome depends on how the power is exercised (Figure 8.3).

Power: Ability to Influence
- Influence = Having Power + Exercising Power
- The key to successful influencing is effective use of power.

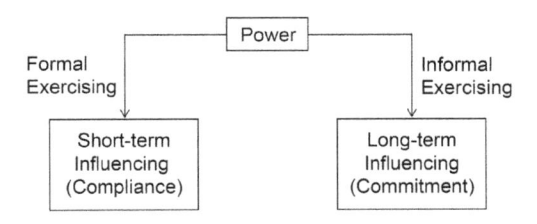

```
                    Power
         ┌────────────┴────────────┐
    Formal                      Informal
    Exercising                  Exercising
         ↓                          ↓
   ┌──────────┐              ┌──────────┐
   │Short-term│              │Long-term │
   │Influencing│             │Influencing│
   │(Compliance)│            │(Commitment)│
   └──────────┘              └──────────┘
```

Communication is the key to successful influencing.

Figure 8.3. Influencing by using power.

We can see the relationship between power and influence in Figure 8.3 and, even more important, the difference between unsuccessful and successful influencing. A better way to compare the difference between formal and informal exercising of power is to say that formal exercising of power results in short-term influencing by achieving only compliance. By exercising power informally, a manager can achieve long-term influencing, which results in compliance and commitment, which is much more desirable and effective because commitment leads to higher motivation to produce better results immediately and in the future. Communication is the key to successful influencing because it conveys whether we use our power formally or informally. It shows whether the influencer tries to force their viewpoint or genuinely cares about the other party's opinions and beliefs and listens actively to create a win-win situation.

8.3.2. Circle of influence

You don't have to be a "person of influence" to be influential. In fact, the most influential people in my life are probably not even aware of the things they have taught me.

—Scott Adams

Networking and building relationships are keys to enlarging the circle of influence. However, relationship quality is more important than quantity because the depth of the relationship increases the "real" circle of influence. Three dimensions create high-quality networks and relationships, expanding the circle of influence (Figure 8.4).

1. Enlarge the network (to get more allies).
2. Strengthen the network (depth of relationships).
3. Validate the network. (Can we get the support when we need it?)

Figure 8.4. Increasing circle of influence.

8–Dynamics of Influencing

Circles of influence in an organizational setting refer to areas in which someone exercises power to influence other people, policies, and decisions. In this sense, there are three types of influence:

1. **General influence:**
   The capacity to influence that works with most people, similar to the formal power people have from their position in an organizational hierarchy.
2. **Situational influence:**
   The capacity to influence particular people across a broad range of issues. It depends on what people want from one another in different situations.
3. **Long-term influence:**
   Influencing others long term, which requires good communication skills and the ability to use power mostly informally. Long-term influencing leads to better commitment to producing high-quality results. Cultivating stronger networks leads to long-term influencing.

This section covered how influence and power interrelate. To influence anyone, we must have power and then use it appropriately. However, to achieve long-term influencing or commitment, we must informally use the power because formally using power only helps get compliance, not commitment.

If project managers have a large circle of influence, they have more wide-ranging power and the ability to sway stakeholders to influence their actions and behavior. Thus, project managers must expand their circle of influence by continually increasing the quality of their network by enlarging, strengthening, and validating their network.

Chapter 8 Summary

Successful influencing requires project managers to understand extrinsic and intrinsic thought levels with planning and executing communication accordingly. The influencing process has three components: (1) the Influencer, (2) the Message, and (3) the Influenced. Successful influencers must pay attention to the influenced's concerns, interests, and thoughts and tailor the message to get the desired effect. In addition, they must recognize and reward the influenced after the desired actions and outcomes are achieved to continue the influencing process.

Influencing is important to project managers for the following seven purposes:

1. Information
2. Resources
3. Agreements
4. Approvals
5. Support and buy-in
6. Problem solutions
7. Positioning for the future from their stakeholders

Stakeholders include top management, project team members, external stakeholders, and functional managers. Project managers need relevant and updated information from all stakeholders to make decisions. They must consider the availability of resources and what skill mix people bring. Project managers can use subject matter training, coaching and mentoring, and visioning and inspiring to improve members' skill levels.

Carrying out agreements is more important than reaching agreement. Success in carrying out agreements requires three conditions: freedom from fear, threat, or coercion; fairness and reasonableness; and mutual understanding. Approvals are important to keep projects on schedule. Project stakeholder support and buy-in lead to more collaboration and cooperation, which leads to better organizational results and greater project manager job satisfaction. Project managers need problem-solving and conflict resolution skills to deal with personality problems, differing perceptions, insufficient information, lack of mutual support, and insufficient teamwork and positive spirit. Positioning for the future is critical to surviving because of ongoing change.

Power provides the ability to influence, and the key to successful influencing is how we use our power. Power has two components: (1) formal or positional power and (2) informal power. Power has eight sources: legitimate (formal), reward (formal), coercive (formal), referent (informal), expert (informal), information (informal), network (informal), and persuasion (informal). For successful, long-term influencing, project managers should focus more on increasing informal power and mostly use power informally.

Commitment leads to long-term influence. Therefore, project managers should strive for commitment rather than just compliance. There are three types of influence: (1) general, (2) situational, and (3) long-term. Three dimensions (enlarging, strengthening, and validating) create high-quality networks and relationships, expanding the circle of influence. Therefore, project managers should use effective networking to increase their circle of influence, and

Leading with Purpose

networking's quality is based on enlarging, strengthening, and validating the network.

Influencing is crucial for successful project management. Influencing involves getting things done by others (especially what we want them to do). It becomes more challenging in project environments where project managers often have much responsibility but not enough direct formal authority over their team members and stakeholders. Therefore, influencing without authority is an essential skill project managers should learn and practice to deliver successful projects.

Chapter 8 Review and Critical Thinking Questions

1. Define influencing and its importance in project management.
2. Describe the process of influencing by affecting thoughts and actions. Describe intrinsic and extrinsic levels of thoughts we need to affect to achieve successful influencing.
3. Explain the three components of the influencing process. Then, describe the guidelines to become sensory sharp to influence effectively.
4. Describe the main purposes of influencing in project management environments. Then, from your project management experience, describe the challenges associated with each purpose and strategies to overcome those challenges.

5. What is the relationship between power and influence? How does the exercising of power affect the influencing outcome?
6. What are communication's role and importance in achieving successful influencing? What important listening strategies would you use to influence your stakeholders effectively?
7. Describe three main dimensions for quality networking, creating better relationships, and expanding your circle of influence.
8. Describe three types of influence typically used in project management. How would you use these types in delivering successful projects?

Leading with Purpose

Chapter 9

Influencing Models, Styles, and Skills

Influencing skills may be the highest level of human skills.

—Vijay K. Verma

Influencing is critical to successful project management. Influencing involves getting things done by others (especially what we want them to do). It becomes more challenging in project environments where project managers often have great responsibility but not enough direct formal authority over their team members and stakeholders. Therefore, influencing without authority is an important skill project managers should learn and practice to deliver successful projects.

Project managers' success in influencing depends on how well they implement their influencing strategies. Communication is the key to successful influencing because it can help convince and connect the stakeholders, depending on the situation. Project managers deal with stakeholders of different characteristics with their personalities, attitudes, and emotions. Therefore, they must understand these characteristics and use appropriate influencing styles and strategies to achieve successful influencing.

This chapter covers two dimensions of influencing (convincing and connecting). It gives an overview of three influencing models and four styles of influencing, depending on the levels of convincing and connecting project managers use through their communication with stakeholders. The first model deals with three types of executive personalities, the second model presents five influencing styles, and the third model presents five characteristics of influencing styles. This chapter also describes a few guidelines for choosing an influencing style appropriate for some situations and relationships.

9.1. Two Main Dimensions of Influencing

Communication is the key to influencing.
It is less about what to say and more
about how to say it.

—Vijay Verma

There are two key dimensions of influencing: (1) convincing (pushing) and (2) connecting (pulling). The success of people's influencing skills depends on how well they implement their strategies. Communication is the key to successful strategy implementation. Two key dimensions of influencing skills can be considered in the two clusters of communication skills (Reed 2010–2023).[1]

A paper on influencing skills contends these dimensions of convincing and connecting are two basic modes of pushing and pulling to influence others, which involve using various approaches, tactics, and behaviors to persuade others (Saylor Foundation 2013).[2] These two modes or approaches are described:

1. **Pushing (convincing):**
   This approach involves using formal power logically. It can be perceived as aggressive and forcing, but it can help achieve solid results if used appropriately.
2. **Pulling (connecting):**
   This approach emphasizes involving and understanding the other party to build genuine working relationships. As a result, it typically leads to collaboration, cooperation, and teamwork.

Influencing styles depend on how much the pushing and pulling approach is used to influence behavior and outcome. The two dimensions of convincing and connecting are described, along with the associated factors.

9.1.1. Convincing (Pushing)

Leadership is influence.
—John C. Maxwell

Convincing is influencing by effectively communicating our beliefs, opinions, and needs. We can view it as influencing through pushing our ideas, not by forcing, but by convincing others by capitalizing on a good understanding of their beliefs and ideas. This knowledge and making the influenced believe their feelings are acknowledged helps us influence successfully. The following six factors contribute to convincing the other party (Verma 2020; Verma 1997–2020; Saylor Foundation 2013; Reed 2010–2023):[3]

1. Proposing (suggesting)
Phrasing a suggestion as a question is a great way to make a proposal to show we value the other party's opinion and input. For example, rather than just saying, "This is a good idea," or "We should add this product," ask, "Do you think this is a good idea?" or "Do you think we should add this new product?" This phrasing allows the other party to share their opinions and feel valued. They still appreciate being asked if we don't take their advice, which helps in convincing because the other party gets good vibes that they and their opinions are valued.

2. Proving (supporting the proposal)
Proving emphasizes the importance of supporting a proposal by using evidence to prove a proposal is a good idea. Examples of evidence include facts, statistics, experience, and expert references. Sometimes, we can use informal sources, such as anecdotes, stories, analogies, similes, and metaphors, as peripheral and indirect support for the proposal to help convince the other party.

3. Asserting (affirming)
Asserting refers to skills we use to state an idea, not as a proposal but as an expectation. Asserting involves changes in context, which can be done

paraverbally or nonverbally. For example, a desire to start a meeting early can be expressed as "I think we should start at 8:30 tomorrow" or "We need to start the meeting at 8:30 tomorrow." This phrasing conveys the message assertively and convincingly.

4. Correcting (giving and taking feedback)

Correcting refers to taking and giving feedback, which should be done in a specific way we link behavior to consequences. For example, if we are unhappy with someone's behavior, a template of what we could say might be: "When you (other's behavior), I feel (our feelings), because (describe consequences or impact of other's behavior). I would like (describe how we would like others to behave) because (describe the new behavior's benefit). What do you think?"

When we are clear and open about our feelings and expectations, the other party is more likely to respond than if we tell them how to act. This allows the other party to give their input or feedback and explains the influencer's expectations, subtly suggesting they are correct in that context and should be followed.

5. Reaching Agreements (finding win-win solutions)

The point of convincing someone is to reach agreement. If this is accomplished, managers use their influencing skills successfully. Senior management wants project managers who *get things done*; they are rarely interested in excuses or reasons for failure. Thus, reaching agreement is

Leading with Purpose

the goal of convincing, and variables such as the time to agree and the happiness of both parties with the result can be used as measuring sticks for success once an agreement is reached.

Although it is useful to agree, implementing agreements is even more critical. Therefore, it is important to convince the other party by communicating and paying attention to each party's beliefs and opinions so the agreement is implemented without problems.

6. Forcing (imposing)
Forcing refers to pressure tactics. Pressuring people can be subtle and implicit, such as saying, "If we don't agree, we won't meet the deadline." It can also be explicit: "If you don't agree, I will give the job to someone else," but this is not usually advisable. More so than other tactics, pressure tactics often result in undesirable consequences, especially when used explicitly. Managers who constantly use this strategy are certain to get a negative reputation among subordinates and superiors, so it should be used sparingly.

9.1.2. Connecting (Pulling)

Kind words can be short and easy to speak, but their echoes are truly endless.
—Mother Teresa

Connecting refers to influencing by paying attention to the other party's (influenced) interests. It emphasizes the importance of listening, supporting the influenced's feelings, and building genuine rapport and relationships. It is pulling people up and engaging with them in a way they feel inspired and motivated to act in our desired direction, much like using an emotional appeal, both personally and inspirationally.

Connecting comprises these three ideas:

1. Communicating interest in and attention to the other party
2. Acquiring information about the other party's opinions, ideas, and needs
3. Showing the other party's value

These three ideas are critical for connecting with project stakeholders genuinely, which is useful in convincing them. It leads to better working relationships and long-term collaboration and support. Take an interest in others first and then communicate our excitement about their needs and interests (Carnegie 2011). It is a basic truth of life that most people want to talk about their interests rather than others' interests.[4]

The following five factors contribute to connecting and engaging with others (Verma 2020; Verma 1997–2020; Saylor Foundation 2013; Reed 2010–2023):[5]

- **Building rapport (establishing positive relationships)**

  Managers must have skills that help others feel comfortable and like them. Creating connection and emotional affinity leads to reciprocal states and behaviors. Neuro Linguistic Programming asserts the key to building rapport is to enter someone's world by assuming a similar mindset to see things from their perspective and feel how they feel (internal processes), which exemplifies the importance of empathetic listening. These internal processes are communicated by both verbal and nonverbal components of communication that make effective communication and active listening essential to understanding the other party.

- **Listening (paying attention)**
  As with building rapport, empathetic listening is a key skill we must use. Doing so shows understanding rather than simply hearing, a passive physiological process. Listening helps us engage in several behaviors: encouragement, restatement, paraphrasing, summary, clarification of feelings, and questioning.

  Active listening is the key to absorbing and retaining the complete message conveyed in the communication process and helps develop a better understanding and relationship in the short and long term. Verma (2020; 1996, 40–49) explained the importance of effective or active listening, verbal and nonverbal listening behaviors, barriers to effective listening, and guidelines for active listening.[6]

- **Supporting (encouraging)**
  The ability and willingness to offer encouragement and reassurance, clarify others' feelings, and provide supportive feedback are great ways to boost team members' confidence and motivation and strengthen relationships. For example, if we provide positive feedback by saying, "I thought

your team-building session was great, Linda," Linda will be proud and pleased with our feedback and strive to do just as well or even better. She is also more likely to provide us with good feedback and support.

- **Revealing (disclosing information)**
  This behavior strengthens relationships by showing a willingness to open up to others, but it must involve appropriate self-disclosure. Others feel uncomfortable if the information is too personal or too much. On the other hand, the relationship can't grow if people share little. Self-disclosure should not be based on business or personal issues; hobbies, interests, and anything else appropriate are encouraged. If done properly, sharing with others encourages them to do the same, which enhances trust and strengthens the relationship.

- **Linking (pointing out similarities and agreements)**
  By building on similarities and agreements, which may be done by pointing out common points, one shows shared support for ideas and proposals. For example, we might say, "One thing we can both agree on is that we should give this task to Maria to meet our deadline," or "Order from outside rather than doing it in-house." We develop a greater team mentality by exemplifying links through matching behaviors and actions. When we reach agreements by linking, support is further entrenched, and we can build on this mutual support even more for future projects.

Leading with Purpose

The factors for the two dimensions of influencing, including convincing and connecting, are shown in Figure 9.1.

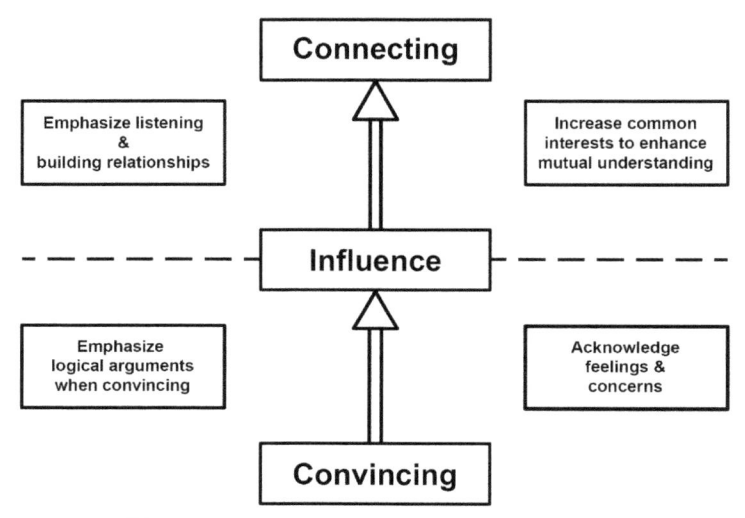

```
                        Connecting
                            △
                            │
┌─────────────────┐         │         ┌─────────────────┐
│ Emphasize       │         │         │ Increase common │
│ listening &     │         │         │ interests to    │
│ building        │         │         │ enhance mutual  │
│ relationships   │         │         │ understanding   │
└─────────────────┘         │         └─────────────────┘
─ ─ ─ ─ ─ ─ ─ ─ ─ ─ ─ ─ ┤ Influence ├ ─ ─ ─ ─ ─ ─ ─ ─ ─ ─
                            │
┌─────────────────┐         │         ┌─────────────────┐
│ Emphasize       │         △         │ Acknowledge     │
│ logical         │         │         │ feelings &      │
│ arguments       │         │         │ concerns        │
│ when convincing │         │         │                 │
└─────────────────┘         │         └─────────────────┘
                        Convincing
```

Figure 9.1. Two dimensions of influencing.

To deliver successful projects, project managers must recognize the two main dimensions of influencing—convincing and connecting. Convincing refers to meeting our objectives by convincing others rather than enforcing, which involves capitalizing on understanding where the other party is coming from. Connecting refers to paying genuine attention to the other party's interests. Listening to and supporting the other party's feelings to build good relationships is the key to connecting.

9.2. Overview of Influencing Models and Styles

As social beings, we are moved in the relations with our fellow beings by such feelings as sympathy, pride, hate, need for power, pity and so on.

—Albert Einstein

People have different personalities, attitudes, and emotions. How they feel depends on their interactions with various people. Therefore, people influence others, and others influence them. The following are influencing models and styles to explain the influencing process and strategies:

9.2.1. Model 1. Three types of executive personalities

Influence is when you are not the one talking and yet your words fill the room; when you are absent and yet your presence is felt everywhere.

—Temit Ope Ibrahim

This model is based on the work of R. W. Wallen (1963), a clinical psychologist.[7] It describes three types of executive personalities. It suggests that each personality uses a different style of influencing, and each must be influenced in particular ways:

Leading with Purpose

1. Tough battlers
Tough battlers have the drive, energy, and commitment to win and get things done in their way by using formal power and positional power leverage. They typically influence by giving orders, offering challenges, threatening and forcing, asserting, and repetition. Typically, these people are not well-respected, but if they use their strategies well, they achieve their objectives.

2. Friendly helpers
Friendly helpers are friendly, open, trusting, hopeful, sympathetic, and cooperative. They have an integrative view of the world, like to include people in resolving issues by appealing to emotion, and influence people by appeasing, appealing, exchanging favors, and developing friendships and positive relationships.

3. Logical thinkers
People with this personality are logical, calm, organized, and thoughtful. They believe the world is based on rationality emphasizing understanding, logic, and knowledge. They use logical arguments and debates based on facts and information and appeal to common sense. They typically influence people with logic, facts, and details, and by quoting rules and regulations and using the hierarchy.

This model is simple to understand and has the advantage that often, we can find others' preferred style and adjust our influencing style. These are the key questions:

- What is our natural influencing style—the one we feel comfortable applying?
- What is the natural influencing style of the party to be influenced?
- Do both styles match or clash?
- If there is a personality clash, are we willing to adjust to influence the other party effectively, and if so, how?

Project managers and leaders should ask these questions and adjust their influencing strategy to the people and situations.

9.2.2. Model 2. Five influencing styles based on personality

Influence does not require position.

— Richie Norton

Musselwhite and Plouffe (2012) described this model in the *Harvard Business Review*, indicating the following five influencing styles managers can use based on their personality:[8]

1. **Rationalizing:** Uses facts, logic, examples, and experiences.
2. **Asserting:** Uses formal power and pressure to convince others.
3. **Negotiating:** Uses compromise and a collaborative approach to develop win-win solutions.
4. **Inspiring:** Uses stories and emotional appeal, focusing on building trust and rapport.

5. **Bridging:** Emphasizes synergy and teamwork to achieve goals.

Good project managers know people differ. So, they take time to understand their stakeholders and use the influencing style they are comfortable with that suits the situation and the people they try to influence. Logical thinkers prefer rationalizing, negotiating, and asserting, whereas friendly helpers prefer inspiring and bridging.

9.2.3. Model 3. Five characteristics of influencing styles

True leadership cannot be awarded, appointed, or assigned. It comes only from influence, and that cannot be mandated. It must be earned.

—John C. Maxwell

This model described by Reynolds identifies five characteristics of influencing styles used by many people, and they can be compared with leadership styles:[9]

1. Tell
Project leaders or managers use their formal or positional power to tell people what is to be done. They impose their ideas and decisions. This style is like the Tough Battler personality and is perceived as dictatorial. Such leaders often encounter resistance and achieve compliance mostly because of fear of threat or coercion but seldom commitment.

2. Sell
This style resembles a salesperson and emphasizes relationship orientation. The leaders with this style find their people's needs and interests and work together to gain their buy-in to develop creative solutions to meet the objectives.

3. Negotiate
Negotiating is a way to get what we want. In this model, negotiation refers to making deals and bargains to meet our goals. It leads to better outcomes and positive relationships if we think and develop a win-win approach.

4. Problem-Solving
This style emphasizes mutual goals and relationships. Such leaders focus on developing common or shared interests and work together to find a suitable solution. It is like a principled negotiation that combines hard and soft negotiation to find creative solutions.

5. Coach/Facilitator
This style encourages people to analyze their problems and develop solutions to the main issues and the situation. People take ownership of their problems and actions. Leaders offer their expert guidance and genuine support throughout this process.

This model highlights the need to understand and analyze stakeholder personalities and then choose a style to influence them to get desired outcomes.

The following are a few common influencing skills also used by managers and leaders:
- **Lead by example:** Be positive and emphasize the importance of relationships.
- **Emphasize/import rules:** Emphasize following rules and regulations, especially regarding safety and health issues.
- **Active listening:** This is the key to effective influencing. Good leaders are active listeners; when interacting with others, they analyze the situation and see things from others' perspectives. Active listening involves listening to both the verbal part (words) and the nonverbal part (vocal tones and body language).
- **Charisma:** Confident, energetic, vibrant, enthusiastic, and courageous people inspire others, propagate powerful positive energy, and influence people to achieve desired outcomes.

Project managers must consider their stakeholders' personalities, attitudes, and emotions when interacting with them to achieve successful influencing. They must understand three influencing models: (1) three types of executive personalities, (2) five influencing styles, and (3) five characteristics of influencing styles. They can determine others' preferred style by asking key questions and adjusting their influencing style accordingly.

9.3. Influencing Styles Based on Convincing and Connecting

> *Think twice before you speak, because your words and influence will plant the seed of either success or failure in the mind of another.*
>
> —Napoleon Hill

Influencing styles are based on the level of convincing and connecting necessary. Project managers must assess situations, relationships, and personalities to determine an appropriate influencing style. Different people require different influencing strategies, so project managers must be able to adapt influencing styles to affect the influenced. Factors must be taken into account to assess which style is appropriate.

9.3.1. Influencing styles

> *We never know which lives we influence, or when, or why.*
>
> —Stephen King

Influencing styles depend on the level of two key dimensions of influencing—convincing and connecting. These styles indicate how each party views the relative emphasis on goals versus relationships, power differences, and mutual trust. The collaborative influencing style is the most successful because it uses high levels of convincing and connecting. Project managers must adapt and use an appropriate influencing style depending on situations, relationships, and personalities.

Leading with Purpose

Influencing styles can be divided into these four categories, as shown in Figure 9.2, depending on the success in connecting with and convincing the other party, and Figure 9.3 shows when to use these different influencing styles (Reed 2010–2023):[10]

- Style 1: Disengaging (low in convincing, low in connecting)
- Style 2: Supportive (low in convincing, high in connecting)
- Style 3: Persuasive (high in convincing, low in connecting)
- Style 4: Collaborative (high in convincing, high in connecting)

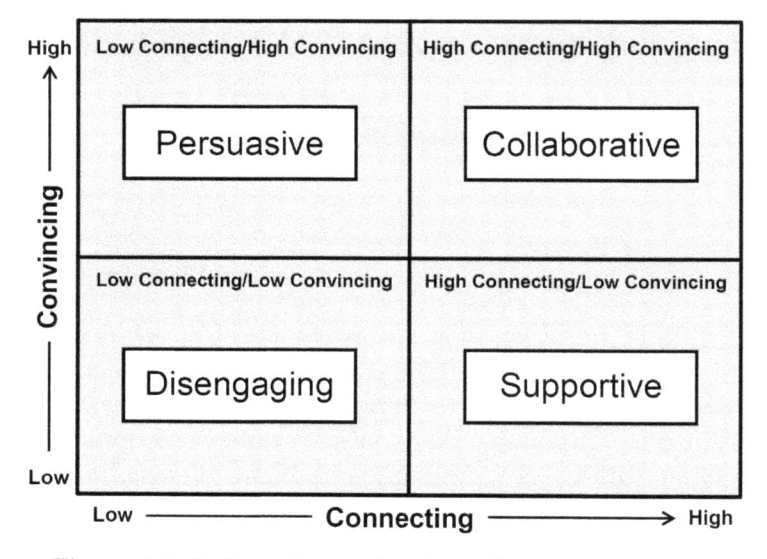

Figure 9.2. Influencing styles depending on connecting and convincing.

9–Influencing Models, Styles, and Skills

Because communication is key to the influencing process, the influencer must pay special attention to many factors that affect their communication's effectiveness with the influenced. The influencer should use an appropriate style, depending on mutual understanding, the level of openness in communication, relationship depth, and trust with the influenced.

The following are a few guidelines about which style should be used in different circumstances to increase the success of the influencing process:

Disengaging: This shows a lack of focus on both goals and relationships. (Low Convincing/Low Connecting)

- When neither the issue nor the relationship is important to us
- When emotions are volatile, and a cooldown is warranted
- When a status change that might shift power in our favor is imminent

Supportive: This is a good style for a relationship's effective, long-term maintenance. (Low Convincing/High Connecting)

- To build rapport or enhance the relationship
- To better understand the other party's needs or issues
- When the value of the relationship outweighs the importance of the issue to us
- When we might be at a significant power disadvantage
- To deposit in the network account to establish currency credit

Leading with Purpose

Persuasive: This emphasizes achieving our objectives more than the value of relationships. (High Convincing/Low Connecting)
- When the importance of the issue outweighs the value of the relationship
- When we already have a clear picture of the other side's needs and issues
- When we have established rapport
- When time is of the essence
- When a value or past agreement has been violated

Collaborative: This emphasizes collaborating and maintaining good relationships to achieve desired results. (High Convincing/High Connecting)
- When there is mutual trust and credibility
- When there is enough time for joint solutions
- When both the relationship and the issue are important
- When the other side is equally interested in working jointly with us

Figure 9.3 shows the situations under which the four influencing styles should influence people long term.

9–Influencing Models, Styles, and Skills

Convincing (Low → High) vs **Connecting** (Low → High):

- **Persuasive** (High Convincing, Low Connecting)
  - The issue is more important than the relationship.
  - Aware of other party's needs & issues.
  - Time is of the essence.

- **Collaborative** (High Convincing, High Connecting)
  - Both the issue & the relationship are important.
  - Mutual trust & credibility.
  - Adequate time for joint decisions.

- **Disengaging** (Low Convincing, Low Connecting)
  - Neither the issue nor the relationship is important.
  - Too emotional, needs cooldown.
  - Possible power shift.

- **Supportive** (Low Convincing, High Connecting)
  - Relationship is more important than the issue.
  - To enhance relationship.
  - Possible power disadvantage.

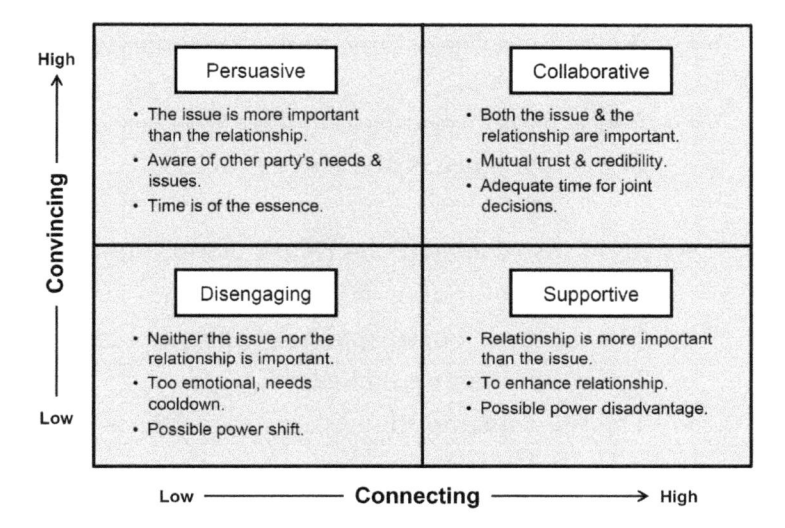

Figure 9.3. When to use different influencing styles.

9.3.2. Adapting influencing styles and techniques

Strength lies in differences, not in similarities.
—Stephen R. Covey

Different people respond differently to influencing strategies. Therefore, to succeed, the influencer must understand what motivates the influenced. Thus, adaptability is essential to influence different people's behavior effectively.

Style adaptability differs from one situation to another, so there are certain factors to consider when choosing an influencing style:

- The other party's personality and communication preferences

Leading with Purpose

- Our personality, skills, and communication preferences
- The way our organization does things
- The importance of the issue at hand

We must also consider the relationship's nature
- Our understanding of their needs and issues
- Our currency power (power of our concessions)
- The relationship's emotional state
- The relationship's long-term importance

Connecting pulls people toward our side, whereas convincing might be viewed as pushing them to accept our goals. Depending on the levels (high and low) of convincing and connecting, there are four influencing styles: disengaging, supportive, persuading, and collaborative. Project managers must analyze and evaluate situations to determine the most appropriate influencing style. They should further recognize the importance of being flexible and adapt their influencing style and strategies to the relationship, personalities, and interests of both parties and their communication styles.

Chapter 9 Summary

Successful project management requires influencing—getting people to do what we want. Project managers must learn to influence without authority because they often lack direct formal authority over team members and stakeholders.

The two key dimensions of influencing are convincing (pushing) and connecting (pulling). Pushing (convincing) involves using formal power logically, whereas pulling (connecting) emphasizes involving and understanding the other party to build genuine working relationships. Convincing tactics include proposing (suggesting), proving (supporting the proposal), asserting (affirming), correcting (giving and taking feedback), reaching agreements (finding win-win solutions), and forcing (pressure tactics). We connect by paying attention to the other party's interests, which means communicating interest and attention in the other party; acquiring information about the other party's opinions, ideas, and needs; and showing the other party's value. Tactics used in connecting are building rapport (establishing positive relationships), listening (paying full attention), supporting (encouraging), revealing (disclosing information), and linking (pointing out similarities and agreements).

This chapter introduced three influencing models: (1) three types of executive personalities, (2) five influencing styles, and (3) five characteristics of influencing styles. The first model describes three executive personalities (tough battlers, friendly helpers, and logical thinkers), suggesting each uses a different influencing style. For example, tough battlers typically influence through orders and threats. Friendly helpers influence through inclusion and relationship development. Logical thinkers influence with logic and facts. By asking key questions, we can determine others' preferred styles and adjust our influencing style.

The second model indicated five influencing styles: (1) rationalizing with facts and logic, (2) asserting with formal power and pressure, (3) negotiating with compromise and collaboration, (4) inspiring with stories and emotional appeal, and (5) bridging with synergy and teamwork. The third model identified five characteristics of influencing styles that compare with leadership styles: (1) tell, which uses formal or positional power, (2) sell, which emphasizes relationship orientation, (3) negotiate, which uses deals and bargains, (4) problem-solving, which emphasizes mutual goals and relationships, and (5) coach/facilitator, which encourages people to analyze the problem and develop solutions. Managers and leaders also influence by leading by example, emphasizing/importing rules, active listening, and charisma.

Based on the two dimensions of influencing (convincing and connecting), influencing styles can be divided into these four categories: (1) disengaging (low in convincing, low in connecting), (2) supportive (low in convincing, high in connecting), (3) persuasive (high in convincing, low in connecting), and (4) collaborative (high in convincing, high in connecting). The disengaging style shows a lack of focus on both goals and relationships. The supportive style focuses on effectively maintaining relationships. The persuasive style emphasizes achieving objectives over valuing relationships. Finally, the collaborative style emphasizes collaboration and maintaining good relationships.

Project managers need to adapt influencing techniques because different people respond differently to influencing strategies. Therefore, certain factors and the nature of the relationship must be considered when choosing an influencing style.

Chapter 9 Review and Critical Thinking Questions

1. Describe two main dimensions of influencing. Give examples of each.
2. Describe the main factors that contribute to convincing (pushing) your stakeholders. In your project management experience, how did you use these factors, and how was the outcome?
3. Describe the main factors that contribute to connecting (pulling) your stakeholders. In your project management experience, how did you use these factors, and how was the outcome?
4. From your project management experience, describe the main challenges encountered in pushing and pulling to influence your stakeholders. Then, how would you overcome those challenges?
5. Describe three types of executive personalities and their respective influencing styles covered in this chapter.
6. Describe the main influencing styles based on the dimensions of connecting (pulling) and convincing (pushing). What are the strengths and challenges of using each style?
7. Describe the five characteristics of influencing styles covered in this chapter. Describe the influencing skills used by managers and leaders in project management.

Leading with Purpose

8. Describe the main factors and situations to consider when choosing different influencing styles. For example, which influencing style do you typically use, and which one do you use when you are stressed?

Chapter 10

Achieving Successful Influencing

Let no man imagine that he has no influence. Whoever he may be, and wherever he may be placed, the man who thinks becomes a light and a power.

—Henry George

Project managers often have enormous responsibility but limited formal authority over their project stakeholders. Therefore, they need to learn the art of influencing to get things done by others (especially what they want them to do). They need cooperation from their stakeholders throughout the project life cycle (PLC). Project managers need help from their stakeholders continuously for various purposes and positioning for the future (when restructuring happens because of mergers and acquisitions).

Leading with Purpose

The dynamics of influencing are complex because they require the project manager to understand extrinsic (expectations, opinions, beliefs) and intrinsic (emotions, feelings, attitudes) thought levels and then use an influencing strategy appropriate to the people and situations. After understanding the dynamics and importance of influencing in project management, project managers must identify and evaluate strategies to influence their stakeholders successfully.

This chapter describes what influencing strategies must be evaluated and used with the situation, how power and influence interrelate, and how project managers should use their power to achieve commitment (long-term influence) rather than just compliance (short-term influence).

10.1. Influencing Strategies

The only way on Earth to influence other people is to talk about what they want and show them how to get it.

—Dale Carnegie

Project managers use different strategies to influence their stakeholders. However, because of the complex dynamics of influencing, they should evaluate and use appropriate strategies because people respond differently to different strategies. What might work exceptionally well for one person might insult another, so influencers must understand the people they try to influence as much as possible. We cannot understate the value of learning their extrinsic and intrinsic thoughts and motivations through empathetic listening. Project managers should understand their stakeholders well and then choose an appropriate influencing strategy for different situations. These are the nine most used strategies:

10.1.1. Gathering information

*Three keys to more abundant living:
caring about others, daring for others,
sharing with others.*

—William A. Ward

If people make a concerted effort to understand their organization as much as possible, they have valuable organizational awareness (or agility). If we make ourselves experts on organizational plans and policies and the strengths of key people, we can rally support and build successful coalitions easily when the occasion arises. To do this, project managers must develop their information power by studying and understanding how the organization works and developing relationships with key influencers.

Project managers should know the social relationships and organizational dynamics to understand who influences whom and how things work (compared with how they should work) in their organizations. This information provides extra power to project managers to build support for their plans and projects, which becomes even more important when support from key stakeholders falls off.

10.1.2. Developing strong network power

True relationships show up during hard times.
—translated from the famous Chinese proverb

Sometimes, project managers must go through others to influence stakeholders to achieve outcomes, meaning that their ability to influence also depends on how well they influence these intermediate people along the path to influence the final stakeholders. Project managers build good relationships and network with people, such as executive assistants, who can help them achieve senior management's attention to discuss important issues about their programs and projects. Therefore, building a strong network is a great way to increase our influence. By accumulating valuable contacts and working on relationship building, project managers extend their network to create strong support and a wealth of information from which to draw.

People want to be with and do things for people they like. Therefore, the larger our network with sincere relationships, the more we can expect to receive through reciprocity. Moreover, creating these networks is especially valuable long term. Once a significant network exists, it leads to more connections and contacts and increased support, reciprocity, power, and influence.

One practical strategy to develop quality networks is to nurture and feed the network. Nurturing refers to keeping our contacts alive and staying in touch. To maintain relationship quality and depth, project managers must feed their network, which means they should provide information, templates, and ideas as people in their network request. This response requires effort or research, but maintaining quality relationships is a good investment. In today's environment, significant communication takes place by email. Although face-to-face communication is better than email, frequent informal email, indicating how we can help each other and how much we care for the other's interests, is useful.

Frequent and valuable contact with people makes it easier to ask for help when needed. We should also offer help to others promptly (for example, sending an article they are looking for or writing a reference letter) rather than procrastinating, which makes a deposit first in our network account. Otherwise, our checks bounce when we request favors from people in our network.

10.1.3. Learning facilitating skills

Be around people who have something of value to share with you. Their impact will continue to have a significant influence.

—Jim Rohn

Facilitating skills present ideas convincingly and use powerful language or evidence to support a proposal. It involves understanding others' interests, where they come from, and why. Project managers make a good impression on others using effective presentation skills with proper analogies and metaphors to paint pictures with words. By empathetic listening and appreciating project stakeholders' ideas without judgment, project managers show their stakeholders they respect them and their ideas. Project managers should follow this advice—"first seek to understand others and then be understood"—to facilitate and solve problems that satisfy common and conflicting interests (Covey 2013).[1]

Influential leaders such as Mahatma Gandhi, J. F. Kennedy, Mother Teresa, and Martin Luther King believed in practicing their preachings. They cared for others genuinely and made them feel important while facilitating or convincing others. They emphasized active listening and finding common ground rather than enforcing their viewpoint.

With good listening and special emphasis on effective presentations, project managers influence key stakeholders to gain support for their programs and projects. Therefore, they must develop effective facilitation skills to find common interests and ideas and gain support from their project stakeholders.

10.1.4. Using logical reasoning

> *Children are more influenced by sermons you act than by sermons you preach.*
>
> —David McKay

This influencing strategy is easy to understand; the trick is knowing when best to use it. By basing arguments and discussions on facts and making points backed up by rational points and convincing evidence, this strategy is often the most effective tool for influencing certain groups of people.

It might be a generalization, but certain professions, such as engineers and scientists, often have personalities based on rational thought and logical reasoning. Therefore, emotional appeals or negotiation alone do not easily convince them. Instead, they are most impressed by the thinking they apply in their careers. Therefore, speaking to them in their language (logical reasoning) makes it much easier to gain respect, followed by compliance or commitment. Therefore, we must know our audience's personality and ways of thinking and doing things, which helps tailor the message to achieve successful influencing.

10.1.5. Understanding others

The most basic of all human needs is the need to understand and be understood. The best way to understand people is to listen to them.
—Ralph Nichols

Understanding often results from a strong interpersonal awareness, achieved by identifying others' needs and concerns. This awareness could also be knowing their concerns and interests and looking after them, depending on the situation, which requires asking the right questions and listening actively. Project managers enhance their interpersonal awareness by listening actively and putting themselves in others' shoes.

Empathetic project leaders identify closely with their team members. They must not be perceived as better than those around them. By showing humility and refraining from stealing praise or deflecting blame, managers demonstrate that they are not just trying to use others for their selfish goals or desires. The best way to wield power is to not brag about it, especially for a project leader looking to gain others' respect and admiration (Cialdini 2006, 171–204).[2]

Ultimately, project leaders are responsible and accountable for a project's success and stakeholders' satisfaction. For example, if some team members devise a creative idea to reduce overall project duration and free resources for other high-priority projects, project leaders should give them credit and mention words of appreciation to senior management. If the project team overlooked some risk items and could not manage them in time, leading to a modest increase in project cost, project leaders should take the blame and accept accountability.

By following this practice, project managers increase mutual trust and empower team members to work harder and meet project objectives. As a practice, project leaders and managers should create high-performance teams by providing opportunities for their team members to learn new things and nurture creativity and innovation. They should show trust and confidence in them and provide visible support when needed, then give them proper recognition and praise for their efforts and results.

10.1.6. Using emotional appeal

The greatness of the man is not how much wealth he acquires, but in his integrity and his ability to affect those around him positively.

—Bob Marley

Emotional appeal is a logical fallacy whereby a debater tries to win an argument by getting an emotional response from the opponent and audience (Boundless Communications 2015).[3] A project manager can emotionally appeal to someone positively. One effective strategy is to use empowerment.

Empowerment involves others and seeks their input, making them feel valued and respected. Once we define goals, empowerment means giving others more autonomy to determine how things should be done. This autonomy leads to acceptance, as people see themselves more as team members and less as independent individuals. When we recognize their ideas and contributions, we increase their feeling of ownership over their work, giving them increased pride and motivation to enhance their output quality.

We can divide emotional appeal into these two categories:

1. Personal appeal:
Personal appeal refers to appealing to a person's feelings, drawing on loyalty and friendship. People want to do things for good friends and feel loyal to project managers they respect. Once influencers know how strong those feelings are, they can appeal to people to do what they want. We should be careful about cashing in on personal appeal because it only takes us so far, especially without doing something in return.

2. Inspirational appeal:
Inspirational appeal refers to intrinsic feelings about people's values, ideals, beliefs, and aspirations. Inspirational appeal's purpose is to raise the person's enthusiasm to do what we want to influence them to do. It is all about connecting to their values and aspirations, which inspires them to do their best to achieve the desired outcome.

When done genuinely, this powerful strategy lives beyond the influencer! If we leave, they are still inspired to do things, not just because they liked us and wanted to do us a favor, but because they believe in our vision and want to contribute to meeting it.

Project managers/leaders can use emotional appeal by expressing humility and sharing their experiences and lessons learned. For example, if project managers wish to point out or correct a mistake made by team members, they could first talk about their similar mistakes. By doing this, criticized team members do not think they are being blamed or belittled. On the contrary, team members appreciate that their project managers help them avoid mistakes they made in the past (Carnegie 2011).[4] Project managers lessen the negative impact by praising team members and discussing their mistakes constructively. Project managers should show confidence in team members' ability and potential to create high performance.

10.1.7. Mastering the art of negotiation

> *Negotiation is the exchange of ideas for the purpose of influencing behavior . . .*
> *Wishes are converted into reality through the process of bargaining.*
>
> —Vijay K. Verma

Some people think of negotiation as bargaining, but the aim of bargaining should also be finding win-win solutions. Bargaining is an exchange for mutual

10–Achieving Successful Influencing

benefit where both parties (influencer and influenced) collaborate to meet each other's needs. Bargaining involves offering favors or resources valuable to the influenced in exchange for some desired actions and resources important to the influencer.

Some people think of bargaining as negative, but in a project environment, which can be political, bargaining is called *currency exchange*. Currency exchange can be immediate or an IOU to be taken care of in the future. Managers should follow the law of reciprocity to create situations that allow the mutual exchange of things valuable to both parties.

Negotiation is another useful strategy to influence, which relates to creating a network for the reciprocity it brings. Through bargaining, people persuade others to alter their original position on an issue by giving them something they desire in exchange. Often, this need not be a win-lose scenario; we might achieve a win-win result if we negotiate effectively.

Negotiation is one of the most tangible but difficult skills to master. However, this option satisfies both parties and creates a long-term relationship in which the parties help and support each other whenever possible. Skilled negotiators are often great communicators. They can best identify what others desire and how best to appeal to them to achieve a mutually beneficial solution.

Skilled negotiation is based largely on general concepts such as being a great communicator and identifying others' desires and motivations. However, negotiators might use several more specific tactics to obtain their desired result. For example, one effective technique to reach a win-win solution is to move away from positions and focus on the other party's interests

(Fisher & Ury 2011).[5] Most negotiating strategies are based on good communication and interpersonal skills. Once these foundations are in place, project managers put themselves in a great position to improve their negotiation skills by walking their talk and delivering what they commit.

The key to successful negotiation is focusing more on interests than positions (Verma 1996, 145–173).[6] Sometimes, negotiations become difficult because people take a position, dig in their heels, and stick to it. The strategy to influence them in such cases is to learn their interests by identifying their hopes and desires and work hard to determine how to meet their interests, which helps them focus on what they specifically want rather than being only concerned with not backing down from an overall position.

This technique facilitates the desired outcome by helping people move away from their position and satisfying both parties' interests. When influencing by successful negotiations, people do not lose face when they alter or modify their positions because the focus is on interests, not positions. We can identify interests by asking open-ended questions, such as these:

- What do you feel is most important?
- Why do you want this?
- What concerns you the most?
- How are you going to use it?
- Where are you going to use it?
- When are you going to use it?

Open-ended questions encourage people to communicate and expand on their interests without making them defensive. These questions lead to collaboration because the influenced believes the influencers are trying to deal with the influenced's concerns and interests rather than push their agenda. It also helps develop better long-term working relationships. The focus here is to master the art of win-win negotiations.

10.1.8. Developing a common vision

> *Alone we can do so little;*
> *together we can do so much.*
> —Helen Keller

Much as how enthusiastic team members are more effective workers, when managers align their ideas with broad organizational goals and values to establish a common vision, they find themselves better motivated and producing higher-quality outputs. This is especially true when dealing with upper management as if ideas are framed in the organization's context and goals. They are much more useful for linking ideas to organizational values and higher-level principles such as fairness or sustainability.

Common vision refers not only to aligning personal visions with broader organizational goals. Although that is the core meaning, a common vision can also refer to the belief that we can reach a win-win alternative in any situation. When a disagreement or obstacle splits opinion, it is much more effective to approach the situation so it focuses on determining which outcome works best for all parties involved rather than just one party. If people show willingness from the start to achieve a mutually beneficial

Leading with Purpose

solution, negotiations and collaboration quickly solve the matter amicably, whereas if both look for a win-lose scenario, both sides fight tooth and nail indefinitely and likely leave the table unsatisfied. Covey, the author of *The 7 Habits of Highly Effective People* (2013), perhaps says it best when discussing win-win scenarios: "It's not your way or my way; it's a better way, a higher way."[7]

Common vision helps achieve concurrence, but real synergy comes from the process used to develop common visions. It is not only about the destination but also the journey to reach that destination. To get real commitment to a common vision, the effective manager uses these steps:

1. Develop vision, strategies, and goals.
2. Communicate them clearly to stakeholders.
3. Get their input and address key concerns.
4. Be flexible in making necessary modifications.

Managers should ensure they *genuinely* seek stakeholders' input rather than give lip service. In addition, using open communication to deal with concerns and opinions leads to common visions toward which stakeholders are committed to work, which leads to real teamwork and synergy.

10.1.9. Using expertise effectively

> *The only way in which one human being can properly attempt to influence another is by encouraging him to think for himself, instead of endeavoring to instill ready-made opinions into his head.*
> —Leslie Stephen

Managers with expertise in certain areas are usually sought for their opinion and referred to when opinions differ. We perceive managers as experts based on their knowledge of specific issues or fields. The more issues on which we are an expert, the more opportunities we have to exert this power to influence people and discussions the way we want. This does not mean we should take advantage of perceived expertise for personal gain, only that it is much easier to gain willing compliance from subordinates if they believe the project manager has expertise. This compares with managers making a request but being unable to back it up sufficiently and give proper guidance based on expertise and experience.

When a project manager is not an expert, it is effective to contact other project managers or functional managers with more expertise in those areas and then recognize them for their help and expertise. Appealing to someone's ego and perceived expertise leads to positive influencing and enhances mutual trust and respect.

We can summarize these influencing strategies nicely in the acronym INFLUENCE, shown in Table 10.1, which effectively captures the keywords and practical concepts to influence. It is clear from Table

10.1 that most of the nine influencing strategies involve informal powers. When we use these concepts effectively, the goal should be to use them appropriately to achieve compliance and commitment.

Chapter 10 Summary

The complex dynamics of influencing require project managers to understand both extrinsic and intrinsic thought levels. They should identify and evaluate influencing strategies successfully. These are the nine most useful strategies:

1. Gathering information
2. Developing strong network power
3. Learning facilitating skills
4. Using logical reasoning
5. Understanding others
6. Using emotional appeal
7. Mastering the art of negotiation
8. Developing a common vision
9. Using expertise effectively

Project managers must study and understand their organization and develop relationships with key influencers to gather information to provide extra power. Knowledge of social relationships and organizational dynamics is essential for project managers to understand who influences whom and how things work in their organizations.

Project managers must sometimes go through others to influence stakeholders to achieve outcomes. Project managers do this by building good

	Keyword	Type of Power	Focuses On
I	Information about Organization	Information (Informal)	Knowing organizational policies and procedures and manner in which organization works
N	Networking	Network (Informal)	Creating collaborative relationships
F	Facilitating	Persuasion (Informal)	Putting together a clear and convincing message
L	Logical Reasoning	Persuasion (Informal)	Presenting factual and detailed information with clear and logical explanations
U	Understanding	Persuasion (Informal)	Listening actively, knowing the other parties, and earning their respect
E	Emotional Appeal	Referent (Informal)	Appealing to personal values
N	Negotiation	Persuasion (Informal)	Reaching win-win solutions
C	Common Vision	Referent (Informal)	Leading stakeholders to achieve synergy and unity of purpose
E	Expertise	Expert (Informal)	Having the right combination of knowledge, experience, skills, and an ability to empower others

Table 10.1. Influence (in a Nutshell).

relationships and networking with people. Maintaining frequent and valuable contact with people and promptly offering help to others makes it easier to obtain help when needed.

Facilitating skills present ideas convincingly and use powerful language or evidence to support a proposal. Project managers must develop effective facilitation skills to find common interests and ideas and gain support from their project stakeholders.

Using logical reasoning means basing arguments and discussions on facts and making points supported by rational thinking and convincing evidence. Rational thought and logical reasoning are necessary to convince some people, so we must know our audience's thinking and tailor our message accordingly.

A strong interpersonal awareness, achieved by identifying others' needs and concerns, often results in understanding. We enhance interpersonal awareness through active listening and empathy. Project leaders and managers should create high-performance teams by providing learning opportunities and nurturing creativity and innovation.

Empowerment, involving others and seeking their input, is an effective strategy for project managers to emotionally appeal to stakeholders positively. Emotional appeal falls into two categories: (1) personal appeal, which appeals to a person's feelings, and (2) inspirational appeal, which appeals to people's values, ideals, beliefs, and aspirations. In addition, project managers use emotional appeal by expressing humility and sharing experiences and lessons learned.

Negotiation aims to bargain for win-win solutions, exchanging for mutual benefit. In a project environment, bargaining is known as *currency exchange*, in

10–Achieving Successful Influencing

which project managers follow the law of reciprocity. Most negotiating strategies are based on good communication and interpersonal skills, followed by project managers walking their talk and delivering what they commit. Successful negotiation focuses less on positions and more on interests, which we can determine through open-ended questions.

Especially when dealing with upper management, project managers find themselves better motivated and produce higher-quality outputs when they align their ideas with organizational goals and values to establish a common vision. Beyond that, a common vision is a belief in win-win outcomes. To gain commitment to a common vision, effective managers develop vision, strategies, and goals; communicate them clearly to stakeholders; get input and address key concerns; and are flexible in making necessary modifications.

Managers with great knowledge of specific issues or fields are considered experts, sought for their opinions, and referred to when opinions differ. This expertise provides opportunities to influence people and discussion the way we want. Conversely, in areas where we are not experts, we should contact other managers with more expertise and recognize them for their help.

Project managers often have enormous responsibility but limited formal authority over their project stakeholders. Therefore, they need to learn the art of influencing to get things done by others (especially what they want them to do).

Chapter 10 Review and Critical Thinking Questions

1. Describe the nine strategies of influencing covered in this chapter. Which strategies do you typically use, and which do you use when you are under stress?

2. Describe the challenges you encountered in your project management experience using the following nine influencing strategies. How would you overcome those challenges? Give examples based on your practical experience of influencing your stakeholders.

    i. Gathering information
    ii. Developing strong network power
    iii. Learning facilitating skills
    iv. Using logical reasoning
    v. Understanding others
    vi. Using emotional appeal
    vii. Mastering the art of negotiation
    viii. Developing a common vision
    ix. Using expertise effectively

3. What are the keywords to describe influencing in a nutshell? What type of power do those keywords represent, and what do they focus on?

Chapter 11

Influencing by Increasing Power

Achievement is a WE thing, not a ME thing, always the product of many heads and hands.
—J. W. Atkinson

Power and influence interrelate. Teamwork is crucial to managing projects successfully. Project managers must increase their total power package as a first step and learn to use their power more effectively to influence their stakeholders, build effective teams, and maintain high teamwork levels throughout the project life cycle (PLC).

Sometimes, a few team members might not be active team players or be barriers to teamwork. However, effective teams have crucial characteristics to create real teamwork. Project managers must understand the characteristics of teams and practical guidelines for effective team building. They must use their influencing strategies and adapt their influencing style to motivate their team members. They must use an appropriate mix of convincing and connecting to influence reluctant team members to contribute and inspire others to increase overall cooperation and performance.

Project managers must strive to increase their overall power to effectively influence their stakeholders long term. Eight sources of power include three formal and five informal components. Project managers should focus on informal power components because they are more permanent, increase personal strength, and cannot be taken away, even if the project managers change departments or organizations. Moreover, informal powers make people more confident and able to help others. When using their power, project managers should recognize the importance of using their power informally to achieve successful and long-term influencing, leading to more cooperation and better working relationships. However, they should not hesitate to use their formal power formally, but only as a last resort.

This chapter describes eight important characteristics of an effective team that are crucial to creating synergy. Project leaders and project managers must create an environment to foster these characteristics and encourage all team members to learn, teach, and practice these characteristics to achieve extraordinary performance. They must select an appropriate influencing strategy to build effective and high-performance teams.

The more power we have and know how to use effectively, the better we can influence our stakeholders and build high-performance teams to increase overall performance. This chapter describes ten guidelines to increase power and, hence, the ability to influence.

11.1. Influence in Team Building

Finding good players is easy. Getting them to play as a team is another story.

—Casey Stengel

The team approach harnesses the members' collective skills, strengths, and energy. It is all about everyone working together and being committed to achieving common and shared goals. An effective team displays the synergy that comes from a whole being greater than the sum of its parts, especially when referring to project teams.

Table 11.1 shows keywords for teamwork that emphasize that project leaders use their influencing skills to create a desire among team members to help one another, take ownership of team goals and results, share knowledge to enhance one another's skills, and recognize their achievements to keep them motivated. All these keywords lead to true teamwork, and then we have a TEAM, which stands for Together Everyone Achieves More (Verma 1997, 37–38).[1]

When focused on win-win scenarios, a team with strong foundations of trust, communication, and empathetic leadership shows elite motivation and potential. Likewise, when a skilled and motivated team has mutually beneficial goals, continued open communication leads to high, self-sustaining levels of creativity and high-quality outputs.

Successful influencing is an important characteristic of a leader. In project environments, leaders must influence their team members to expand their potential, creativity, and commitment. They must use their influencing skills to build effective teams and

Leading with Purpose

			Emphasizes
What Is a Team?	**T**	Together	Combining knowledge and experiences of all team members.
	E	Everyone	Including *all* team members.
	A	Achieves	Accomplishing team goals rather than just doing tasks.
	M	More	Achieving synergy (1 + 1 > 2).
What Creates Teamwork and Synergy?	**W**	Willingness	Creating desire to help others with technical and personal issues.
	O	Ownership	Taking ownership of team goals, tasks, and results.
	R	Reward	Recognizing accomplishments and rewarding objectively.
	K	Knowledge	Sharing knowledge to enhance team members' skills.

Table 11.1. Teamwork (in a Nutshell)

continually inspire and motivate team members to produce high-quality results. They must be genuinely interested in helping their team members grow.

Effective teams have several task-related and people-oriented characteristics. Task-oriented characteristics directly measure project performance by focusing on tasks and results. People-oriented characteristics contribute indirectly to project performance by improving the working relationships among team members. Project managers use their influencing skills to enhance the people-oriented characteristics of effective teams. These characteristics also enrich team members' experience and contribute to their self-development. This section focuses on the people-oriented characteristics of effective teams.

11.1.1. Understanding effective team characteristics

Everyone has to work together; if we can't get everyone working towards a common goal, nothing is going to happen.

—Harold K. Sperlich

Project managers and team leaders must understand team characteristics to influence team members to meet organizational goals and strategies and work together as an effective team. It helps them use an appropriate communication style and influencing strategies to create synergy among team members. Besides project team members' interdependence and the satisfaction and pleasure they derive from their association with the team, project managers must ensure they understand team characteristics and encourage all team members to understand these characteristics and dynamics to optimize one another's performance. Verma (1997, 37–38) described an effective team's important people-oriented characteristics.[2] Table 11.2 shows the eight characteristics and associated influencing strategies.

Leading with Purpose

	Team Characteristics	Associated Influencing Strategies
1	High involvement, energy, and interest	• Gathering information • Learning facilitating skills • Developing a common vision
2	Good communication	• Learning facilitating skills • Understanding others
3	Positive and cooperative team atmosphere	• Learning facilitating skills • Understanding others • Developing a common vision
4	Mutual trust among team members	• Understanding others • Using emotional appeal • Mastering the art of negotiation
5	Self-development of team members	• Using emotional appeal • Using expertise effectively
6	Capacity to solve conflicts	• Learning facilitating skills • Using logical reasoning • Understanding others • Mastering the art of negotiation
7	Effective organizational interface	• Gathering information • Developing strong network power • Developing a common vision • Using expertise effectively
8	High need for achievement and growth	• Gathering information • Using emotional appeal • Developing a common vision

Table 11.2. Team Characteristics and Associated Influencing Strategies

The eight team characteristics and associated influencing strategies are described:

1. **High involvement, energy, and interest**
   In many companies and teams, project team members are given tasks and complete them adequately, doing what is asked of them on schedule and within budget. This might be acceptable for many teams, but if we strive toward creating a highly effective team, it is not!

   When employees are highly involved and interested in their work to achieve high-quality results, they are dissatisfied with acceptable outputs; they take challenges and go the extra mile. By empowering employees, giving them suitable tasks in which they are interested, and creating a high-energy atmosphere where team members feel involved and motivated, they own their tasks, leading to higher productivity and employee satisfaction.

   A great way to get a team involved and interested from the project start is to create a vision and mission statement that everyone helps create and can get behind without pressure. By showing team members their opinions are valued and expected, especially in creating a statement representing the belief system, managers show they value every person's input. We must establish a strong base of shared values and collaboration from start to finish. High involvement, energy, and interest are essential for a team to function efficiently. By demonstrating that these traits are highly valued, a manager quickly gains an advantage over others who overlook the importance of empowering their team members.

Leading with Purpose

2. Good communication
This simple characteristic is an easy way to increase a project team's effectiveness, yet we often overlook it. Every person has unique strengths and weaknesses, which is why teams are assembled and should be viewed as a cohesive unit. Team members must draw on other members' strengths to gain advice and input into decisions. This creates a system of checks and balances to avoid mistakes and realize possible improvements. Additionally, open communication increases a team's unity, leading to higher motivation for joint success and gains through synergy as team members learn of their peers' capabilities.

Project managers should be assertive to achieve effective team communication. We must ensure communication is shared in a manner that builds trust and cooperation, not only through words but also through vocal tones and body language (Verma 1996, 40–49; Quick 1992, 55–66).[3]

3. A positive and cooperative team atmosphere
An actively and openly communicating team effectively creates increased motivation for joint success. Therefore, it is essential to ensure team members commit to the team concept rather than just individual outputs. Members must realize that they all benefit when they work together, and high intragroup interaction helps develop mutual understanding.

Prima donnas divide a team, cause conflict, and weaken essential communication lines through group segmentation and working in silos. We must avoid this, as team members must accept group accountability for success or failure. If we do not achieve this, people fight to take credit or pass blame, which decreases unity, productivity, and the happiness and motivation of all team members. A great way to ensure a cooperative team atmosphere is to develop the project plan carefully as a team where everyone feels involved and takes ownership of outcomes (Verma 2006–2018; 2013; Stuckenbruck & Marshall 1985, 16–24).[4]

4. Mutual trust among team members

As specified, when communication lines are open, team members work to neutralize individual weaknesses through others' strengths, but this depends on mutual trust among team members. Through a positive and healthy team atmosphere, teams must develop a sense of belonging in their team based on respect and cooperative interaction among team members. Employees feel empowered if members learn to be open to healthy conflict and listen to and value other team members' ideas and opinions, even when they differ from their viewpoints. In addition, when they think they are heard and respected, they get more involved, share ideas, and communicate openly with one another, leading to increased mutual trust. Building and maintaining trust is gradual and requires high action and involvement for success (Verma 2006–2018; 2013; Bartolomé 1989, 135–142).[5]

5. Self-development of team members

Although we should focus on developing a team mentality among team members, it does not mean individual improvement is not valuable. Conveniently, the more empowered and committed team members are, the higher their motivation is to increase their productivity. With increased responsibility and desire for team success come increased aspirations for earning even more responsibility and contributions to team success. By working closely with other team members, individuals learn from these members' strengths and opinions and overcome their weaknesses. In addition, they gain new insights and any personal improvements they make, such as increasing their informal power.

6. Capacity to solve conflicts

When a team is full of interdependent, open, and motivated members, it becomes much easier to resolve conflicts when they arise. Most teams recognize that conflict is expected and even encouraged among team members, so managers must be able to resolve it as needed. Through their actions, project managers must show that everyone can share opinions and suggestions. They must show consistency and not favoritism when differences of opinion arise.

If a manager is perceived as fair and just, there will be little to no resentment and bitterness when final decisions are made, which is essential so teams move forward, harboring no hard feelings toward other team members or the manager. Thamhain and Wilemon (1975, 31–50) contended many teams commonly experience seven sources of conflict (Verma 2013; 1996, 98–109; Posner 1986, 207–211):[6]

1. Schedules
2. Priorities

3. Human resources
4. Technical issues
5. Administrative problems
6. Personality
7. Cost

Effective project managers who are also good team builders properly identify the sources of conflict and take corrective actions to resolve them successfully to maintain high team performance.

7. Effective organizational interface
Teams are composed of members with different backgrounds and expertise from different departments or units in the organization. As a result, project managers must recognize different ways of doing things in various departments, often leading to inefficiency or even friction and conflict.

Project managers must also have sufficient organizational awareness to figure out how to interface with different departments and integrate their efforts effectively to meet project and overall organizational objectives. In addition, they must recognize the importance of people skills and team dynamics to achieve this effective organizational interface, enhance all team members' potential, and achieve maximum synergy.

8. High need for achievement and growth
An underlying theme throughout these points is that if team members feel more empowered and committed, they have an increased desire for team success and the need for higher achievement and

growth. This need is a characteristic of effective teams. No matter how motivated, cohesive, mutually trusting, or committed team members are, they must always strive for improvement. The hallmark of the most effective teams is that results can always be improved upon, individually and as a team.

A tendency to "think outside the box" and always working to increase efficiency and outputs distinguish between stagnation and complacency and growth and excellence. Teams that become satisfied with just acceptable results see their motivation and productivity slowly dwindle. In contrast, the team that constantly sets challenging goals and high expectations sees an energetic team constantly improving its strengths and shoring up its weaknesses.

There are always team members who are not overambitious and uninterested in taking on more responsibilities. They might be happy keeping the status quo for their job and feel no need to expand their roles. For example, some team members are less interested in project work and happy to do operations work. Project and functional managers must recognize this situation and allocate roles and responsibilities accordingly.

This section covers an effective team's eight important characteristics crucial to creating synergy and real teamwork. Project leaders and project managers must influence their team members to create an environment to foster these characteristics and encourage all team members to learn, teach, and practice them to achieve extraordinary performance and create high-performance teams long term.

11.2. Ten Guidelines to Increase Power and Influence

> *Great minds must be ready not only to take opportunities, but to make them.*
>
> —Colton

Power refers to the ability to influence. The more power project managers have and know how to use effectively, the better they can deliver successful projects. The best strategy to influence successfully is to focus on increasing informal personal power, as these powers influence people sustainably and practically with more long-term benefits. Project managers should use these ten guidelines to increase their power and ability to influence stakeholders long term. Table 11.3 shows the ten guidelines with associated power sources to increase power and influence.

11.2.1. Develop a sense of obligation

> *I have just three things to teach: simplicity, patience, compassion. These three are your greatest treasures.*
>
> —Lao Tzu

Senior management wants to develop a sense of obligation in their program managers, functional managers, and project managers. In addition, they strive to develop a sense of obligation among their team members, major vendors, suppliers, and contractors to enhance their potential and increase

Leading with Purpose

	Ten Guidelines	Associated Power Source
1	Develop a sense of obligation.	Referent and Network
2	Develop a reputation as an expert.	Expert and Network
3	Rely on successful track record.	Expert
4	Create a sense of identification (with the project and the project team).	Referent
5	Get stakeholders' commitment.	Referent and Persuasion
6	Increase knowledge about organizational procedures and policies.	Information
7	Develop and strengthen network power.	Network
8	Develop interpersonal skills.	Referent, Expert, and Persuasion
9	Increase project profile.	Referent and Network
10	Build a high-performance team.	Referent, Expert, and Persuasion

Table 11.3. Ten Guidelines to Increase Power and Influence

overall performance. Largely, this implies creating an environment where people want to do tasks assigned rather than think they must do those tasks. This is the main component to gaining ownership and buy-in from all stakeholders. Therefore, senior management should create this as a culture in the organization.

As a first step to developing a sense of obligation among stakeholders, project managers should genuinely involve them in developing plans, processes, and logistics to gain full acceptance. They develop this sense of obligation by accommodating reasonable and justifiable changes in specifications/scope, providing genuine support to team members, and ensuring they get recognition for their efforts. They should establish better rapport with stakeholders and create accountability among team members, functional managers, contractors, vendors/suppliers, and clients by negotiating effectively and encouraging them to work as a team.

Project managers earn a sense of obligation from team members by making them believe the project managers care for them as individuals, respect their ideas and interests, and empathize with their problems and obstacles. Managers strengthen bonds of trust and fellowship with them by using this approach in dealing with team members, even if it simply involves listening to them. Team members give their best efforts because they think their project managers value them, their ideas, and their desires (Carnegie 2011).[7]

11.2.2. Develop a reputation as an expert

How you think is influenced by what you read, what you listen to. Reading books that have a positive influence on your thinking can truly change your life.

—Catherine Pulsifer

Perception is everything with power and influence. Thus, if the project team believes their project manager has high expertise, it increases management's confidence in the project manager. A good way to do this is by project managers contributing significantly with expertise and ensuring contributions are visible and valued by senior management. In addition, others in the organization readily accept their expert power if project managers share their knowledge and experience to help solve difficult issues and problems.

Following this, project managers must make themselves accessible and reliable. To be perceived as having expertise in some areas, project managers cannot rely on just one or two contributions. Instead, they must consistently show they are knowledgeable and can be relied on to successfully resolve complicated problems.

Some scholars, such as Greene (2000), believe the best way to build a strong reputation is to initially focus on one outstanding, unique quality and then make it well known to others, subtly and humbly.[8] In project environments, that quality might apply to project managers' jobs, skills, and knowledge.

After ensuring they become well known for this quality, project managers have a reputation as experts. It is much easier to expand this reputation by sharing knowledge because the more people who share this power, the more they get. To develop a strong reputation such as this, managers must ensure they are dependable so management considers them first when assigning important, high-profile tasks.

11.2.3. Rely on a successful track record

Results speak louder than words.
—Vijay K. Verma

Like motivation, reliability comes from within. Some people feel obligated to perform, whereas others do not. Project managers rely on those who feel obligated because they have a good record of delivering on their promises. Sometimes, project managers lack direct knowledge of potential team members' reliability and the time to supervise everyone on the project. Therefore, project managers must trust their team members to do their tasks.

A person with authority and responsibility is reliable when they are worthy of confidence and can be trusted. Reliability is associated with moral qualities and judgment, knowledge, skills, and habits. A good record of accomplishment and high-quality work over the long term are two important factors in increasing and maintaining high reliability.

Project managers usually prefer to delegate important tasks to those with strong records of accomplishment. In addition, project managers must rely on records of accomplishment because they often lack time to test team members' reliability. In such cases, actions speak louder than words, and records of accomplishment help build self-confidence and increase management's confidence.

Project managers should rely on a successful record of their accomplishments valued by top management. Project managers should uphold the same standards they expect from their team members. As expected by management, they should deliver results consistently long term to increase their ability to influence and gain support from senior management and other stakeholders. This earns top management's confidence and makes them more valuable.

11.2.4. Identify with the project and the project team

> *If you want to be successful, find someone who has achieved the results you want and copy what they do and you will achieve the same results.*
>
> —Anthony Robbins

If team members identify with the project and the project team, they are much more closely tied to the project's success or failure, and thus, they are more likely to put forth greater effort. In addition, the more committed team members are to one another and the project, the more interested they are in their performance because project failure will be more closely associated with personal failure and disappointment. Conversely, team members take pride and satisfaction in a job well done.

As with successful sports teams that require teammates to identify with a team/goal-oriented strategy (for example, play for the logo on the front of the jersey, not the name on the back), the best teams are made of a cohesive unit rather than self-interested individuals. The more unified and committed the team is, the higher the quality of their outputs, which reflects the project manager.

Project managers should identify with the project and project team by aligning the project stakeholders' benefits with the organization's goals and objectives.

This way, people want to be associated with those project managers because it creates more visibility. Besides the importance of having team members identify with one another and the project, they must identify with the project manager, who symbolizes both.

A manager can increase this identification in many ways, such as behaving in a way others respect, espousing goals, values, and ideals others hold, and creating a vision to inspire people for higher performance. When a manager commits to the project and the team, it rarely goes unnoticed. By showing dedication and a strong will to succeed, a manager sets an example for team members to follow, which causes them to want to identify with their manager even more. Besides this, the more closely project managers identify with high-profile projects and influential people in the organization, the more powerful others will perceive them.

11.2.5. Get stakeholders' commitment

I have learned that people will forget what you said, people will forget what you did, but people will never forget how you made them feel.

—Maya Angelou

As with developing a sense of obligation and identification, gaining the stakeholders' commitment requires motivating team members by increasing their feeling of responsibility to the team and the project. If we encourage participation and involvement in a project team, workers own the project rather than just work on it, leading to more commitment and motivation to produce high-quality results.

Developing a sense of obligation through gaining more commitment and motivation is explained in more detail at the end of this section. At the core, project managers gain team members' commitment when they motivate them. Motivation is a complex driver of human actions, but there is no debate about its usefulness, as motivated people are energized and better equipped to handle obstacles, especially political, bureaucratic, and barriers to change.

Harnessing employees' motivations benefits not only the project manager but also the team members. This is enough to develop a sense of obligation, as they realize the manager helps them reach their goals and objectives. By leading and communicating effectively, project managers motivate their team members and create a work environment that optimally allows psychological, social, and economic satisfaction (Cleland & Ireland 2006; Certo, Appelbaum & Divine 1993, 387–395).[9]

Besides the importance of gaining team members' commitment, never overlook that upper management is made of stakeholders. The more committed management is to a project, the more resources and support the project receives, which leads to better results and even more commitment and support. The management support here also refers to effective workload management to allocate properly skilled resources and the timing needed to meet project objectives.

11.2.6. Increase knowledge about organizational policies and procedures

You people are telling me what you think I want to know. I want to know what is actually happening.

—Creighton Abrams

Although all managers are expected to know a company's written policies and procedures, the subtle nuances unique to companies, divisions, project teams, and even individuals are all important aspects of "organizational knowledge." Not just knowing how organizations should work through their formal processes but also knowing how they function is invaluable. Managers who take it upon themselves to be aware can answer many important questions, for instance:

- What shortcuts can be taken?
- Who are the real decision-makers?
- Where are the gaps in hierarchal communication?
- Which people are more likely to support and which types of initiatives?

Knowing the answers to these questions gives project managers an advantage over their counterparts who never bother digging deeper than company manuals and formal policies.

11.2.7. Develop and strengthen network power

The only difference between where you are right now and where you will be next year at this time, are the people you meet and the books you read.

—Charlie "Tremendous" Jones

We cannot overemphasize the importance of increasing network quantity and quality. Project managers should focus not just on quantity but also on the quality of their network because just one valuable contact is worth a hundred mediocre ones. Aspiring managers should constantly add to their network. Organized managers should learn to prioritize and update their network contacts regularly.

However, although it would be great to keep in touch with hundreds of acquaintances, this might not be practical. Power players such as Dilenschneider (2007, 125–138) argue that you must "Keep growing your network by shaving it. There is no substitute for a powerful network that embraces you and even nurtures you. You cannot do it alone."[10]

In his book *The Little Black Book of Connections*, Gitomer (2006, 16) presented excellent strategies to increase network power. He suggested the four following questions that open the door to growth and success in effective networking.[11]

1. Whom do you know?
2. How well are you connected?
3. Do you know how to make a connection?
4. Who knows you?

Two key elements to increase network power are the following (Verma 2018, 246–248):[12]

1. Nurture the network.
2. Feed the network.

We should be in touch with our contacts regularly and know of any major changes in their lives. We must continually feed the network by doing favors for people who ask and new people we meet. They might need specific information about the products, suppliers, vendors, or project management techniques and tips, and our prompt help will be greatly appreciated. Eventually, others might reciprocate favors we do because "what goes around comes around."

People appreciate it if we respond to them promptly and give them resources they can use to find the answers to their questions independently if we cannot. Doing favors for others first is like depositing in the bank and then writing checks so our checks do not bounce. The simple phrase "give and take" means we should give before we hope to get anything in return.

11.2.8. Develop interpersonal skills

I will pay more for the ability to deal with people than any other ability under the sun.

—John D. Rockefeller

By improving interpersonal skills, managers set themselves up for increased success. Perhaps the most obvious example is the importance of strong communication skills. When we give team members clear, consistent, and thoughtful instructions and feedback, they much better understand what we expect from them and how to fulfill their responsibilities. Conversely, unclear or contradictory messages from managers result in confused, frustrated employees who often deliver outputs that do not match the original intention and might even need to be redone.

Fair and constructive feedback is another area where managers with strong interpersonal skills shine. Team members appreciate a manager who takes the time to help them understand their tasks and improve their ability to produce higher-quality outputs. In addition, by being empathetic listeners, we can better understand others' motivations and learn to adjust their behaviors to suit the unique personality of whomever we deal with. In this sense, project managers must be more sensitive to others' feelings and flexible enough to use the appropriate techniques for specific people and circumstances.

Communication is not the only area in which interpersonal skills are useful. Most project managers recognize they also need increased influencing, negotiating, conflict management, and facilitating abilities. These skills help them gain support from management, keep stakeholders in harmony, steer discussions in progressive directions, and make more effective presentations.

11.2.9. Increase project's profile

Do not go where the path may lead. Go instead where there is no path and leave a trail.
—Ralph Waldo Emerson

The more closely managers identify with high-level organizational strategies, high-profile projects, and influential people, the more powerful others perceive them. Thus, increasing our project's profile is a desirable strategy because higher-profile projects often get more resources and support from upper management. The more resources and support a manager has, the higher the potential for success and the greater opportunity to create and manage a high-performance team effectively.

To increase the project profile, managers must convince upper management of its value and importance. Perhaps the most effective way to do this is to relate our project to the organization's long-term strategies. To do so, project managers should become involved with the organization's central planning, such as having influential people as their mentors and champions, becoming members of important committees, and participating in and contributing to planning processes. By doing this, managers become more familiar with the organization's core direction and more convincingly align their project goals to organizational goals.

When we show a strong desire for increased responsibility that comes with a higher-profile project, management recognizes we have ambition and confidence, two of the most treasured traits high achievers possess. Therefore, increasing our project profile and

Leading with Purpose

the quest for working with high-profile people and projects increases our power and ability to influence others.

11.2.10. Build a high-performance team

> *There are four ways, and only four ways, in which we have contact with the world. We are evaluated and classified by these four contacts: what we do, how we look, what we say, and how we say it.*
>
> —Dale Carnegie

Teams are composed of people with diverse skills, backgrounds, and interests. Project managers need people committed to consistent, accurate, and high-quality results. Thus, the difference between good and high-performance teams is important. Once a team is assembled and performing effectively, effective project managers must follow the following four guidelines to build high-performance teams (as shown in Table 11.4).

11–Influencing by Increasing Power

	Guidelines	**Associated Strategies**
1	Support the team.	• Perform proper risk analysis. • Credit others and take the blame. • Discuss important information one-on-one to resolve ambiguities.
2	Provide opportunities to team members.	• Provide training to enhance technical, interpersonal, and conceptual skills. • Encourage team members to attend conferences. • Work with team members on progression plans.
3	Demonstrate trust and confidence in team members.	• Do not micromanage, • Show confidence in team members' abilities. • Empower team members.
4	Nurture creativity and innovation.	• Encourage team members to think "outside the box." • Support psychological and intellectual enrichment. • Be willing to experiment with ideas.

Table 11.4. Four Guidelines to Build High-Performance Teams

1. Support the team.

All teams need appropriate support from management. Managers can do the following to provide genuine support to their teams:

- Ensure proper risk analysis is performed.
- Give credit to others and take the blame themselves.
- Discuss important information one-on-one to resolve ambiguities.

2. Provide opportunities to team members.

Team members always look for opportunities to learn and grow in the organization. Team members will believe their managers care for their future and will be motivated to expand their potential. Project managers can provide opportunities to help team members gain new skills and knowledge by doing the following:

- Provide training to enhance their technical, interpersonal, and conceptual skills.
- Encourage team members to attend conferences to learn from experts and network.
- Work with team members on their progression plans.

3. Demonstrate trust and confidence in team members.

Team members will take on new challenges, but they could fear failure. So, project managers must believe in their team members' abilities. They should do the following to show trust and confidence in their team members to accept new challenges.

- Not micromanage, especially when they do new tasks.
- Show confidence in team members' abilities.
- Empower team members to increase their skills and confidence.

4. Nurture creativity and innovation.

High-performance teams thrive on thinking "out of the box." Project managers can do the following to expand their team members' potential and nurture

creativity and innovation:
- Encourage team members to think "outside the box" to develop creative solutions.
- Support psychological and intellectual enrichment.
- Be willing to experiment with ideas.

We cannot take high-performance teams for granted. If managers assemble first-rate teams and coax them to produce consistently high-quality output, they must not slide into complacency or risk losing what they built. Effective leaders are humble and realize their team is their most important power base.

Managers should give credit to their team and celebrate small wins. Nothing tears a team apart faster than lack of recognition, demonstrating selfish behavior, and unjustly taking credit that should be shared. Similarly, managers should never deflect blame on their team. In the same way as giving credit to their team, managers should take the blame and deflect attacks on their team. Team members go to any extent for a leader who stands up for them and does not hesitate to allow them to share any earned success.

We must constantly challenge team members to sustain a high-performance team's high self-motivational level. Confident and motivated workers perform their best when they know their actions are appreciated and rewarded. By increasing the visibility of a team and their project, project managers gain more resources and support (as described in the guideline for increasing project profile), leading to higher levels of team commitment to deliver

Leading with Purpose

extraordinary results. High-performance teams have pride and unity that, if properly harnessed by the project manager, produces results far exceeding others' expectations.

As shown in Figure 11.1, the following are the three important characteristics of high-performance teams:

1. Trust and confidence
2. Creativity
3. New opportunities

Figure 11.1. Three characteristics of high-performance teams.

Good project managers recognize the importance of these elements, provide full support, and gain support from senior management to ensure all these elements are nurtured and supported for team members. They must provide support at the professional level (to provide new opportunities), organizational level (to provide proper guidance and empowerment to demonstrate trust), and personal level (to coach and inspire to nurture creativity and innovation).

Chapter 11 Summary

As power and influence interrelate, project managers must increase their power and use it to influence their stakeholders, build effective teams, and maintain high levels of teamwork. They must combine convincing and connecting to influence their team members and increase cooperation and performance.

Eight sources of power include three formal and five informal components. Project managers should focus on informal powers because they are more permanent, increase personal strength, and cannot be taken from them. However, as a last resort, they should not hesitate to use their formal power formally.

An effective team displays the synergy from a whole being greater than the sum of its parts, with all team members working together to achieve goals. TEAM stands for Together Everyone Achieves More.

Effective teams have several task-related (a direct performance measure focusing on tasks and results) and people-oriented characteristics (improved working relationships among team members). An understanding of the following important people-oriented team characteristics by project managers and team members is critical to optimizing performance:

1. High involvement, energy, and interest
2. Good communication
3. A positive and cooperative team atmosphere
4. Mutual trust among team members
5. Self-Development of team members
6. Capacity to solve conflicts

7. Effective organizational interface
8. High need for achievement and growth

Project managers should use these ten guidelines to increase their power and ability to influence stakeholders long term:

1. Develop a sense of obligation.
Senior management must gain ownership and buy-in from all stakeholders. They do this by creating an environment where people want to do tasks assigned to them instead of thinking they have to do the tasks. To develop a sense of obligation among stakeholders, project managers should genuinely involve them in developing plans, processes, and logistics. Team members feel obligated when they think the project managers care for them, respect their ideas and interests, and empathize with them.

2. Develop a reputation as an expert.
By contributing their expertise valuably and visibly, project managers create perceived expertise among their team members and increase management's confidence in them. However, this perception also requires accessibility, reliability, and consistent contribution. Some scholars believe the best way to build a strong reputation is by becoming well known for one outstanding and unique quality. The reputation as an expert can then be expanded by sharing knowledge.

3. Rely on a successful track record.

Project managers should rely on a successful record of their accomplishments valued by top management, holding themselves to the same standards they expect from their team. Consistent delivery of results increases their ability to influence, gain support, earn top management's confidence, and increase their value in the organization.

4. Identify with the project and the project team.

Identification with the project and the project team ties team members more closely to the project's success or failure, making team members more likely to put in a great effort. Project managers should identify with the project and project team by aligning the project and stakeholders' benefits with the organization's goals and objectives.

5. Get stakeholders' commitment.

Stakeholder commitment is gained by increasing team members' feelings of responsibility to motivate them. Motivation benefits the project managers as well as the team members. Never overlook that upper management is made of stakeholders; therefore, the more committed management is to a project, the more resources and support the project receives.

6. Increase knowledge about organizational policies and procedures.

The subtle nuances unique to companies, divisions, project teams, and even individuals are important aspects of "organizational knowledge." This knowledge gives project managers an edge over those who do not dig more deeply into organizational policies and procedures.

7. Develop and strengthen network power.

Aspiring managers should constantly add to their network. Two elements to increase network power are nurturing and feeding the network. Do favors for others first.

8. Develop interpersonal skills.

In addition to communication, project managers need to increase their skills in influencing, negotiating, conflict management, and facilitating to gain support from management, keep stakeholders in harmony, steer discussions progressively, and make more effective presentations.

9. Increase the project's profile.

Higher-profile projects often get more resources and support from upper management. Upper management must be convinced of the project's value and importance to increase the project profile. The responsibility of a higher-profile project shows management that the project managers have the ambition and confidence of high achievers.

10. Build a high-performance team.

Project managers must follow four guidelines to build high-performance teams: (1) support the team, (2) provide opportunities to team members, (3) demonstrate trust and confidence in team members, and (4) nurture creativity and innovation. Trust, confidence, creativity, and new opportunities characterize high-performance teams. In addition, project managers must provide support at the professional and organizational levels, provide proper guidance and empowerment, and coach and inspire.

Chapter 11 Review and Critical Thinking Questions

1. Describe the eight people-oriented characteristics of an effective team and influencing strategies associated with each characteristic.
2. How are power and influence interrelated? How would you achieve the desired influencing outcome long term?
3. What are the role and importance of communication in influencing your project stakeholders?
4. Following are the ten guidelines to increase your power and influence. From your project management experience, describe the challenges encountered in using each of these guidelines and strategies to overcome those challenges:
    i. Develop a sense of obligation.
    ii. Develop a reputation as an expert.

iii. Rely on a successful track record.
iv. Identify with the project and the project team.
v. Get stakeholders' commitment.
vi. Increase knowledge about organizational policies and procedures.
vii. Develop and strengthen network power.
viii. Develop interpersonal skills.
ix. Increase project's profile.
x. Build a high-performance team.

Postscript

No problem can be solved from the same level of consciousness that created it.

—Albert Einstein

What should we do if the world changes suddenly? Things that were important before 2020 were not as important in 2020 and 2021. Most of us would have never believed it if anyone had told us such changes might happen as early as February or March 2020.

Some changes worldwide included the following (BK Center 2020):[1]

- We were locked down and asked to stay home except for essential things.
- Airplanes stopped flying.
- Universities, schools, public parks, playgrounds, and libraries closed.
- We couldn't go to our offices (we had to work from home).

Leading with Purpose

- Shopping malls, movie theaters, concert halls, and restaurants closed.
- Cities that never sleep became silent.
- Highways and roads were empty (hardly any traffic and cars on the road).

As we all know and have experienced firsthand, these changes happened around March 2020 with the worldwide spread of the coronavirus (COVID-19). The World Health Organization at the United Nations declared it the most serious pandemic since the Spanish flu in 1920. The news reports called it the major global crisis of the century because it had no boundaries. It rapidly spread worldwide without discrimination toward culture, nationality, gender, age, or color. By April 26, 2022, there were 510,620,922 confirmed cases and 6,224,259 deaths globally2 (Johns Hopkins). The world's scientific community researched to understand more about this virus regarding its genetic code, cause, spread, precautions, measures to prevent and stop its spread, and cure.

All nations' leaders established regulations and laws for physical safety, such as lockdowns, hand-washing (properly and regularly), wearing face masks, and social distancing. Medical staff and frontline workers were required to use special personal protection equipment (PPE). The increased demand for such articles created a worldwide shortage and competition to procure these things.

All national leaders and research scientists worked hard to find solutions to this global crisis. For every country, the challenges involved establishing special public health and safety protocols, health facilities with health care workers, and PPE and other resources. For individuals, the challenges related to

Postscript

mental health cases, domestic violence, job loss and working from home, financial difficulties and uncertainties, and the inability to see family and friends. Most people felt frustrated and helpless. They complained about "why me" and wondered how long they had to face these difficulties.

Fortunately, pharmaceutical companies developed a vaccine for this virus with the government's help in expediting the project in December 2020. A portion of the North American population received a double dose of the vaccine by mid-2021. Still, this problem became even more challenging because of new variants of coronavirus, such as Delta and Omicron, that were quite transmissible. All national leaders faced the public safety issues and economic challenges caused by this pandemic.

The major issue is that no one knows how long it will last and how to handle it. After thinking calmly about this crisis, there had to be a new way of thinking, doing, and being during these unprecedented and challenging times. We had to do more than manage the crisis as a project surrounded by many uncertainties. Political leaders felt pressure from various economic sectors and began to lift restrictions toward the end of 2021. Leaders of many nations had to use their power, influence, political strategies, and spiritual wisdom to deal with this crisis with calmness, kindness, and cooperation.

To meet the health, safety, and economic challenges COVID-19 caused, we needed extraordinary leadership at personal, organizational, national, and international levels. We were "all in it together" and therefore had to work as a team. National leaders had to use their power (formal and informal), influencing, and organizational skills, and take actions based on scientific evidence. However, it was not enough. This crisis inspired them to look at this challenge holistically and develop solutions that would benefit everyone worldwide. They needed to use their skills and spiritual wisdom with compassion and calmness to ensure economic and physical safety for their people. Everyone recognized the need to respect the environment, understand themselves, care for others, and appreciate the value of service to others. All leaders understood better the importance of the triple bottom line (TBL), which focuses on people, the planet, and profits. We learned many spiritual lessons, summarized in this postscript, to deal with such a difficult global crisis, which inspired us to write another book about next-generation leadership.

1. Dealing with This Change and Crisis

You must be the change you wish to see in the world.

—Mahatma Gandhi

Besides implementing regulations and laws for public and health safety, vaccine research, and government financial help, people thought there must be a new way of thinking, doing, and dealing with this crisis. The whole world was worried and nervous about this global crisis because of the following issues:
- How long would it last?
- What would the outcome be?
- How could spirituality and spiritual wisdom help in these uncertain times?

- How could I help my family, friends, and myself?
- How could we help one another, our communities, nations, and the globe?
- What should our leaders do in these unprecedented and difficult times?

This crisis created public health and safety emergencies and economic challenges. However, we looked at this positively—an emergency comes from the word *emergence*. This implied that we must use our intellect and creativity during an emergency and emerge with a new opportunity to cope. Many believed the solutions would be found by understanding ourselves and nature and finding harmony between the two.

The following were choices to deal with this change:

• Accept reluctantly and deal with resistance.
This choice was bad for us because it causes mental and physical stress, anxiety, fear, frustration, and financial difficulties. These lead to more of the same and harm us physically and mentally long term.

• Embrace this change, adapt, and ride through it with calmness, courage, and unity.
This choice required spiritual strength, self-realization, and the need to capitalize on our internal powers. We needed to be more compassionate toward others. Many of us observed the following during this difficult time:

- People were more aware of others' suffering.
- We could simplify our needs and do with much less (food, gadgets, comforts . . .).

- We didn't need too much entertainment, traveling, and eating out.
- We are a global family, and we are all in it together.
- Our actions affect others (washing hands, creating masks, social distancing, etc.).
- We could share a lot even if we couldn't meet physically (using technology to connect).
- The best of human nature comes out, including compassion and kindness.
- We must protect our environment.

We rode through these difficult times by following the second option and embracing this change with calmness, compassion, and unity. This choice created positive thoughts, and we helped and supported others better.

2. Spiritual Lessons

All the initiatives taken by many governments at all levels related to establishing protocols for public and health safety and economic stimulus were necessary, but they were not enough. All these initiatives could create serious short-term and long-term health and economic challenges globally. Therefore, we needed to look inside and reflect in silence to increase our spiritual strength and deal more effectively with challenging times. Our leaders had to use their power and politics positively, use influencing and teamwork skills with sincerity, and develop self-inspired leadership (SIL) skills to guide us properly. At the same time, we needed to increase our spiritual strength and internal powers to deal with the present challenges with calmness, kindness, compassion, and unity.

This section covers the spiritual lessons with their associated virtues that could be most effective in dealing with this crisis and unpleasant times and creating a new normal we can all handle happily and effectively. We and self-inspired leaders must use power and influence appropriately and follow important lessons and SIL's main elements based on spiritual wisdom:

1. Stay calm and have a clear vision.
   (Associated Virtues: Self-realization, Introspection, Life Purpose, Focus on Being, Silence, and Positive Thinking)
   To stay calm, we must practice the art of self-realization by using silence, stillness, and introspection. The language of silence is loud enough to reach our minds and create positive and elevated thoughts. We must simplify our needs and learn to do with much less (food, gadgets, comforts, and material things . . .). We don't need too much entertainment, traveling, and eating out. We need to slow down to hear the voices of others who cannot express themselves in words because of mental, physical, or financial stress. As Mahatma Gandhi said, "There is more to life than increasing its speed."

2. Communicate with compassion for impact and success.
   (Associated Virtues: Compassion, Empathy, Harmony, Understanding, and Active Listening)
   Communicate with compassion, not just empathy, because too much empathy risks over-involvement, which clouds your

Leading with Purpose

objectivity. Engage all stakeholders and listen to them actively. Communicate to influence by using power positively and establishing and communicating protocols.

3. Analyze and decide carefully.
(Associated Virtues: Knowledge, Insight, Accuracy, and Discipline)
Develop a clear mind to analyze situations and evaluate options. Use stillness to sharpen your intellect. Look at the big picture (iceberg concept).

4. Increase your resilience (be courageous and creative).
(Associated Virtues: Creativity, Faith, Freedom, Confidence, Determination, and Courage)
Be creative and capitalize on technology and people to think "out of the box." Have faith in yourself, people, and nature (nature balances things). Convert threats into opportunities. Challenges increase our strength and let us experience difficult situations. Evaluate long-term and short-term economic issues. Consider the TBL—people, planet, and profits.

5. Synergize yourself and others.
(Associated Virtues: Collaboration, Cooperation, Sharing, Openness, Teamwork, and Respect)
Achieve collaboration and teamwork; we are all in it together because the virus does not discriminate. Frontline responders show their kindness and compassion by risking their safety, so our moral responsibility is to

support them. Share knowledge, information, resources, and solutions. Treat others and their ideas with respect.

6. Inspire yourself and others.
   (Associated Virtues: Servant Leadership, Empowerment, Inspiration, Visioning, Enthusiasm, and Potential)
   Follow the concept of servant leadership. Inspire people to expand their potential. Have faith in people and their potential to inspire and empower them.

7. Connect and strengthen relationships.
   (Associated Virtues: Respect, Appreciation, Sharing, Helping, Trust, and Politeness)
   Nurture relationships by helping one another. Respect others.

8. Learn to withdraw and stay positive.
   (Associated Virtues: Tolerance, Acceptance, Detachment, Discipline, Contentment, and Positivity)
   Detach from the situation, observe, analyze, plan, and act. Accept people and situations as they are, with their strengths and weaknesses. Free yourself from external negativity (news media and social media). Stay positive (create positive thoughts and send positive vibrations).

We must share calmness instead of fear because fear is our greatest enemy. We can infect others more severely by fear than by the coronavirus. In addition, staying calm increases our emotional stability and enables us to help others. Therefore, calmness within is an important skill we must develop to cope with the present times. For example, when a social worker or a counselor must deal with serious family problems, and psychiatrists and psychologists need to resolve their patients' problems, they use these steps:

- Ask yourself, who am I, and what is my primary responsibility?
- Bring yourself out of the situation and examine it by staying calm. This detachment from the situation prevents you from being caught up and entangled in the situation, which reduces your ability to analyze and plan properly.
- Analyze the situation objectively, evaluate various options, and decide the best option to resolve the situation.
- Bring yourself back into the situation and implement the best option by working with the family or the patient.

Calmness reduces our fear, anxiety, and tendency to react. It helps us sharpen our intellect and make good decisions by following a three-step approach of think, plan, and act (TPA). A crisis is an awakening that strengthens us to face future challenges and experience unpleasant circumstances with courage.

During this pandemic, some people believed it is difficult to stay calm because of mental and physical stress, lack of connection with family and friends, and financial hardships. As a result, they felt a strong urge for quick action without using a proper TPA approach. Their inability to stay calm reduced their spiritual strength, capacity, and potential to do their best. Under these circumstances, it is better to develop gratitude and be grateful for what we have, even in the most difficult situations. Gratitude creates positive energy.

On a personal level, we can become calm by meditating regularly. Meditation helps us master our thoughts and manage our internal world by creating positive and elevated thoughts. It is interesting to note that thoughts are our constant companion, and no one can take our thoughts away from us. Therefore, learning to master our minds increases our spiritual strength and helps uplift us and others.

We all operate in our lives at three levels, which we can compare to three concentric circles: (1) being (innermost circle), which focuses on who I am and what I can do for others; (2) doing (middle circle), which deals with roles and responsibilities in work and relationships; and (3) having (outermost circle), which means going after materialistic things (fame, success, wealth). Sadly, most of us live our lives from the outside in. To deal with this crisis and beyond, we must change our mindset and learn to live our lives from the inside out. One important piece of spiritual wisdom is to think of ourselves as a trustee rather than an owner because we can't lose what we don't own.

The authors hope readers will consider the wisdom put forth here to enrich their lifestyle and people skills. Just as they were inspired to write this book and the next one, they sincerely hope everyone reading them will be inspired to develop spiritual strength to sustain themselves and the planet.

Leading with Purpose

Appendix: Case Studies and Exercises

Case Study 1: For Part I (Chapters 1–3): From Strategies to Results
(Understanding the importance of people skills and the dynamics of power and influence)

Preamble
This case study illustrates the importance of people skills in project management to meet organizational strategies and goals. It deals with these issues:

1. **Translating organizational strategies into results**
   It deals with the importance of using the Management by Projects (MBP) approach to meet organizational goals and understand the technical and holistic perspectives of projects and project management.

2. **A model for achieving the most from people**
   It deals with four key people skills and the roles of power, politics, and culture in getting things done and completing internal and external projects successfully.
3. **The importance of people, project structure, and project processes**
   It deals with the importance of having the right people (project champions, project managers, and team members), project structures, and project management tools.

Stakeholder: Nik

Nik has been the Ultimate Motorcycle Incorporated (UMI) president for the past five years. He received his MBA from Harvard in strategic planning and international relations. He has worked at UMI for fifteen years and progressed rapidly to become president after leading many successful projects. He worked for Harley-Davidson for three years before joining UMI. He strongly believes MBP is one of the most effective strategies to manage a business organization successfully and meet global competition.

He has traveled extensively and is interested in interacting with people from different cultures and backgrounds. He believes a leader must continuously look for new opportunities and challenges and develop good leadership, communication, negotiation, and team-building skills to meet challenges. In addition, leaders must think holistically to focus and achieve emotional stability.

Stakeholder: Neel

Neel has been the executive vice president at UMI for the past three years and is responsible for the engineering and project management groups. He is a mechanical engineer with an MBA and has worked at UMI for ten years. Neel believes managing programs and projects successfully is the key to meeting organizational strategies and goals. He recognizes that people are the backbone of projects. Therefore, it is important to have good team-building, leadership, and communication skills. Both leadership and management are important, and achieving a balance between the two is critical to achieving success.

Stakeholder: Rohn

Rohn is a mechanical engineer who worked for four years with Ford before joining UMI. After working for three years as an engineer, he chose project management as his career. Rohn got a Project Management Professional (PMP)® certification from the Project Management Institute (PMI) and an executive MBA. He has managed large and complex projects for more than five years at UMI. He believes people, not software packages, do projects; therefore, he developed good interpersonal skills, especially communication skills, with stakeholders. He is always keen on using his creativity and people skills to meet new challenges and opportunities. He understands the dynamics of power and influence in getting things done through others.

Leading with Purpose

Setting

UMI is a California-based company with more than two hundred employees. UMI prides itself on delivering top-quality custom vehicles, especially motorcycles, for the film industry.

UMI received a proposal from a highly valued customer, Century Films Ltd., that often uses unique vehicles on movie sets. Century Films requested a proposal from UMI to build five unique motorcycles to perform stunts. UMI accepted the proposal from Century Films and agreed to meet all specifications and delivery time for this project, called Stunt Motorcycles (SM), to meet the filming date deadline. Nik, the president of UMI, viewed this as an excellent opportunity to expand UMI's business. He believes that after completing this project successfully, UMI can enter a similar business for the Bollywood film industry that could benefit UMI in the long term.

However, given this project's tight delivery schedule, Nik took this opportunity as a personal challenge and wanted to get this project completed as a high priority and on time. In addition, he believes MBP is an effective business strategy for managing business organizations in a globally competitive environment. Therefore, he thinks this is a good opportunity to implement MBP at UMI.

He prepared the overall business plan and discussed it with Reyva and Rahi, the well-respected board of management (BOM) members, before formally presenting it to the BOM. After some discussions in the meeting and support from Reyva and Rahi, the BOM approved the business plan. Nik hired Neel as executive vice president to help him implement MBP at UMI and oversee the special programs and projects to completion to meet overall organizational strategies and goals.

Appendix–Case Studies and Exercises

After discussions with other members of senior management, Neel proposed Rohn as the best person at UMI to manage this critical project because of his excellent project management skills and people skills. Rohn was highly qualified with a P.Eng. license, an MBA, PMP® certification, and eight years of experience with the company. Rohn also has an excellent reputation for completing complex projects on time and within budget.

On the recommendations of leadership team members, Nik approached Rohn:

Nik: Hello, Rohn; I need your help. I would like you to be the SM project manager. This is an excellent opportunity for UMI to grow its market internationally. I have heard many good things about you from many leadership team members. Your track record for completing projects on time and within budget over the past three years is impressive. I would like you to become the SM project manager.

Rohn is pleasantly surprised by this request from Nik and responds:

Rohn: Nik, I am flattered that you chose me to take this responsibility. If you don't mind, I would like to consider it for two days.

Over the next two days, Rohn thought about the dynamics of power and influence and wanted to clarify two things:

1. Who would be his champion?
2. Which team members would be critical to completing this project successfully to have the right skill mix for the project?

Rohn came back to Nik after two days and said:

Rohn: Nik, after considering your request, I would happily accept the project manager role for the SM project if you can assign Jaya and Veeyan as engineers to this project full-time. I have worked with them on many projects, and we can apply our team synergy effectively. They have always been my top performers.

Nik talked to Jaya and Veeyan's manager and got them assigned to the SM project to work with Rohn. Rohn worked hard, and Neel oversaw the progress regularly. Rohn also presented the project status to the steering committee and identified any problems and risks. He believed Neel and Nik supported him and the project as good champions. As a result, all motorcycles were completed and tested, and the project was completed three weeks early.

UMI established a good reputation in this area and received a request from Creative Films (CF), one of the biggest production companies in Bollywood, India, to supply six motorcycles like the ones manufactured for the SM project with a delivery time of fifteen months for $150,000. UMI completed this project successfully within time and budget constraints and established an international reputation in this market.

Questions

1. Describe the systematic process to achieve successful results from the vision and organizational strategies using the MBP approach.
2. Describe the three skills for effective project management integration.

Appendix–Case Studies and Exercises

3. What did Rohn understand about the dynamics of power in his communication with Nik?
4. Briefly describe the four key people skills to deliver successful projects.
5. Describe external influences Neel and Rohn must know to successfully manage the SM project. For example, describe the main elements of culture they must consider to do international projects.
6. What is the difference between a leader and a manager? Which is more important, and when and why during the project life cycle (PLC)?
7. What are the three main components of communication? How can Rohn improve his skills in listening and nonverbal communication?
8. Briefly describe the three stages, four principles, and three common negotiation methods. What strategies should Nik and Neel use to negotiate a win-win situation with CF?
9. What are a champion's key roles? What steps should Rohn take to find and sustain a champion? What positional power should a champion have to help him deliver successful projects?
10. What makes a successful project manager? Identify five key roles and responsibilities of a project manager.
11. What does "having the right team members" mean in a project environment? Who gets the best people and why? How can project managers increase the skills of their team members to achieve high performance?

Leading with Purpose

Case Study 2: For Part II (Chapters 4–7): Evaluating Power Level and Strategies to Increase Your Power

Richard is a well-known professional engineer respected by senior management at the robotics company Automatech. Richard holds a Bachelor's in Electrical Engineering with a Master of Science in Robotics and completed an executive MBA. He worked in industry for five years before joining Automatech, where he has worked on several projects over five years. During his work experience at Automatech, he understood the dynamics of departments and overall organization in its policies and procedures and the dynamics of power among stakeholders.

Richard frequently exercises his natural talent for networking and people skills to deliver successful projects. In addition, he visualizes the big picture and pays attention to detail. Often, other project managers come to him for advice on their projects. Because of his excellent conceptual, people, and project management skills, Richard is frequently assigned to lead complex projects, as he is skilled in a wide range of disciplines and is an excellent troubleshooter.

Richard attended a trade show on medical robotics and got an idea for a leg-strengthening apparatus to rehabilitate patients with leg injuries. Richard met Nicholas, vice president of R&D at Automatech, at the show and discussed this idea. The prospect excited Nicholas, who told Richard it would be good for his career progression within Automatech. Nicholas recognized Richard's passion for R&D and excellent engineering knowledge and experience and suggested he should prepare a business case with a high-level project plan and estimated resource requirements for presentation to senior management to secure project funding.

Richard prepared the project charter and a detailed project plan with the specific resource requirements and risk analysis. Nicholas reviewed Richard's project plan and arranged a meeting with the steering committee responsible for selecting R&D projects and approving funding to present the business case. Richard presented his project plan, which was well-received by all steering committee members, who gave the project the green light in principle. After one month, the project was formally approved with the required funding, and Nicholas would champion this project and oversee the project to completion.

Richard appreciated the project's complexity and wanted to secure the best resources right from the beginning. He knew a heavy R&D component could necessitate financial support and properly skilled people on a timely basis to meet project milestones. Richard met with Nicholas, the chief financial officer, and Joan, the head of the engineering division, to discuss resource requirements (people and money). Richard recognized that he would need the cooperation of both Thomas (to get funds as needed) and Joan (to get the best engineers and technicians) for his project.

Richard assembled his team of eight full-time equivalents (FTEs) after getting the required resources with the help of Nicholas and Joan. He prepared the project plan with a detailed schedule, resource requirements, and cost estimates. He did the risk analysis and thought of risk management strategies. Joan realized that Edward, one of her best engineers, had just finished another project and could be assigned to a new one. He has a Master's in Electromechanical Engineering with five years of practical experience working on such projects. Joan and Richard felt that Edward would be the best choice for the lead design engineer and take responsibility for the overall design work package with three other engineers: Fred, Gina, and Cyrus.

Richard realized that Edward had strong technical skills but little supervisory experience. But he believed Edward had good people skills, and he could mentor Edward as needed to interact with stakeholders effectively. Richard was also happy to have Nicholas as his mentor for properly using his various types of powers (formal and informal) to fit the people and situations. He was confident Nicholas and he could work together and satisfy both identified and unidentified needs of the steering committee at Automatech (internal client) to ensure the project would be done on time and within budget with a sound plan to get it to the market quickly to secure significant market share.

Richard recognized the need for healthy working relationships with all important stakeholders to meet project objectives. Richard would require Nicholas to continue being his project champion to remove obstacles as they occur throughout the project life cycle (PLC).

Questions

1. Why was Richard chosen as the project manager? What informal powers does he have?

Appendix–Case Studies and Exercises

2. Evaluate each power level on a scale of 1–10 for Richard.
3. Why was Edward chosen as the lead engineer? What informal powers does he have?
4. Identify the lowest two sources of power for Richard and Edward and their impact on the project.
5. How can Richard increase all eight sources of his power?
6. What issues should Richard remember for using his power effectively?
7. What are the main issues related to power and influencing for overall project success?
8. Describe two main leadership skills related to power and influencing Nicholas and Richard must have and use effectively.

Case Study 3: For Part III (Chapters 8–11): Influencing in Project Management

Summary of Smith and His Team Members

Project Manager: Smith
Smith is an electronics engineer with an MBA in strategic management. He has worked for five years with a company developing products that involve mechatronics systems. After that, he joined Energy Solutions Inc. (ESI) and has been involved in product development for ten years. In the past five years, he has managed three projects that involved innovative projects for the health care and defense industries.

Smith is good at building relationships with internal and external stakeholders. He has good conceptual skills and interpersonal skills. He has mentored a few project managers at ESI and helped them advance. Because of his good communication and influencing skills, he has led and completed several complex projects successfully ahead of schedule and under budget.

Electrical Engineer: William
William completed his Bachelor's in Electrical Engineering and a Master's in Circuit Design and Sensors. He has a good sense of conceptualizing the product. He believes in working collaboratively with his teams.

Mechanical Engineer: Paul
Paul is logical and analytical. During his bachelor studies, he worked on many projects that required creative solutions. He has a passion for machine dynamics and energy efficiency.

Appendix–Case Studies and Exercises

Quality Control: Ken
Ken is a mechanical technologist who has worked in quality assurance departments in several manufacturing industries, giving him a diverse background in product development. He believes in following policies and procedures. He conducts himself formally and always wants to refer to proven statistics in decision-making.

Controls and Software: Bruce
Bruce is a technologically apt programmer. He has a natural talent for logical thinking. He has developed a strong, patient work ethic and can focus on a project for hours. Bruce is a free-flow person and doesn't like schedules imposed on him.

Production: Phil
Phil is a production manager who has been working for the company for fifteen years. He has developed manufacturing, inspection, and assembly guidelines for the organization, which require various levels of reviews and approvals. Many people find him difficult to work with because he tends to micromanage the manufacturing process. He strongly believes that following standard policies and procedures improves product quality.

Marketing: Tyler
Tyler has a degree in arts and an MBA in Marketing. He has worked with the company for ten years and has been respected by senior management for increasing the market share in Europe and Asia. He is interested in meeting and networking with people to establish good working relationships. He is

collaborative and supports the R&D group in developing new products. He can visualize the broader scope of complex projects and create effective presentations to sell stakeholders new ideas.

Setting

ESI is involved at the forefront of innovative products for personal trainers and hikers. Recently, the company's CEO had the vision to develop a wearable battery-charging device. This product could have a large market for technology users in remote regions for extended periods, such as hikers and military deployments. He presented this vision to the leadership team. The team was excited at this idea and anticipated great potential. They agreed that it was important to capitalize on marketing opportunities by going from idea to market as soon as possible. In addition, it was important to select a professional with good project management skills and experience in an R&D environment to lead this project. The CEO assigned Jason, executive vice president, to become this project's champion/sponsor.

Jason presented a high-level business case and project plan with risk analysis and opportunities to the leadership team. The team approved the project in principle and the hiring of a new project manager. Jason talked to a few colleagues who highly recommended Smith as a project manager. Smith was eager to accept the position and developed a detailed project plan with proposed key team members. Smith realized that it is important to know the strengths and weaknesses of his team members and their personalities to work together to deliver a successful project.

Questions

1. What is the process for influencing team members?
2. Why should Smith influence his team members?
3. Which influencing strategies should be used with each team member and why?
4. Describe the advantages and disadvantages of the four influencing styles described in this part of the book.
5. Which influencing style should he use with all six team members and why?

Case Study 4: For Part III (Chapter 11): Team Dynamics of a Dragon Boat Team

Profile of Key Team Members

Roger has watched many dragon boat races and hopes to become a drummer for a team. He has a Bachelor's in Sports and Fitness Leadership and has loved sports since childhood. He has been on soccer and rowing teams throughout his high school and university years. He volunteered for three years in dragon boat festivals and met many coaches. He showed keen interest in becoming a drummer, and finally, he was offered a position, which was a dream come true.

Tom has been interested in dragon boat races for many years. He saw several friends from his kinesiology degree participating in dragon boat teams and joined a team one day. Tom is highly goal-oriented and persuasive. He has also practiced drumming in a band for five years. He believed he could become a good drummer on a dragon boat team based on his skills and physique.

Ryan and Kyle are the lead paddlers for the Vancouver team. They have been interested in rowing for years and have developed considerable upper-body strength. They have both been personal trainers for many years at local gym facilities. They participated in college rowing teams throughout their university years.

Kyle has a degree in oceanography. He is an outdoor person who has loved sailing since he was young. He enjoys camping and hiking to exercise his sense of direction and quick thinking. He is fit and trains regularly with Ryan and Kyle at the gym.

Setting

There is an annual dragon boat festival in the summer in Vancouver, British Columbia, on the West Coast of Canada. Last year, ten teams participated in the competition. The Vancouver team trained hard to take first place in the competition. Unfortunately, they lost to the California team by a narrow margin.

After celebrating the close final race, the team and the coach met to reflect on what could be improved for next year's competition. They studied the other team's performance and found that the other competitor's synchronization was superior. The coach thought there was a need for improvement in coordinating the paddling with the drumming. After the kickoff meeting, team members concluded they liked their positions and would like to train harder to improve their performance. The coach emphasized that the team's key to winning next year's competition is to take ownership of their roles, share knowledge and information, and work together to achieve the goal of winning the finals.

The coach established a rigorous training schedule for the months leading to the competition. The team was very committed to training harder. The coach emphasized to Roger, the drummer, that he is the heartbeat of the boat and that his role is to communicate with the lead paddlers, Ryan and Kyle, to maintain the synchronization of the team's strokes and speed.

The team practice was going well, but unfortunately, Roger could not continue as the team's drummer because he broke his arm while playing soccer. His doctor told him he needed several weeks of recovery and could not participate in the competition. The coach was concerned that the team could not enter the competition without a drummer. He approached Tom, one paddler, to be the drummer for the team because of Tom's experience in bands and his educational background. Tom gladly accepted the role and was excited to demonstrate his drumming skills.

Questions

1. Identify team characteristics when:
    a. Roger was the drummer.
    b. Tom was the drummer.
2. Identify the weaknesses and strengths of the team under each drummer.
3. How would you evaluate the overall team characteristics?
4. How can Roger and Tom increase their powers to influence team members successfully?

Notes

Preface

1. Project Management Institute (PMI), *A Guide to the Project Management Body of Knowledge (PMBOK® Guide)*, 7th ed. (Newtown Square, PA: Project Management Institute, 2021).
2. Vijay K. Verma, *The Art of Positive Politics: A Key to Delivering Successful Projects* (Oshawa, ON, Canada: Multi-Media Publications Inc., 2018).

Part I

1. Project Management Institute (PMI), *A Guide to the Project Management Body of Knowledge (PMBOK® Guide)*, 7th ed. (Newtown Square, PA: Project Management Institute, 2021).

Chapter 1

1. Project Management Institute (PMI), *A Guide to the Project Management Body of Knowledge (PMBOK® Guide)*, 7th ed. (Newtown Square, PA: Project Management Institute, 2021).
2. PMI, *PMBOK® Guide*.
3. James Norrie, *Breaking Through the Project Fog: How Smart Organizations Achieve Success by Creating, Selecting and Executing On-Strategy Projects* (Mississauga, ON: John Wiley & Sons Canada, Ltd., 2008), 18–31.
4. Norrie, *Breaking Through the Project Fog*, 18–31.
5. Peter Morris and Ashley Jamieson, *Translating Corporate Strategy into Project Strategy: Realizing Corporate Strategy Through Project Management* (Atlanta: PMI, 2004).
6. Norrie, Breaking Through the Project Fog, 18–31.
7. Morris and Jamieson, *Translating Corporate Strategy into Project Strategy*.
8. PMI, *PMBOK® Guide*.
9. PMI.
10. PMI.
11. PMI.
12. Doug DeCarlo, *eXtreme Project Management: Using Leadership, Principles, and Tools to Deliver Value in the Face of Volatility* (San Francisco: Jossey-Bass, 2004), 28–46.
13. DeCarlo, *eXtreme Project Management*, 28–46.
14. DeCarlo, 28–46.

15. DeCarlo, 28–46.
16. DeCarlo, 28–46.
17. DeCarlo, 28–46.
18. DeCarlo, 28–46.
19. DeCarlo, 28–46.

Chapter 2

1. Vijay K. Verma, *Organizing Projects for Success: Human Aspects of Project Management, Volume 1* (Upper Darby, PA: Project Management Institute, 1995), 32–42.
2. Dave Francis and Don Young, *Improving Work Groups: A Practical Manual for Team Building* (San Francisco: Jossey-Bass/Pfeiffer, 1992).
3. Vijay K. Verma, *Managing the Project Team: Human Aspects of Project Management, Volume 3* (Upper Darby, PA: Project Management Institute, 1997), 89–101, 133–146, 194–195, 214–221.
4. Linn C. Stuckenbruck and David Marshall, *Team Building for Project Managers* (Project Management Institute, 1985), 48–49.
5. Jeffrey K. Pinto and Ido Millet. *Successful Information System Implementation: The Human Side* (Upper Darby, PA: Project Management Institute, 1999).
6. Vijay K. Verma, *Human Resource Skills for the Project Manager: The Human Aspects of Project Management, Volume 2* (Upper Darby, PA: Project Management Institute, 1996), 220–230.

7. Vijay K. Verma and Max Wideman, "Project Manager to a Project Leader and the Rocky Road in Between," proceedings of 25th Annual Seminar/Symposium, Project Management Institute, Drexel Hill, PA, 1994, 627-633.
8. Richard W. Sievert, Jr., "Communication: An Important Construction Tool," *Project Management Journal* (December 1986): 77.
9. Verma, *Human Resource Skills*, 24–25.
10. Albert Mehrabian, "Communication without Words," *Psychology Today* (September 1968): 53–55.
11. Verma, *Human Resource Skills*, 40–48.
12. Verma, 40–48.
13. Roger Fisher and William Ury, *Getting to Yes: Negotiating Agreement Without Giving In*, 3rd ed. (New York: Penguin Books, 2011); Verma, 146–153, 161–162.
14. Vijay K. Verma, *The Art of Positive Politics: A Key to Delivering Successful Projects* (Oshawa, ON, Canada: Multi-Media Publications Inc., 2018), 52–53.
15. Verma, 54–61.
16. Verma, 212–241.
17. Verma, 243–302.
18. Verma, 331-413.
19. Adapted from M. Dean Martin, "The Negotiation Differential for International Project Management," *Proceedings of the Annual Seminar/*

Symposium of the Project Management Institute, Project Management Institute, Drexel Hill, PA, 1981: 450–453.

20. Verma, *Managing the Project Team*, 89–100.

Chapter 3

1. Vijay K. Verma, "Power, Influence and Politics in Project Management," Seminars World of Project Management Institute, Newtown Square, PA, 2000–2013.
2. Verma, "Power, Influence and Politics in Project Management."
3. Verma.
4. Verma.
5. Vijay K. Verma, *Organizing Projects for Success: Human Aspects of Project Management, Volume 1* (Upper Darby, PA: Project Management Institute, 1995), 22–27, 109–113.
6. Vijay K. Verma, *Managing the Project Team: Human Aspects of Project Management, Volume 3* (Upper Darby, PA: Project Management Institute, 1997), 120–121.
7. Verma, *Organizing Projects for Success*, 146–161.
8. Verma, 146–161.
9. Verma, 146–161.
10. Project Management Institute (PMI), A Guide to the Project Management Body of Knowledge (*PMBOK® Guide*), 7th ed. (Newtown Square, PA: Project Management Institute, 2021).

Part II

Chapter 4

1. Vijay K. Verma, "Power, Influence and Politics in Project Management," Seminars World of Project Management Institute, Newtown Square, PA, 2000–2013.
2. Stephen R. Covey, *The 7 Habits of Highly Effective People: Powerful Lessons in Personal Change* (New York: Simon & Schuster Ltd., 2013).
3. Max Wideman, "Negotiating for Project Benefit," *Max's Project Management Wisdom*, 1998, http://www.maxwideman.com/papers/negotiating/power.htm.
4. Robert B. Cialdini, *Influence: The Psychology of Persuasion* (New York: William Morrow and Company Inc., 2006).
5. Cialdini, *Influence.*
6. Sally Hogshead, *Fascinate: Your 7 Triggers to Persuasion and Captivation* (New York: Harper Business, 2010).
7. Dale Carnegie, *How to Win Friends & Influence People* (New York: Simon & Schuster, 2011).
8. John P. Kotter, *Power and Influence* (New York: The Free Press, 2008).

Chapter 5

1. Vijay K. Verma, *Organizing Projects for Success: Human Aspects of Project Management, Volume 1* (Upper Darby, PA: Project Management Institute, 1995), 102–105.
2. Robert B. Cialdini, *Influence: The Psychology of Persuasion* (New York: William Morrow and Company Inc., 2006).
3. Robert L. Dilenschneider, *Power and Influence: The Rules Have Changed* (New York: McGraw Hill, 2007), 155–63.
4. Dale Carnegie, *How to Win Friends & Influence People* (New York: Simon & Schuster, 2011) and B. F. Skinner.
5. Albert Mehrabian, "Communication without Words," *Psychology Today* (September 1968): 53–55.
6. S. D. Gladis, "Notes Are Not Enough." *Training and Development Journal* (August 1985): 35–38.
7. Nicole Steckler and Robert Rosenthal, "Sex Differences in Nonverbal and Verbal Communication with Bosses, Peers, and Subordinates," *Journal of Applied Psychology* (February 1985):157–63.
8. Andrew J. DuBrin, *Contemporary Applied Management* (Plano, TX: Business Publications, 1982), 127–34.

Chapter 6

1. Adapted from Robert B. Youker, "Power and Politics in Project Management," *PM Network* (May 1991): 36–40.
2. Bob Nelson, *1500 Ways to Reward Your Employees* (New York: Workman Publishing Company, 2012).
3. Edwin A. Locke, D. B. Feren, V. M. McCaleb, K. N. Shaw, and A.T. Denny, "The Relative Effectiveness of Four Methods of Motivating Employee Performance," *Changes in Working Life*, eds. K. D. Duncan, M. N. Gruneberg, and D. Wallis, (1980): 363–383.
4. Robert Greene, *The 48 Laws of Power* (New York: Penguin Books, 2000).
5. John P. Kotter, *Power and Influence* (New York: The Free Press, 2008).
6. Robert L. Dilenschneider, *Power and Influence: The Rules Have Changed* (New York: McGraw Hill, 2007), 82–88.
7. Dilenschneider, *Power and Influence*, 125–38.
8. Jeffrey Gitomer, *Little Black Book of Connections: 6.5 Assets for Networking Your Way to Rich Relationships* (Austin, TX: Bard Press, 2006).
9. Stephen R. Covey, *The 7 Habits of Highly Effective People: Powerful Lessons in Personal Change* (New York: Simon & Schuster Ltd., 2013).

Chapter 7

1. Paul Hersey, Kenneth H. Blanchard, and Dewey E. Johnson, *Management of Organizational Behavior*, 10th ed. (Glenview, IL: Pearson, 2012).
2. Dale Carnegie, *How to Win Friends & Influence People* (New York: Simon & Schuster, 2011).
3. Bob Nelson, PhD, *1001 Ways to Energize Employees* (New York: Workman Publishing Company Inc., 1997).

Part III

Chapter 8

1. *The Saylor Foundation*, paper on Influencing Skills, BUS208: Principles of Management, 2013, https://learn.saylor.org/course/search.php?q=bus+208&areaids=core_course-course.
2. *The Merriam-Webster Dictionary*, s.v. "influence," https://www.merriam-webster.com/dictionary/influence; and the *Oxford English Dictionary*, s.v. "influence," https://www.oed.com/.
3. Genie Z. Laborde, *Influencing with Integrity: Management Skills for Communication and Negotiation* (Palo Alto, CA: Syntony Pub., 1987).
4. Vijay K. Verma, "Power, Influence and Politics in Project Management" and "Leadership, Power, Influence, Politics, and Negotiations in

Project Management," seminars presented at Project Management Institute (PMI) Seminars World, Project World, and other project management conferences and events (1997–2020).

5. Edwin A. Locke, "Nature and Causes of Job Satisfaction," in *The Handbook of Industrial and Organizational Psychology*, ed. M. D. Dunnette (Chicago, IL: Rand McNally, 1976), 1300.

Chapter 9

1. Joseph Reed, "Influencing without Authority," seminar presented at Seminars World of the Project Management Institute (PMI), 2010–2020; retitled "Influencing without Authority: Skills for Obtaining Resources, Building Relationships, and Getting Things Done," and presented at PMI Training, 2021–2023.

2. *The Saylor Foundation*, paper on Influencing Skills, BUS208: Principles of Management, 2013, https://learn.saylor.org/course/search.php?q=bus+208&areaids=core_course-course.

3. Vijay K. Verma, "Power, Influence, and Politics in Project Management" and "Leadership, Power, Influence, Politics, and Negotiations in Project Management," seminars presented at PMBA Conference (2018–2020), Project World, and other project management conferences and events (1997–2020); Saylor Foundation, paper on Influencing Skills; Reed, "Influencing without Authority."

4. Dale Carnegie, *How to Win Friends & Influence People* (New York: Simon & Schuster, 2011).
5. Verma, "Power and Influence"; Verma, "Power, Influence, and Politics in ProjecManagement"; Saylor Foundation, paper on Influencing Skills; Reed, "Influencing without Authority."
6. Verma, "Power and Influence"; Vijay K. Verma, *Human Resource Skills for the Project Manager: The Human Aspects of Project Management, Volume 2* (Upper Darby, PA: Project Management Institute, 1996), 40–49.
7. R. W. Wallen, "Three Types of Executive Personality," 1963, in Lindsay-Sherwin, "Consultancy Skills Toolkit," 2005.
8. Chris Musselwhite and Tammie Plouffe, "What's Your Influencing Style?", *Harvard Business Review* (January 13, 2012), https://hbr.org/2012/01/whats-your-influencing-style.
9. Larry Reynolds, "Influencing Styles," *The Twenty-first Century Leader Training Manual*, Trainer Active.
10. Reed, "Influencing without Authority."

Chapter 10

1. Stephen R. Covey, *The 7 Habits of Highly Effective People: Powerful Lessons in Personal Change* (New York: Simon & Schuster Ltd., 2013).
2. Robert B. Cialdini, Influence: The Psychology of Persuasion (New York: William Morrow and Company Inc., 2006), 171–204.

Leading with Purpose

3. Boundless Communications, "Defining Emotional Appeal," *Lumenlearning.com*, July 21, 2015, https://courses.lumenlearning.com/boundless-communications/chapter/emotional-appeals/.
4. Dale Carnegie, *How to Win Friends & Influence People* (New York: Simon & Schuster, 2011).
5. Roger Fisher and William Ury, *Getting to Yes: Negotiating Agreement Without Giving In*, 3rd ed. (New York: Penguin Books, 2011).
6. Vijay K. Verma, *Human Resource Skills for the Project Manager: The Human Aspects of Project Management, Volume 2* (Upper Darby, PA: Project Management Institute, 1996), 145–173.
7. Covey, *The 7 Habits of Highly Effective People*.

Chapter 11

1. Vijay K. Verma, *Managing the Project Team: Human Aspects of Project Management, Volume 3* (Upper Darby, PA: Project Management Institute, 1997) 37–38.
2. Verma, *Managing the Project Team*, 37–38.
3. Vijay K. Verma, *Human Resource Skills for the Project Manager: The Human Aspects of Project Management, Volume 2* (Upper Darby, PA: Project Management Institute, 1996), 40–49; and Thomas L. Quick, *Successful Team Building* (New York: AMACOM, American Management Association,1992), 55–66.
4. Vijay K. Verma, "Power and Influence in Project Management," seminar presented at Project World Conferences, 2006–2018; Vijay K Verma,

"Creating High-Performance Teams for a Global Economy," seminar presented at Seminars World of Project Management Institute (PMI), 2013; Linn C. Stuckenbruck and David Marshall, *Team Building for Project Managers* (Project Management Institute, 1985), 16–24.

5. Verma, "Power and Influence in Project Management"; Verma, "Creating High-Performance Teams for a Global Economy"; Fernando Bartolomé, "Nobody Trusts the Boss Completely: Now What?", *Harvard Business Review* 67 (1989):135–142.

6. Verma, "Creating High-Performance Teams for a Global Economy"; Verma, *Human Resource Skills*, 98–109; Barry Z. Posner, "What's All the Fighting About? Conflict in Project Management," *IEEE Transactions on Engineering Management* EM-33, no. 4 (November 1986): 207–211; and Hans J. Thamhain and David L. Wilemon, "Conflict Management in Project Life Cycles," *Sloan Management Review* 12, no. 3 (1975): 31–50.

7. Dale Carnegie, *How to Win Friends & Influence People* (New York: Simon & Schuster, 2011).

8. Robert Greene, *The 48 Laws of Power* (New York: Penguin Books, 2000).

9. David Cleland and Lewis Ireland, *Project Management: Strategic Design and Implementation*, 5th ed. (McGraw Hill, 2006); and Samuel C. Certo, Steven H. Appelbaum, and Irene Divine, *Principles of Modern Management*, 4th ed. (Scarborough, ON: Prentice-Hall Canada, Inc., 1993), 387–395.

Leading with Purpose

10. Dilenschneider, *Power and Influence*, 125–138.
11. Jeffrey Gitomer, *Little Black Book of Connections: 6.5 Assets for Networking Your Way to Rich Relationships* (Austin, TX: Bard Press, 2006), 16.
12. Vijay K. Verma, *The Art of Positive Politics: A Key to Delivering Successful Projects* (Oshawa, ON, Canada: Multi-Media Publications Inc., 2018), 246–248.

Postscript

1. BK Center, twenty-one master classes in new consciousness, moderated by Philippa Blackham, 2020.
2. Johns Hopkins University & Medicine Coronavirus Resource Center, "COVID-19 Dashboard by the Center for Systems Science and Engineering (CSSE) at Johns Hopkins . . .," April 26, 2022, https://coronavirus.jhu.edu/map.html.

References

Bartolomé, Fernando. "Nobody Trusts the Boss Completely: Now What?" *Harvard Business Review* 67 (March 1, 1989):135–142.

BK Center. Twenty-one master classes in new consciousness. Moderated by Philippa Blackham. 2020.

Boundless Communications. "Defining Emotional Appeal." *Lumenlearning.com.* July 21, 2015. https://courses.lumenlearning.com/boundless-communications/chapter/emotional-appeals/.

Carnegie, Dale. *How to Win Friends & Influence People.* New York: Simon & Schuster, 2011.

Certo, Samuel C., Steven H. Appelbaum, and Irene Divine. *Principles of Modern Management.* 4th ed. Scarborough, ON: Prentice-Hall Canada, Inc., 1993.

Cialdini, Robert B. *Influence: The Psychology of Persuasion.* New York: William Morrow and Company Inc., 2006.

Cleland, David and Lewis Ireland. *Project Management: Strategic Design and Implementation.* 5th ed. McGraw Hill, 2006.

Covey, Stephen R. *The 7 Habits of Highly Effective People: Powerful Lessons in Personal Change.* New York: Simon & Schuster Ltd., 2013.

DeCarlo, Doug. *eXtreme Project Management: Using Leadership, Principles, and Tools to Deliver Value in the Face of Volatility.* San Francisco: Jossey-Bass, 2004.

Dilenschneider, Robert L. *Power and Influence: The Rules Have Changed.* New York: McGraw Hill, 2007.

DuBrin, Andrew J. *Contemporary Applied Management.* Plano, TX: Business Publications, 1982.

Fisher, Roger and William Ury. *Getting to Yes: Negotiating Agreement Without Giving In.* 3rd ed. New York: Houghton Mifflin, 2011.

Francis, Dave and Don Young. *Improving Work Groups: A Practical Manual for Team Building.* San Francisco: Jossey-Bass/Pfeiffer, 1992.

Gitomer, Jeffrey. *Little Black Book of Connections: 6.5 Assets for Networking Your Way to Rich Relationships.* Austin, TX: Bard Press, 2006.

Gladis, S. D. "Notes Are Not Enough." *Training and Development Journal* 39, no. 8 (August 1985): 35–38.

Greene, Robert. *The 48 Laws of Power.* New York: Penguin Books, 2000.

Hersey, Paul, Kenneth H. Blanchard, and Dewey E. Johnson. *Management of Organizational Behavior*. 10th ed. Glenview, IL: Pearson, 2012.

Hogshead, Sally. *Fascinate: Your 7 Triggers to Persuasion and Captivation*. New York: Harper Business, 2010.

Johns Hopkins University & Medicine Coronavirus Resource Center. "COVID-19 Dashboard by the Center for Systems Science and Engineering (CSSE) at Johns Hopkins . . .." December 8, 2020. https://coronavirus.jhu.edu/map.html.

Kotter, John P. *Power and Influence*. New York: The Free Press, 2008.

Laborde, Genie Z. *Influencing with Integrity: Management Skills for Communication and Negotiation*. Palo Alto, CA: Syntony Pub., 1987.

Locke, Edwin A. "Nature and Causes of Job Satisfaction," in *The Handbook of Industrial and Organizational Psychology*. Ed. M. D. Dunnette. Chicago, IL: Rand McNally, 1976.

Locke, Edwin A., D. B. Feren, V. M. McCaleb, K. N. Shaw, and A.T. Denny. "The Relative Effectiveness of Four Methods of Motivating Employee Performance." *Changes in Working Life*. Eds. K. D. Duncan, M. N. Gruneberg, and D. Wallis, (1980): 363–388.

Martin, M. Dean. "The Negotiation Differential for International Project Management." *Proceedings of the Annual Seminar/Symposium of the Project Management Institute*. Project Management Institute, Drexel Hill, PA, 1981.

Mehrabian, Albert. "Communication without Words." *Psychology Today* (September 1968): 53–55.

Morris, Peter and Ashley Jamieson. *Translating Corporate Strategy into Project Strategy: Realizing Corporate Strategy Through Project Management*. Atlanta: PMI, 2004.

Musselwhite, Chris and Tammie Plouffe. "What's Your Influencing Style?" *Harvard Business Review*. January 13, 2012. https://hbr.org/2012/01/whats-your-influencing-style.

Nelson, Bob. *1500 Ways to Reward Your Employees*. New York: Workman Publishing Company, 2012.

———*1001 Ways to Energize Employees*. New York: Workman Publishing Company Inc., 1997.

Norrie, James. *Breaking Through the Project Fog: How Smart Organizations Achieve Success by Creating, Selecting and Executing On-Strategy Projects*. Mississauga, ON: John Wiley & Sons Canada, Ltd., 2008.

Pinto, Jeffrey K. and Ido Millet. *Successful Information System Implementation: The Human Side*. Upper Darby, PA: Project Management Institute, 1999.

Posner, Barry Z. "What's All the Fighting About? Conflict in Project Management." *IEEE Transactions on Engineering Management* EM-33, no. 4 (November 1986): 207–211.

1. Project Management Institute (PMI). *A Guide to the Project Management Body of Knowledge*: (*PMBOK® Guide*). 6th ed. Newtown Square, PA: Project Management Institute, 2017.

References

Quick, Thomas L. *Successful Team Building*. New York: AMACOM, American Management Association, 1992.

Reed, Joseph. "Influencing without Authority." Seminar presented at Seminars World of the Project Management Institute (PMI), 2010; retitled "Influencing without Authority: Skills for Obtaining Resources, Building Relationships, and Getting Things Done." Seminar presented at PMI Training, 2021–2023.

Reynolds, Larry. "Influencing Styles." *The Twenty-first Century Leader Training Manual*. Trainer Active.

Saylor Foundation, The. Paper on Influencing Skills. BUS208: Principles of Management. 2013. https://learn.saylor.org/course/search.php?q=bus+208&areaids=core_course-course.

Sievert, Jr., Richard W. "Communication: An Important Construction Tool." *Project Management Journal* (December 1986): 77–82.

Steckler, Nicole and Rosenthal, Robert. "Sex Differences in Nonverbal and Verbal Communication with Bosses, Peers, and Subordinates." *Journal of Applied Psychology* (February 1985): 157–63.

Stuckenbruck, Linn C. and David Marshall. *Team Building for Project Managers*. Project Management Institute, 1985.

Thamhain, Hans J. and David L. Wilemon. "Conflict Management in Project Life Cycles." *Sloan Management Review* 12, no. 3 (1975): 31–50.

Verma, Vijay K. "Power and Influence in Project Management," "Power, Influence and Politics in Project Management," "Power and Influence: Mastering Organizational Politics to Deliver Successful Projects," "Creating High-Performance Teams for a Global Economy," and "Leadership, Power, Influence, Politics, and Negotiations in Project Management." Seminars presented at Project Management Institute (PMI) Seminars World, Project World, and other project management conferences and events (1997–2020).

———*The Art of Positive Politics: A Key to Delivering Successful Projects*. Oshawa, ON, Canada: Multi-Media Publications Inc., 2018.

———*Managing the Project Team: Human Aspects of Project Management, Volume 3*. Upper Darby, PA: Project Management Institute, 1997.

———*Human Resource Skills for the Project Manager: The Human Aspects of Project Management, Volume 2*. Upper Darby, PA: Project Management Institute, 1996.

———*Organizing Projects for Success: Human Aspects of Project Management, Volume 1*. Upper Darby, PA: Project Management Institute, 1995.

Verma, Vijay K. and Max Wideman. "Project Manager to a Project Leader and the Rocky Road in Between." *Proceedings of 25th Annual Seminar/Symposium*. Project Management Institute, Drexel Hill, PA, 1994.

Wallen, R. W. "Three Types of Executive Personality." 1963. In Lindsay-Sherwin. "Consultancy Skills Toolkit," 2005.

Wideman, Max. "Negotiating for Project Benefit." *Max's Project Management Wisdom*. 1998. http://www.maxwideman.com/papers/negotiating/power.htm.

Youker, Robert B. "Power and Politics in Project Management." *PM Network* (May 1991): 36–40.

Leading with Purpose

About the Authors

Vijay K. Verma, PMP, MBA, PEng, PMI Fellow

Vijay K. Verma is an internationally renowned speaker and author. He wrote a three-volume series on the Human Aspects of Project Management published by the Project Management Institute (PMI)— *Organizing Projects for Success, Human Resource Skills for the Project Manager*, and *Managing the Project Team*—and a fourth book, *The Art of Positive Politics: A Key to Delivering Successful Projects*, published in June 2018 by Multi-Media Publications Inc. Vijay received the 2009 PMI Fellow Award (one of the highest and most prestigious awards presented by PMI), the 1999 PMI David I. Cleland Project Management Literature Award (for his book *Managing the Project Team*), and the 1999 PMI Distinguished Contribution Award for sustained and significant contributions to the project management profession.

Vijay has given many keynote presentations at various conferences. He has authored and presented many papers at national and international conferences on the Human Aspects of Project Management and Managing Cross-Cultural Teams. He has presented several workshops on project management in the United States, Canada, Europe, Australia, South Africa, China, and India with participants from various industries. More than four thousand professionals working in project management have attended his presentations to enhance their skills and confidence in managing projects effectively.

Mr. Verma worked for forty years at TRIUMF (TRI University Meson Facility), Canada National Research Laboratory. Here, he provided project management services for projects varying in size, complexity, and diversity. Mr. Verma served as president of the West Coast BC Chapter (1988–1989). He is a professional engineer with an MSc in Electrical Engineering from DalTech, Halifax, and an MBA from the University of British Columbia, Vancouver, Canada. He lives in Vancouver with his wife, Shiksha, enjoying life with seven grandchildren.

About the Authors

Shiksha Verma, B.Ed.

Shiksha Verma is the cofounder, with her husband Vijay K. Verma, of Samanda Enterprises Inc., a company based in Vancouver, British Columbia, Canada, primarily involved in project management and leadership training, and real estate development. She has been involved in charitable activities and community projects for many years.

Shiksha holds a Bachelor's in Education and taught at a high school in India for many years. After marrying Vijay in 1976, she migrated to Canada and stayed home to raise three children. She supported Vijay in all his professional, teaching, and writing endeavors, giving him fresh ideas and helping him develop seminars and keynote presentations for project management conferences in the United States, Canada, Australia, and India.

While collaborating with Vijay on this book, she was committed to adding value by ensuring that serious messages and results are delivered through easily remembered and sustained stories and examples. In this book, she included her common-sense approach to lead with purpose, influence people, and create a compelling desire in them to expand their potential and meet their personal and organizational visions.

Shiksha Verma is a proven natural project manager and thought-provoking leader. Although she does not have formal designations in project management, she leads with management and leadership principles in everything she does, from real estate development to planning and organizing their children's weddings. She can identify risks and develop risk management strategies for small and large challenges in life.

Shiksha is driven by a belief in lifelong learning and everyone's ability to fulfill their potential and make positive life changes. She understands the importance of people feeling valued and engaged at work. She loves to help others change their people skills to produce big results.

In the past ten years, Shiksha has developed a keen interest in exploring the role of spirituality in leadership. She firmly believes the spirituality component provides leaders with strong conviction, commitment, and empathy, which are necessary to lead purposefully and with people in mind. She believes in leading life with high moral values and developing internal powers, whether to raise a family or lead a business organization.

She lives in Vancouver with her husband, Vijay, enjoying life with seven grandchildren.

About the Authors

Jaimini Thakore, MBA

Jaimini has worked in the health care field for more than twenty years. He has experience in project management and obtained his PMP in 2008. Jaimini contributed to the *PMBOK® Guide* 4th edition and was a PMI West Coast Chapter instructor for several years. He joined the Cardiac Services BC team at the Provincial Health Services Authority (PHSA) in 2021 after many years with PHSA's Trauma Services BC, where he led the transformation of the Trauma Registry, including the reporting and analytics infrastructure. Before PHSA, Jaimini ran the Project Office and Performance Measurement with Vancouver Community Services. During his few years in Ontario, he also worked at the Canadian Institute of Health Information.

Jaimini holds a degree in Health Information Science and a Master's in Business Administration. He is father to three very energetic children, aged 13, 11, and 8, who are busy with soccer, basketball, and music.

Krupal Patel, MBA, PMP

Krupal Patel earned a Bachelor of Science in Industrial Engineering and Management Information Systems from the University of Central Florida and completed his MBA with the University of Victoria. He received his PMP certification from PMI in 2013.

Krupal is an associate faculty member at Royal Roads University focusing on Operations Management and Supply Chain Management. He has worked with BC Pensions, creating and developing an Operations Excellence Program. His experience in manufacturing and supply chain has ranged in projects worldwide, including the United Arab Emirates, Australia, Germany, and the United States, with many initiatives focused on improving efficiency and creating sustainable systems. Krupal has spent the last fourteen years delivering projects that have a lasting impact on operations and lead to significant improvements for clients.

Did you like this book?

We hope you enjoyed it as much as we enjoyed creating it and making it available to you.

In today's world, nothing is more helpful to us than readers taking the time to write online book reviews. Every review helps make others aware of this book, spreading the message. Also, the authors take the time to read reviews to motivate them to create new books.

If you enjoyed this book, please take the time to write an online review at the site where you purchased it, or at Amazon.com.

If you want more information on the topic of this book, the author is available for training and consulting engagements through Procept Associates Ltd.

Precision meets Expertise.
Procept
ASSOCIATES LTD.

Procept delivers management training and consulting services across North America and around the world. Its award-winning trainers and consultants deliver services customized to your industry or your own company's challenges, processes and culture. Find out more at:

www.Procept.com

The Art of Positive Politics: A Key to Delivering Successful Projects

by Vijay K. Verma

No matter how well you estimate and schedule a project, or how well you plan for risks, project success will depend upon the cooperation of people who have their own hidden agendas, who have conflicting motivations, or who have past unresolved conflicts with each other. Getting people to work together effectively is one of the key challenges in project management.

This fascinating book looks at how to manage the people who influence our project outcomes by examining their overt (and covert) motivations. Carefully navigating this minefield of conflicting interests (or "office politics") surrounding a project will allow you to better support and motivate external stakeholders and team members to take action to help your project succeed.

Full of useful tips and sound, practical advice, this book distills decades of research on the topic into actionable steps you can take today to improve your success as a project manager.

ISBN: 9781554891771

Available in paperback and ebook formats.

Milton Keynes UK
Ingram Content Group UK Ltd.
UKHW022029230824
447344UK00012B/836

9 781554 891818